DIVINE DIVORCE

HOW TO MAKE
A GREAT
ADVENTURE
OUT OF THE
WORST DISASTER OF
YOUR LIFE

Jacque Small

Catalyst Press | Victoria, British Columbia

Printed in the United States of America
First Printing, 2014

Book design by
Shannon McCafferty Design

978-0-9918242-0-5

Catalyst Press
Victoria, British Columbia
www.YourDivineDivorce.com

Names and details of stories related here have been changed
to protect privacy. This publication is not intended as a substitute for
medical advice. Please consult your physician before applying the
emotional release methods outlined in this book.

THIS BOOK IS DEDICATED TO
PHYLLIS VALLENCE SMALL
MY MOTHER, BEST FRIEND,
AND GUARDIAN ANGEL

Acknowledgments

HEARTFELT THANKS TO ALL of my teachers, specifically those who assisted me to fully experience and grow through major transitions in my life: T. Harv Ecker, Jack Canfield, Satyen Raja, Tom Stone, and Michael Stratford. Transformation occurs in community, of course, so I am also grateful to my fellow personal development learners who undertook their own transformation, kindly providing me with support and a mirror for my transformation. I am also very appreciative of Cheryl and Robert Smith who invited me into their beautiful home during my transition to single life, and as this book began to take shape. To the many friends who offered their support, both while my relationship came to an end, and while writing this book: I can't thank you all enough. I am doubly grateful for the invaluable guidance of my editor, Ceci Miller, who has been with me every step of the way. Finally, I would like to thank those men who have been a mirror for my learning in intimate relationship — especially you, Milo.

Contents

Introduction   *11*

Chapter 1 A Travel Guide to Happiness   15

PART ONE | *The River Adventure*
Chapter 2 Wonderful Excursions   29
Chapter 3 Major White Water   48
Chapter 4 New Tools for My Backpack   59
Chapter 5 Shock and Awe   83
Chapter 6 Capsized in the Current   97

PART 2 | *Heading Out on My Own*
Chapter 7 Separate Ways   129
Chapter 8 Looking Back up the River   155
Chapter 9 Do I Enter the Jungle?   182
Chapter 10 The Jungle Looms   205
Chapter 11 Emotions, Dark and Light   215
Chapter 12 Entering the Jungle of Emotional Conditioning   235
Chapter 13 Cutting Through the Jungle of Feeling   263
Chapter 14 Clearing My Path Vine by Vine   275
Chapter 15 Tilling the Soil   304
Chapter 16 Planting Seeds for a Magical Life   328

Bibliography   *341*

Introduction

I HAD DREAMED OF A HAPPY and blissful marriage, and while I ended up in a long-term common law relationship, I thought we were going to live "happily ever after," paddling our kayak down the river of life. I imagined traveling with the love of my life down one big long river that flowed for hundreds of miles through a variety of geographies, and experiencing all sorts of different adventures. In my story we grew old together and reminisced about all the wonderful days and nights we had spent on the river, laughing at our mistakes and telling the tales of our adventures. We would stand beside each other in old age as the river of our life poured out into the sea.

This all changed when the tropical storm of 2008 hit, with violent winds and torrential rain swelling the tranquil jungle river that we had been traveling down. We had weathered storms before, but nothing like this storm that blew up seemingly from nowhere.

1. A Tropical Storm Hits

It is a beautiful sunny day in Vancouver. Summer is finally here; the rain has stopped pouring outside. I am looking forward to the weekend. My husband, Milo, and I are in the living room. The sun is shining in through the blinds, creating a warm glow. I am sitting on our old couch. Milo is standing and looking quite nervous.

"Jacque, I want to talk to you," he says.

A feeling of sickness lurches up in my stomach. This sick feeling is very familiar. It happens whenever I think someone is angry with me and I have made a mistake of some sort. For the life of me I have no idea where I might have screwed up.

"Jacque, I want to leave."

I am in utter shock. How could he want to leave me? Why would he want to leave me? I have been working so hard to become happy, going to workshop after workshop, applying as much of my learning as possible. I know I am changing; I am starting to become a really wonderful person. I am starting to experience myself as a lovable woman, and I am building great relationships with other people. How can he not see how much I am changing? Doesn't he know how much I love him? Why would he want to leave me?

I feel the shock in my heart. Tears well up in my eyes and begin to roll down my cheeks. My chest is constricted and I can feel a pain stabbing me in my right breast. It is like there is a huge thundercloud overhead; the skies have opened up and threaten to wash away everything that I hold dear. How could this be happening to me?

Milo is sitting at the other end of the couch with a look of pain and concern on his face. I slide over to him so he can put his arms around me and hold me. I want him to comfort me and tell me this is not really happening. The little girl in me wants this all to go away, so that everything will be OK again. He holds me and I sob in his arms. In the far reaches of my mind I can hear the distant murmur of his voice.

Milo assured me that it was nothing I had done. I had always been very good to him. I had saved him from the depths of depression and unhappiness when we met. He said he had fallen in love. He had never felt happy, and now he had met someone that he knew he could be happy with. This might be the only chance that he would ever get. How could he pass it up?

Claire, a friend from public speaking classes, had moved in on my relationship without me even knowing it. My head felt like it would explode with rage and fury when I thought about how she had betrayed me. How could someone do this? I shook as the rage boiled throughout my body. I had been so wronged. This was the worst thing that ever happened to me. Milo was my best friend in the whole wide world. He held me every night when we went to bed and helped to make me feel safe. Now I was going to lose him. What was I going to do?

I had lost my mother three years earlier, at ninety-one years of age, and I was devastated by her parting. We had been wonderful friends. I had been her caregiver and she had been my confidant. There was a big hole in my life, and I had moved closer toward Milo to fill the gap that my mother had left.

I was now losing everything. Lying in bed I felt the crushing weight of fear and devastation. Everything that I had worked for was being washed away by a torrential rainstorm. Milo would be gone. I would have no one to golf with, no one to ski with. Who would go camping with me? We went camping every summer for our holidays. Packed the camping gear and our golf clubs in the car and headed off to explore another part of beautiful British Columbia. I always felt a sense of peace when we were out in the lush green forest, with no one else around for miles. Now I wouldn't be able to do what I loved best.

I would lose my house and the beautiful elaborate gardens I had built, which burst full of color every spring and summer. For sixteen years, I had toiled in those gardens. The gardens were a labor of love, the plants were my children, and I nurtured them and took care of them. Now it would all be gone.

2. The Aftermath of the Storm

As with any major storm, trees were blown down, branches were strewn everywhere, and the calm river we were on was all of a sudden swollen with water. The current was taking us downstream at an uncontrollable pace. I was hanging on to the boat for dear life, with terror in my eyes and fear in my heart.

Our toughest tests come when we have to respond to an event like this. What do we do? Do we get caught up in the drama that our partners have wronged us, that they promised to be with us "till death do us part"? Do we stand in the place where we have been wronged and believe the only solution is retribution? Or do we take a hard look at our lives and how we got here in the first place? I decided to take a look at myself and see what I could learn. I decided to go back in time and see how I got here.

CHAPTER 1

A Travel Guide to Happiness

THERE IS A TIME BEFORE we take action where we dream and contemplate what it is we want, whether an adventure holiday or the ideal life partner. We pore through travel magazines and search the Internet for the ideal holiday destination, and then imagine and dream about the adventure that we want to go on. Finding a life partner is much the same—we have dreams of the ideal partners that we would like to meet, we dream about them when we go to bed at night, we agonize about finding the right person when we talk to our friends. Will we ever find that person? The last thing we want is to be alone. Then we see someone. Excitement, giddiness, and the thrill of anticipation strike with the electrical charge of lightning. Could this be the right one?

When I met Milo, it felt like I was setting out on the adventure of a lifetime. I was excited and nervous like a young schoolgirl. My whole life, I had been looking forward to meeting a kind, intelligent, witty man who was excited to be with me. I dreamed of being with a man who loved the outdoors and was physically active. When I met Milo I knew he was the one, and we embarked on what I was sure would be a wonderful journey together.

The dream I had in my head was like the perfect adventure holiday, and as I lay in bed at night and dreamed about our relationship it was nothing short of thrilling. We would have times of tranquility: lying in a hammock, swaying in the breeze, looking out over the turquoise blue waters of the Caribbean Sea, feeling the bliss in our hearts. We would go on adventures: scuba diving or snorkeling and exploring the underwater mysteries of the sea.

We would hike through the jungle and listen to the sounds of the wildlife. We would be awed as we watched a river cascade over the edge of the falls, thundering and splashing many feet below as it made its way to the sea. I imagined a white-water kayaking trip, sleeping out in the jungle at night—oh, I so loved sleeping out underneath the stars. And we would explore ancient ruins, reviewing our past relationships and family history. At times I was giddy as I imagined being on the adventure of a lifetime, and at other times I felt like I was floating along on a tranquil river marveling at the fluffy white clouds overhead. Oh sure, I knew there would be some difficult times—one could get malaria out in the jungle, but I was taking malaria pills for that! I knew there was a distinct possibility of getting hurt, and I did the wise thing to protect myself. I bought insurance to medevac out of the jungle if I ran into problems. I had taken care of everything; all I had to do was buy the tickets and I would be off on my dream adventure.

I was innocent and naïve; I had no idea that when it comes to heartbreak I could be incapacitated for a long time if I was not healthy and strong. I thought I could endure anything with my partner; all we needed was to love each other. With love we would paddle our kayak bravely on the river called life, over waterfalls and through the boiling white water of the rapids. We would pitch a tent to weather any storm and string up tarps to keep our campsite perfectly dry. Together we could deal with whatever life presented us. Nothing would get in our way. I imagined our lives would be filled with smiles, happiness, fun, and adventure, just like in the movies.

But real life is not quite like the movies or the fairy tales that our parents read to us. Our conditioning began when we were young children, and it taught us to believe in the fairy princess who finds her Prince Charming and "lives happily ever after." The problem is that we are not fairy princesses. As for the guys, once they have hunted and bagged a bride and gotten her to the marriage throne, they set their sights on new game. Guys forget all about being Prince Charming once they're married. After all they have serious work to do; they need to feed and look after a bride and family, and then they relax with other men to release the stress. This is what has been conditioned into men for thousands of years: providing for and protecting a family.

Modern-day fairy tales do not prepare us for the difficulties we will face in marriage, never mind divorce. Over time the white knight's armor becomes tarnished and rusty, and needs a little polish and oil. We might have the tendency to stamp our feet like children and demand that our partners be the way we want them to be. Unfortunately we can't change our partners—we can only change ourselves. Relationship challenges are a great place for us to stop blaming, look inside ourselves, and ask, "Am I being who I want to be?" The prospect of separation and divorce presents us with a compelling opportunity to take a close look at what we want and to make proactive choices that prepare us to have a magical life in the future.

The Adventure Begins

This is a real-life adventure story. It chronicles my quest to find my own happiness. Just as happiness comes within my grasp, disaster strikes, and the looming prospect of divorce is in front of me. This is a story of passion, tenacity, and love, as I persistently cut through all the emotional drama of divorce. When I reach safety on the other side, I sit down for a moment to breathe, and I notice I am different. My journey has given me new strength, confidence, and skills to start preparing for another great adventure—living into my dream life.

As you can see, I love adventure, so I have crafted this story as a jungle adventure trip. Marriage is much like a jungle: beautiful and challenging at the same time. Serious disaster can strike very quickly in the jungle and result in grave danger, just like divorce. You get to choose right now whether relationship challenges and possible divorce will be a great adventure or your worst nightmare. Ask yourself:

- How long will I spend in the jungle of a broken relationship?
- How long will I insist that my relationship kayak should not have crashed against that big rock?
- How long will I grieve about my possessions being swept away down the river of life?
- When will I quit blaming my partner for crashing the kayak?
- Do I have the courage to enter the jungle and cut down the thorny emotional vines that have plagued me all my life?
- Am I ready to drop off my emotional baggage and travel lighter?
- Would I sooner just curl up and go to sleep in the perceived safety on the riverbanks of yet another relationship?
- Why should I even bother to try and make it out of the jungle?
- What is important enough that I am willing to take a stand?
- Am I willing to take a stand for myself and love myself first?

Many of us live our lives and engage with our partners on autopilot. We meet our partners, decide they're the right one for us, get married, and have children. In the meantime we work hard to find the right job, buy a decent car, buy a house, furnish it, and create a nest for our lives. We buy car, home, and medical insurance, and we think we are protected. We work hard to do all the right things to have a good life and a good marriage.

We Aren't Prepared for the Storm

We did our research. We bought beautiful kayaks for our relationship journeys and kitted them out for the adventure of our lives. We were ready to run the smooth-flowing waters of our relationships, and we felt well prepared to paddle hard in the white waters of fast-flowing rapids. Our love was strong and we felt it would get us through any bad weather that might come our way.

Were we really prepared for life, however, or were we living in illusion, unaware of what would be required to weather, learn, and grow from the storms in our relationship?

Though we bought the medevac insurance, we never really imagined that our beautiful kayaks would one day smash up against rocks in the river of life, or that our relationships would be pulled down under the hydraulic power of a waterfall and smashed to smithereens. At the outset and during the daily life of our relationships, it seemed unreal that we could lose all the precious camping gear we had acquired with loving care. It was hard to imagine everything being swept downstream by a river which had no attachment as to where it scattered our treasured possessions. How could the intimacy of our relationships be washed away by the powerful currents of betrayal, deceit, or even apathy? The beautiful, peaceful river on which we shared our life adventure suddenly turned dangerous and hostile, as the thunderous clouds of separation and divorce loomed over our heads.

Tapping into the deep love that we have for ourselves gives us inner strength, which inflates like a life vest to buoy us up when we are in turbulent waters. Love supports us as we swim to shore and save our own lives, and maybe our relationships at the same time. Medevac insurance meant to take us off the river and out of the jungle is useless if we drown when the kayak capsizes. Sadly, when it comes to divorce, many families drown in anger and bitterness, each of us blaming our partners for being someone other than the person we dreamed of in our fairy-tale stories.

I'm in Turbulent Waters — HELP

I know you are not living a fairy-tale life. In fact if you are reading this book, you already know that your princess has warts and the armor of your prince is rusty. So what do you do to inflate your life vest, get out of this turbulent water, and get to shore before you drown?

In my kayak I had this beautiful, blue backpack full of tools that I pulled out and used in the storm of separation. During the happier days of my journey down the river with Milo, when we stopped and made camp together on the shores of the river, I would often wander off down a path into a nearby village and listen to the elders share their wisdom. At first I was afraid to go alone, but Milo did not want to go, and I found these talks gave me all sorts of ideas on how to be happier in life.

I spent six years participating in personal development workshops and listening to various people speak, and I gathered a lot of tools for my backpack. Many of these became favorites, and I made it a habit to use them on a regular basis to build up my inner resourcefulness.

Contrary to popular belief, we are not hardwired to be the way we are. We can change our thinking, our behaviors, and the frequency and velocity of our emotional reactions. We can choose who we want to be in every moment. I used the tools in my backpack to start choosing to be a new Jacque. The old one I called Bulldozer Beatrice; she stepped on too many people's toes and she needed to go! The tools in my backpack allowed me to inflate a bright yellow life vest of resourcefulness, which saved me from drowning in fear, depression, and anger.

We are often in denial about what is actually occurring in our relationships. Sometimes we are floating around in circles in an eddy on the side of the river, and everything feels calm and safe. I knew things weren't perfect, but I was willing to accept and love Milo for the way he was. His armor was a little rusty, but after all, we had been on our adventure trip for eighteen years. A little rust was bound to accumulate! At the same time, I could sense the beautiful, gentle man who was inside the armor. I loved him, and I would love him for the rest of my life. I was ready to settle for good enough. Apparently he wasn't; his unhappiness was prompting him to look for a woman with fewer warts!

Who Will Save Me Now?

It is shocking to be thrust into the uncharted wilderness of divorce. The unthinkable is happening — my partner is leaving. As I stood shivering on the banks of the river wondering what to do next, I was bombarded by all the fears of being single once again, terrified of being alone and not being loved by anyone. Looking into the foreboding, dark jungle of divorce, I had to face myself and the huge void I felt inside. Now that I no longer had the safety of marriage, I had to face life head on. Facing separation and divorce felt like having to walk alone down an overgrown, hostile path in the jungle. The only thing for me to do was to pluck up my courage, walk out of the jungle, and find safety in a local village.

The jungle felt very dangerous as I ventured in underneath its beautiful but ominous canopy. The jungle, like life, has no shortage of big vines hanging down covered with sharp thorns, trees that are poisonous when you cut into their bark, and powerful jaguars that will take a bite out of you if they are hungry.

One factor in divorce is the emotional baggage we have been hauling around since childhood. As we move into adulthood, traumatic situations occur in our lives. It is very difficult to make it through the jungle when we're hauling all this baggage. Many people try, and they have vicious scars to prove the arduousness of their journey around the thorny vines of their emotions. I say, cut those thorny vines down — it's easier and it hurts less!

In my hour of greatest need, I discovered a machete had been discarded at the base of a tree. I picked up the machete and started hacking away at the thorny emotional vines that blocked my way out of the jungle. I chopped at anger, fear, loneliness, and any other negative emotion that threatened to strangle me. As I cut down the thorny vines of my emotions, I noticed that my emotional hot buttons started to disappear — I became calmer and less frightened. Then I noticed that I was hauling less and less baggage around with me; I was having fewer emotional reactions. Finally I noticed the simplicity of what the machete was allowing me to do, and that was to simply *feel*. Feeling helped me drop off the heavy baggage so I could travel lighter in life. Now I wouldn't have to add the bitterness of divorce to my emotional baggage and carry around even more harmful energy.

Opportunity in the Midst of Crisis

When it came to divorce I adopted the attitude that if I was going to go through this event, then I was going to get something valuable out of it. I was going to turn the worst disaster of my life into a great adventure from which I would receive value. Based on this attitude, I made a powerful commitment to myself about how I would be as I passed through divorce. I set the intention to bring my relationship to a close with grace and ease. I did not want to have a divorce that was bitter and cruel. Milo was a man whom I loved deeply, and I had stated forcefully that "I will love you no matter what happens." I learned how powerful it is to take a stand in my own life for who I wanted to be. I came to understand what it means to create my own reality.

Too many of us are living in a jungle, weighed down by our emotional baggage—as is evidenced by the increasing rates of stress-related illness, prescriptions for depression, and heart attacks and other illnesses. The quality of everyday life is declining due to stress and our struggles to cope. As you may already know, an unhappy relationship is a very big stressor that detracts from all areas of our lives, including our ability to focus and be productive at work. I discovered that we can use our relationship challenges, especially divorce, to lighten the load of our emotional baggage, to start living the life we really want, and to improve our health—all at the same time. Not a bad outcome for what might seem to be the worst disaster of our lives!

When we drop off our emotional baggage, we also become more resourceful in our future relationships. People often attract the partner that creates the most learning; hence if we learn whatever it is this time around, we won't have to learn it next time. Being as emotionally grounded and as centered as you can be will serve you well as you go through this turbulent time, and any challenging times you have in the future.

How to Use This Book

I learned about the tools, principles, and techniques in this book in the approximate order that I have written about them here, but that is certainly not the only way to learn them. You may want to read the conclusion of this book first so that you will have the end of this leg of the trip within sight. Chapters 11 through 14 will take you through the world of emotions and how to permanently resolve the emotional turmoil you are feeling now. You might as well be cutting down the vines in your emotional jungle as you take the time to read this book. Chapter 7 will give you the principles by which I have learned to live. Every day I practice embracing these principles to have a happier and consistently more spectacular life. Chapters 4 and 6 will give you what you need to start building your own backpack of tools to assist you to become more resourceful, especially in your thinking. When you change your thinking, life starts to become easier. If you read the book in this order, you will be changing your thinking in two ways. First, by letting go of your emotional baggage, you let go of the old memories and stories that are attached to the old emotions. Second, the tools will directly assist you to change your thinking.

The self-reflection questions you'll find in every section will likely provoke a whole host of emotional reactions that you can work on resolving. As you go through the book, you can start cutting down your own emotional jungle and experience the true miracles that life has to offer. Then when life presents you with more opportunities to learn, you will be fully prepared. The tools, principles, and techniques form a dynamic system to support you as you begin to live into a magical life.

Come Soar with Me

When you decide to step into the jungle of all the turmoil and horrible emotions that you feel right now, you will be taking a stand for your life. You get to choose to let go of the hurt of your inner child, so that child can grow up to be a healthy, strong adult person. You can reclaim your power. You can finally have the confidence to be your authentic *you*, to speak what is on your mind without fear. You can live without being controlled by your ego, which is perpetually afraid that bad things might happen or that good things won't happen. You will have the opportunity to purposefully grow what you want to bring into your life.

As you leave the jungle canopy, you might come to the realization that it was your emotional baggage and your partner's that was actually doing the duelling — maybe you really love your partner and the two of you want to stay connected. It may be your emotional baggage that you really need to divorce! Or you might come to the place where you respect your partner's position and recognize that the relationship has run its course and it is time to move on. When a significant amount of your emotional baggage is gone, you will be able to use your intuition, your gut feelings, to help you make this decision. You will no longer be hooked by your ego, having to figure everything out in your mind. You will be able to tap into the much more powerful force of "knowing" that comes from feeling connected to others and to universal energy, which some people call God.

I was extremely grateful to emerge from the thick, dark jungle canopy into an opening that had been cleared by one of the local farmers. I was blessed; I could feel the sunshine on my face. I would be OK. And I had found a resource that I could use for the rest of my life. Now that I was out in the open, all I had to do was to till the soil that I wanted to plant. Then I could decide what I wanted in my life and plant seeds accordingly. New opportunities would present themselves, and I could decide which ones to say yes to. Now, no matter what I grow in my garden, I know weeds will always poke their heads out. But I no longer have to worry about being overwhelmed; I can just dig the weeds out and compost them. Now that my plot of land is relatively weed free, I can manifest what I want with relative ease.

Different varieties of jungle vines block each of us from attracting what we want. Some people can attract lots of money into their lives, but have terrible relationships; others have wonderful relationships and are financially poor. Emotional baggage has an amazing degree of similarity, however, and it can be sorted out and pared down. Hauling around large quantities of baggage is now optional!

If I could do it, you can do it. It doesn't matter if you are male or female, in a gay relationship or a straight relationship, if you are religious, spiritual, or agnostic. Heck, you don't even have to divorce your partner if you don't want to. None of these things are important. What is important is that we all have emotions. As you travel through this book with me, you will realize that the tools I give you here are priceless, especially the emotional clearing techniques included at the end. This book will become your trusted travel guide as you navigate turmoil in your relationship. It will show you how to take every emotional upset that you feel and turn it into gold. Not only is it a travel guide through divorce, but it can be your compass as you embrace your next journey. Before you know it, you will be sharing it with your friends and inviting them to come on this great adventure with you, to divorce your emotional baggage. Come soar with me!

PART
ONE

CHAPTER 2

Wonderful Excursions

ALL ADVENTURE TRIPS REQUIRE some research and careful planning. Part of the excitement of going on an adventure is planning the trip. Where do I want to go, what do I want to see, and what do I want to do? Does this all sound exciting? Dating is like planning a dream adventure; we are keeping our eyes open, looking for what we really want in a partner. As we get to know our partners, we decide if we would like to make a bigger commitment—to travel down the relationship river together. We might choose to acquire a temporary boat to travel in, living together while we decide if this is what we really want. Later we might get the marriage boat of our dreams and make a real long-term commitment to our relationship.

Getting Together

The journey of Milo and Jacque started while I was finishing up my master's degree in economics in spring of 1991. I was doing a research project at the university and would not start working fulltime until October, so I had some free time and was looking forward to a marvelous summer of fun and exploration. I was in Vancouver, British Columbia, a stunningly beautiful city surrounded by lots of inlets and beaches, and set in a lush, green backdrop of mountain peaks. I loved the ocean and this was a whole new playground for me. I decided to learn how to sail.

It was fun and thrilling for a prairie girl to be out on the choppy waters of English Bay, skimming over the waves with the salt wind biting at my face. I learned quickly and was soon able to take a sailboat out on my own with only a small amount of nervousness. I learned all sorts of new skills, like tying knots, rigging the sails, and righting the boat if I flipped it over, which I tried to avoid at all costs as it was not the warmest water to swim in. I loved this new adventure, even though I didn't know any of the people at the sailing club.

One of my buddies, Peggy, asked me if I would like to go sailing, and I was delighted to go out on a big sailboat. It would be so much fun to go out sailing and not get wet, not have to worry about capsizing the boat. The boat was nothing fancy but it had an exciting history: it was a twenty-four-foot, deep-keel sailboat that had been sailed single-handed from Japan.

It was a beautiful sunny day and I could feel excitement and anticipation churning in my belly as I drove toward the marina. We boarded the boat, glided our way out of the harbor, and then set sail. On the big sailboat there was lots of work to do, and everyone was quickly put to work as crew. The concept of sailing a larger boat was the same as for a small one, but the rigging was so much bigger that I felt out of my element and was unsure what needed to be done. Milo, the man who had invited us sailing, was great at explaining what he needed, and I was eager to learn and help.

Once we were under sail and had all the lines coiled away, there wasn't much work to do. We sat in the cockpit talking or lounged on the deck, napping and enjoying the sunshine. Milo looked after most of the sailing; however, he did give me a chance to take the helm and sail the boat. I was thrilled. As the day went along Milo became more comfortable with me. I could tell he was because he started to challenge me to see how much I knew about sailing. Could I coil the lines properly? Did I know how to slab the sail at the end of the day? A dynamic unfolded between Milo and me: he'd set out a challenge and I'd do my best to accomplish the task. He would acknowledge me if I did it correctly and tease me if I didn't quite get it right.

Milo was a very intelligent man, very well read. I was mesmerized as I listened to him talking to my girlfriend about work and science. I loved how smart this guy seemed to be, and I liked that he teased and challenged me. Milo had finished his master's degree in organic chemistry a couple of years before. We were both starting out in our careers, me in corporate finance and he in the production chemistry of pheromones. Talk about chemical attraction, this guy was making the stuff! We were both highly educated people who liked to talk about interesting things. I wondered if this guy would be interested in a girl like me.

Courtship

It only took a couple days. Milo called me and we planned our next excursion together. A houseboating trip on Shuswap Lake in the interior of British Columbia was being organized by some of my friends. I am an exuberant, let's–just–do–it kind of person, so I invited Milo along for the weekend. The more the merrier was my motto. There were two houseboats with eight people on each boat. What I didn't realize about Milo was that he was a loner; he was uncomfortable with strangers and claustrophobic in small spaces. So sixteen people rafted together on two small houseboats was a little overwhelming for him.

When I invited Milo on the houseboating trip, I didn't realize that being with strangers was a challenge for him, and he really didn't know me at all. This was a big risk for a guy who played life safe. Later he told me that he had insisted on taking his car for this trip instead of mine because if things went sideways, he could bail. He said he would have abandoned me and left me behind if necessary, and I didn't know if he was telling the truth or just pulling my leg. Milo made these kinds of statements with such a straight face that I couldn't tell if he was really serious or not.

We got up early, made breakfast on our own boat, and then ventured out onto the lake for the day. We slowly made our way up one arm of Shuswap Lake, which is about twenty miles long. Sometimes we'd stop, raft our two boats together, and go swimming. There was nothing to do but eat, drink, relax, connect with friends, and look at the beautiful, mountainous landscape, covered by coniferous forest. At night we'd make our way to one of the beaches at the end of the lake and beach the boat on the sand. We had bonfires at night on the beach, all of us sitting around chatting and watching the flames dance. When we couldn't keep our eyes open any longer we wandered off to bed, getting up the next day to do it all over again.

We survived the four-day trip together, and Milo drove me back to Vancouver. Would our budding relationship survive a second trip?

I had planned a cycling trip to the San Juan Islands in Washington State at the end of August, with seven friends from university. I asked Milo if he would like to join us on this camping cycling trip. Milo didn't own a bike and hadn't been cycling since he was a teenager. He said he was game to come on the trip, though, so we borrowed a bike and got him some padded cycling shorts.

One friend brought a truck over to San Juan Island with all the camping gear, and the rest of us took our bikes. I was a little concerned for Milo, as San Juan Island is pretty hilly and this wasn't going to be an easy trip for someone who hadn't been on a bike in fifteen years, but Milo assured me he was up for it. We started the trip on a beautiful sunny day, and the views were spectacular from the ferry.

When we got off the ferry, we cycled through rolling fields. The sun shone on our faces and I could feel the tranquility of life on this beautiful Pacific Northwest island. We got down to work, setting up our campsite, making dinner, and settling in for the night. It had been a long, exciting day, and I crawled into my sleeping bag exhausted, looking forward to the rest of the weekend.

Suddenly I could tell that something awful was happening — rain was pelting down on the tent. I unzipped the tent to see a torrential amount of rain falling from the heavens. It was seven in the morning, everything was gray outside, and pools of water were forming everywhere. If we didn't act fast our tents would be drowned in water. Everything would be wet before we knew it. If you have ever gone camping, you know you never want your sleeping bag to get wet; it will ruin the rest of the trip.

I pulled my clothes on and flew out of the tent. The first order of business was to trench our tent to keep it from floating in the small lakes that were forming all around it. The rest of our crew started to emerge from their tents, looking shocked and depressed. Milo proved his worth; it turned out he was a master camper. He strung the tarp over the picnic table so we had a dry place to huddle and cook breakfast. Rumblings were starting to come from some members of the group that they were going back to Vancouver; they weren't going to hang out in this rain.

That's when we did what all great campers do — we went to town. We put our bikes in the back of the truck, piled into cars, and headed in. We wandered through the stores, ending up in the bar playing pool all afternoon. My friends were undecided about staying or leaving, but I really didn't want to go home. I hate quitting early. I had planned this adventure for over a month, and after we left San Juan Island, we were supposed to go to Port Townsend for two days. I asked Milo if he was willing to stay. He said yes, he would stay with me. I was so grateful! We each bought an extra pair of shoes and extra towels and committed to finishing this trip, even if we were the only ones. The rain let up in the afternoon and the sun came out. That evening Milo somehow got a campfire going and built a drying rack for our clothes.

I knew right then this was my kind of guy: someone who loved the outdoors and didn't quit. Milo was the perfect person for me to have an adventure with on the river of life. Not only was he witty and fun, but he was really handy. He could entertain me with his stories when we were on a calm river, and at the same time he was willing to stick with me and look after me when the going got tough. This was a man I could trust.

We finished that camping trip, putting many miles on our bicycles around San Juan Island and Port Townsend. It turned out to be a great trip and a good start to our relationship. I learned that Milo was willing to stick things out, and that he was creative and very handy. He was comfortable and easygoing with my friends.

We moved in together after about six months of dating. Milo was a voracious reader of scientific magazines and science fiction, and he seemed to be able to remember everything that he read. He would entertain me with scientific stories, painstakingly explaining the scientific concepts to me. I loved it. I didn't have to do the reading, yet I was learning. In summer, my girlfriends and I would play tennis by our house, and after dinner Milo would make us all cappuccinos. His sense of humor was offbeat and a bit quirky, always making fun in a way that had an edge to it. He affectionately called the women in my tennis group the sharks. It had a double-edged meaning, as we were all strong, very intelligent women whom he could respect, and at the same time we carried a degree of personal power that was a little daunting and dangerous.

Sunny Skies

Having fun doing things together was a huge part of our relationship. We really had a great time together for many years. The common denominator about the things we loved was that they involved sports and they took place outdoors. Over time the activities changed. Each of us brought something into the relationship that we had done before, and we would both try it out to see if it would stick. Cycling, tennis, sailing, golf, camping, skiing — we tried them all. Sailing, camping, and skiing were the sports that ultimately became important parts of our life together.

Sailing

We really enjoyed sailing during the first several years of our relationship. Milo was a member of the University of British Columbia's sailing club, which gave us access to a keelboat. Vancouver
is right on the doorstep of the Gulf Islands, seven large islands
that stretch over a distance of about seventy miles. This collection
of islands is a sailor's paradise.

Some islands have been made into marine parks. One time
we packed a lunch, rowed ashore, explored an island, and then
strung our hammocks up in between the trees for some much
needed rest. When I got tired of reading my novel in the hammock I went and sat on the shell beach, meditatively watching the
water lap against the shore. In moments like these I found great
peace in my heart. I was grateful to Milo for introducing me to the
wonders of sailing and the ocean.

Not everything was peaceful and magical, however; we
also had some terrifying and hell-raising moments. The worst
was when we sailed into a rainstorm with wind so strong that I
thought we might not make it back to shore alive. It was the first
day of a summer vacation. We had left the harbor slightly later
than intended, under heavy gray skies. We were sailing across
the Strait of Georgia heading for Porlier Pass. As the day wore on,
the sky became darker and a steady rain began to come down. We
had a port wind, coming from the left, which meant that we had
to tack the boat up into the wind fairly often to stay on course,
sailing in a zigzag pattern.

As we started to come in sight of land we were shocked to
discover that we could not see the pass. Where were we? It turned
out the compass mount was slightly bent and we'd missed the
mouth of the pass, so we needed to head a couple of miles back
south. It was late in the day and the storm had strengthened. Milo
was at the helm trying to hold our course as we headed up into
the wind to make a run for the pass. The last thing we wanted
to do was miss slack tide, which is when the water in the pass is
calmest. The boat was heeled over at a steep angle as we crashed

against wave after wave. If the current overwhelmed us at any point, we would be flung up against the rocks, which would likely punch a hole in our hull. We crawled forward slowly, trying to stay in the deepest part of the channel, hoping we would make it through. It was a tense, gut-wrenching time.

Despite the terror I experienced during that trip, we didn't give up sailing; the magic of it outweighed the challenges. Over a seven-year period we experienced many days of beautiful, sunny skies, passing through the blue waters of the Pacific with the high peaks of the Gulf Islands on either side of us.

Camping

When we stopped sailing, a new trend emerged for summer holidays. Each year we headed off to explore the wild backwoods terrain of beautiful British Columbia, loading up our golf clubs, camping gear, sunblock, and mosquito repellent into whatever four-wheel drive vehicle we had at the time. We drove hundreds of miles down winding highways, each time exploring a new part of the province. When we reached our intended destination, we'd turn off the smooth, paved highway and begin ten- to thirty-mile drives on narrow, winding logging roads full of potholes to find our ideal campsite. We always held out for a place where we had the stars in the sky all to ourselves and no other campers around. It was just us, magnificent pine and cedar trees, and a rushing, ice-cold mountain stream. I cooked many a gourmet meal on our Coleman stove. Whenever we moved into a campsite, we set up to stay several days. Milo strung up tarps to keep us dry if it rained, and hammocks in between the trees for our reading pleasure and for my many, many naps. To entertain himself, Milo panned for gold, while I read personal development books in the morning and novels in the afternoon and evening.

The logging roads provided lots of fallen wood for us to collect, and we built huge, roaring campfires to warm us at night when the cold mountain air settled in around us. We'd read in front of the campfire after dinner, and then eventually we'd turn off the Coleman lamp and marvel at the beauty of the millions of stars in the sky. This was heaven for both of us. It rejuvenated our souls and recharged our batteries. It was one of my favorite things to do. In the woods we were two faithful companions together and I couldn't have wished for a better partner.

Skiing

In winter Milo took me into a world where he was very comfortable, downhill skiing. I had been downhill skiing a few times before and spent most of my time being terrified of falling off the edge of something, even if was only my skis! Whenever I was up really high and had to look over an edge, my stomach churned, my legs turned into soft rubber, and my hands would sweat. I definitely was afraid of falling; however this did not stop me from learning how to ski. It was amazing what I was able to do with perseverance, determination, and a lot of ski lessons, plus Milo's support. Milo was a very good skier but a little lazy, so he was quite happy to hang out with me as I valiantly conquered one fear hurdle after another, moving from the easy, green-rated ski runs to the intermediate, blue slopes, and eventually to the more difficult black diamond runs. Each year I got better, faster, and more confident.

Ski weekends were a major part of our social life in winter throughout our whole relationship. We often gathered together with friends and rented a cabin in Whistler, British Columbia, one of the world's top ski destinations. After a couple of years we found the ideal cabin that we'd rent on a regular basis. It was a big, four-bedroom cabin, relatively old, which translated into affordable. It had a hot tub on the deck, which we loved soaking in after a hard day of skiing. It was our perfect winter getaway place. For fifteen winters, every third weekend for the whole ski season, a group of us went up to Whistler and spent the day whooshing our way down the pristine mountain slopes, weaving our way in between the evergreen trees. On sunny days it was glorious, on foggy or cloudy days it was difficult, on rainy days it was downright disappointing and we would sit in the cabin and play Scrabble for hours.

Over the years this group of people became like family. We watched as our friends' children grew into young adults, finding partners and starting their own families. Going to Whistler was a consistent part of our life together. Every third or fourth winter we decided to have a white Christmas at the cabin. I had been used to having a white Christmas growing up on the prairies, so Christmas was extra magical for me when we spent it at Whistler.

What Kind of Boat Will We Travel In?

When we'd been living together for a year, it was time to make a decision. I had finished graduate school and taken a commercial banking position with one of the banks in Canada, and I was about to complete my training program. I had joined this program with the understanding that at the end of it, I would likely be placed in a job outside of Vancouver. If Milo and I were not in a committed relationship, I was going to leave it up to the bank to send me wherever they needed me. If we were, then I would inform the bank that my relationship status had changed and I was not willing to leave Vancouver. I was ready for commitment and wanted Milo to decide what he wanted in our relationship.

Milo was willing to commit to our relationship; however, he was not willing to get married yet. Living together suited Milo just fine. As long as I knew that he was committed to being in a relationship with me, I was willing to wait until he was sure about what he wanted. Besides, living together before marriage was starting to become a trend. It seemed wise to live together for a while before making such a big commitment, so I decided not to push the issue.

The river of life, however, came along and swept us up and away, presenting an unexpected opportunity — we wanted to buy a house. I explained the change in my relationship status to the bank, and they posted me to a position in Vancouver in spring of 1992. That summer my mother came out to visit us from Manitoba, and we started talking about all three of us living in the house together.

Logically it all made sense. Milo and I had just finished graduate school. Both of us had good jobs and we were earning a reasonable income, but house prices in Vancouver were going up faster than we could save money. My mother at seventy-seven had reached the point where she was struggling to keep up her house and yard in the small town of Beausejour, Manitoba. I talked to Milo about asking her if she would like to move to Vancouver to live with us, and Milo agreed.

We looked at houses together to see what all of us liked. The backyard was the most important part of the house for all of us. Also, it had to have two living rooms, one for Mom and one for Milo and me, so we'd all have our privacy. We found the right house, and now Milo and I had a mortgage. Now we had a kayak to travel down the river of our relationship. I was very excited to own my first house, and for the moment the house was a big enough commitment for me.

Now that I had my own kitchen and one more person to cook for, I outfitted myself with great cooking pots, sharp knives, serving pieces, china, and glassware. It didn't matter if I was cooking an everyday meal or if we were having people over for dinner, I always found interesting recipes that were healthy, tasted great, and looked good. I felt very fulfilled being able to feed my family such good food. Because I cooked almost everything, we saved lots of money on groceries by not buying commercially prepared food. I was proud of how my industriousness also allowed me to be very responsible with our money. Preparing elegant dinner parties was a passion for me. Through food, I expressed my love for my family and our friends.

My second passion was gardening. We moved into the house in December 1992, and on a warm, sunny day in January, Mom and I were outside raking the leaves. This was certainly something that we wouldn't have been doing on the prairies in the depth of winter. I was excited about being able to transform our yard with beautiful gardens. I loved the bright-colored flowers that poked their heads through in the spring. Pretty purple and yellow crocuses were followed by yellow daffodils and tulips of all different colors. As we moved into summer, the larger perennials came into bloom: pink peonies, purple irises, white Shasta daisies, and many more flowers, each taking their turn until the cold, wet weather of fall signaled the closing of gardening for another season. In those early years I could hardly wait for spring to come around so I could continue to transform the gardens. They were my way of creating home and beauty in our relationship together.

Children and Family

I can't explain why, but I never had a huge drive to have children. Other women always seemed to crowd around a baby and want to hold it, but not me. I had attracted a group of friends that didn't want children, so it was not surprising that I also attracted a man who didn't want to have children. In fact, Milo was dead set against having children. One of the things that he found endearing about me was that I had no interest in babies when we were around them.

Though we didn't have children, there was one person in our family life who was hugely important to us from early in our relationship—my mother, Phyllis. Mom became my best friend. We went shopping together, we worked in the gardens together, and she talked to me for hours while I cooked those amazing meals. I cooked huge quantities of food on the weekend and froze it for later in the week. Mom was my companion in all these household adventures. I stood at the stove stirring one pot of food while reading the cookbook for the next thing. Mom sat at the kitchen table with the cutting board, ready to chop the next onion or carrot or whatever the recipe called for. As we worked we talked about my work, my friends, or something that was happening in the news. There was no shortage of things for us to talk about. We had a very close mother-daughter relationship.

My mother was very good at staying out of my relationship with Milo. She never spoke badly about him and she never gave me relationship advice. It was really quite amazing that she never interfered, because we certainly gave her opportunities, for example, when one of us was taking a less than flexible position about something. Actually, that would usually have been me! Milo was the one who was quiet and let things slide, keeping the peace in the family.

Mom and Milo developed their own quiet, close relationship. Mom was supportive of him and listened to his many stories about things not going as they should at work. She was never critical, nor did she offer him unsought advice; she was far better at this than I was. When I wasn't home for dinner, Milo helped Mom prepare dinner and they ate together. Mom loved to have a good political debate, but Milo was not interested in politics and was always careful to steer clear of these conversations. I could tell that his relationship with her was very important to him. Mom suffered with osteoarthritis and found it difficult to walk up the stairs in our house. If she needed a hand, Milo was always there to help.

Mom was creative and tenacious. Shortly after moving in with us, she needed to get a walker so she could get outside for walks. Osteoarthritis and osteoporosis made it painful for her to walk with a cane. Eventually these diseases limited her mobility so much it became difficult for her to walk a long distance even with her walker. Together we decided to buy her a lightweight wheelchair so she and I could go for walks together. She pushed the chair until she got tired, and then sat down in it. Then I pushed her until she recuperated and was ready to push the chair again herself.

As Mom's health deteriorated, my role as caregiver increased. She was no longer able to get to doctor's appointments on her own, so I'd take her. Getting to the senior's center had become difficult as her mobility decreased. She started to become a prisoner in our house, which caused her life to center on ours. Eventually she moved into a new assisted living facility, which was like a five-star hotel. Here she once again came alive with all the social stimulation.

When she moved out of our house after ten years together, it was like losing a child. Milo and I had all of a sudden become empty-nesters. Up until then we had only spent one year alone. Now we were together all the time. I only had him to talk to on a daily basis, and he had no one to run interference for him during dinnertime conversation. Mom passed away in 2006 at the age of ninety-one, leaving the relationship after we had all been together for fourteen years. Milo and I lost an important member of our family, and though we didn't talk about it, both of us were devastated. I put on a brave face, not knowing how to deal with the sadness of death. We just tried to pretend that everything was OK.

Careers and Money

Milo and I had spent a long time in university, and now it was time to focus on our careers, earn some money, and get ahead in life. Milo was one of thirteen people in the world who manufactured pheromones, preparing chemical solutions in really small quantities, from a thimbleful to half a cup. He was creative and resourceful at work. Not only was he a chemist, but he had also physically built the lab that he worked in. To say he was handy would be an understatement.

Milo always had a love-hate relationship with work. Being very intelligent, things came to him quickly and he had definite ideas about how things should be done. Unfortunately, others didn't always see things the way he did, or the quality of their work was not up to his standards, and this frustrated him to no end. He generally had someone junior to him working in the lab, who was responsible for making the products and following a well-defined procedure. Often the person would make a mistake somewhere along the way, and the chemical reaction would fail. Milo was amazed and apoplectic about how the person couldn't follow the procedure, about the waste of very expensive chemicals, and about how the mistake caused their production schedule to fall behind. There was always drama at Milo's work, and he came home almost every night with a story or complaint about what stupid thing someone had done.

I had gone into corporate finance and was hired to do small-business banking right out of graduate school. I had always been great with numbers, and working with clients' financial needs was a good fit for me. Banks, however, are full of rules and full of people who are responsible for enforcing those rules, whether the rules make sense or not. It was very frustrating for me, especially when my manager was away and I had to run around getting signatures and making the same explanations over and over again to people who were not directly involved, when I was fully capable of taking responsibility. I was looking out for our clients, but the bureaucratic waste of time made me less effective instead of supporting me.

Work felt like running into one brick wall after another, and I was in alignment with Milo that life would be so much easier if it weren't for some of the people or rules we had to work with. We both felt that people did not appreciate us; we felt both undervalued and afraid to ask for what we wanted. We were caught in the same trap, complaining about work and how poorly things were run. As painful as all our dead-end complaints were, they gave us common ground in our relationship.

After ten years, a crisis at work brought my banking career to a close and sent me out to explore what I was passionate about doing. I spent almost a year deciding what I wanted to do. For my next job, I wanted to be passionate about something. After many months I came to the decision that self-employment was my best option. I registered for the Executive Coaching course at Royal Roads University, and entered into the world of small-business and management coaching. There were all sorts of things to learn about running my own business, about developing confidence in myself and my ability to bring value to my clients. I loved the learning and the challenge, but I was in no hurry to get back into the same stressful rat race. In my own business I was going to work at my own pace, even if that meant I would earn a little less money or that it would take more time to become successful.

I loved having control of my own time. I loved being able to go golfing on a Friday morning at six and start work at eleven. Time freedom and not having to answer to anyone but myself was wonderful. When it came to summer holidays or taking time off, we only had to work around Milo's schedule. Milo always accumulated lots of overtime, so for the first time in our lives we were able to take three-week vacations. We could take more time to go skiing, plus I had time flexibility to take courses whenever I wanted. Basically, Milo and I had more time to play together and enjoy each other's company. Life was so much more pleasant that I never wanted to give this up. I was determined to do whatever it took to be successful in my coaching career.

Though I was now self-employed and making less money, Milo and I had a long history of being good money managers. I was a pragmatist and Milo was a shopping avoider. The term for the two of us was frugal—not cheap, frugal. We only spent money on things we valued. When it came to spending money, I always asked myself the question, "Do I really need this or could I live without it?" I usually chose to live without it.

Upstairs where my mother spent most of her time, we had the antique furniture that she brought with her from Manitoba. In my dressing room was the antique furniture that I bought when I moved to Vancouver to go to graduate school. Our living room was furnished with Milo's furniture that he had bought from an auction house when he finished graduate school. We had the ugliest couch with a wagon wheel pattern on it, but it just wouldn't wear out. That couch was built in the 1970s and the material they used was like steel. I bought only one new car during our whole relationship; I still have that car and likely will have it until it dies. Milo had two new vehicles in eighteen years. The car companies didn't get rich on us. Without even trying, Milo and I had a relatively small environmental footprint.

Milo and I were in alignment when it came to money. We

had established a joint account to pay for household operating expenses, which we split three ways, and Milo and I split the mortgage payment. Otherwise Milo's money was his money and my money was my money. We did spend money on things that we really valued. We always purchased good quality equipment to support our golf and skiing activities. Also, I spent a ton of money on plants and soil for my flower gardens; there I purchased what I wanted and did not worry about whether it was practical. My gardens were like my children: I tended them, nurtured them, and coaxed them to life and beauty. They radiated my love throughout the neighborhood; they were my pride and joy.

Being in the finance industry, I knew the importance of starting to save money for our retirement at an early age. In the early years our mortgage felt really large for us, but we started to put money away on a monthly basis for our retirement anyhow. The only joint asset we had was our house; everything else was separate. Given our natural inclination to being frugal, we didn't argue about money. But then again, when everything is separate, what is there to argue about? Maybe part of the reason that everything was separate had to do with the lack of commitment to get married, rather than simply being a practical way for us to handle money and avoid arguments. There was always a part of me that wanted to be independent, and I wanted to be able to take care of myself.

Romance

What is romance? I had never really thought about whether Milo and I were romantic, but I have come to realize that it is an important part of married life. True romance is doing the small things for our partners that they like, regardless of whether we like doing them or not. Romance is about putting your partner first.

Milo and I were great friends and companions. We spent quality time together and we expressed our love through touch, spending many hours on the wagon wheel couch giving each other foot rubs. I would often fall asleep on a Friday night watching a movie as Milo massaged my feet. This felt wonderful and I felt truly loved. We also gave each other massages, and always had a friendly fight as to whose turn it was to receive the next massage. It was easily settled when we opened the massage table and looked at where the legs were set. At his six-foot-one versus my five-foot-one, there was no doubt as to who had had the last massage!

My passion for cooking and preparing wonderful food was an expression of my love and an act of service to Milo. In hindsight, I likely missed the mark in terms of what Milo wanted to receive. He always said that food was fuel for him; he didn't really care about what he ate. Yet when we had company over for dinner he remarked about how we ate like this all the time, and there was pride in his voice. Whenever I was in Vancouver, I stopped in at a deli on the way home and purchased dessert for him. I knew he had a sweet tooth and loved dessert. Yet I always got the feeling that he never received this gift as an act of love; there was always something not quite right about the dessert. Around food there were mixed signals when it came to romance.

Kayaking down the River of Our Relationship

Milo and I had what felt like a really great relationship. The kayak we chose for our journey down the relationship river seemed to work pretty well for us. We both loved to be outdoors and I loved adventure. Neither of us was interested in accumulating a lot of stuff, so we didn't need a big, fancy motor launch. Nor did we need a big boat for all of our children! We had lots of smooth water during our trip down the river. We lived with ease and in quiet harmony for the most part, doing fun things together. I loved that he was a very intelligent, well-read man; it made for many interesting nights around the campfire when we pulled into shore for the evening. We had a very good life together and I had a ton of fun doing what I loved to do. What more was there to a relationship?

SELF-REFLECTION QUESTIONS

- What expectations did you have about marriage when you first got together with your partner?
- What were you passionate about in your relationship?
- What were the things you loved to contribute in your relationship?
- What do you like to do that fills your soul with joy and happiness?
- What was working in your relationship?
- What did the two of you have in common?
- What is one romantic thing that your partner wanted to receive?
- What is one romantic thing that you wanted to receive?

CHAPTER 3

Major White Water

WHEN I WORKED IN corporate banking the attitude was that when you went to work, you should park your personal problems at the door. Of course, the reality was that I took all of myself to work, and I took all of myself home to our relationship. There was a dynamic interaction between stress at work and stress at home. When things were spiraling down at work they also seemed to spiral down at home. As I felt more stress at work I had less tolerance for all the challenges that Milo seemed to face at work, and I was less willing to listen to his work stories. I often felt frustrated with Milo and wondered why he didn't just go out and get another job. My unhappiness at work and lack of understanding of Milo's situation put significant pressure on our relationship.

Compartmentalizing life between work and home was like trying to paddle my boat down many rivers at the same time. Impossible. Work and home life were intricately connected and could not be separated. The truth is that all the water of our lives, our life energy, flows down one river. What happens in one area affects all other areas. When it was raining heavily and a storm was brewing in one area of my life, there was more rain in all other areas, too. All this rain increased the volume of water flowing down the river of my relationship. The size and speed of the rapids — that is, the emotional turmoil on our relationship river — increased, testing Milo's and my ability to shoot the rapids and keep our kayak upright. To be successful at navigating the fast-flowing river, we needed to be aware of and present to our surroundings, and especially alert to the sky above us. Looking back, we travelled through some very difficult rapids in our emotional life, and went over some very steep waterfalls in our relationship.

I had been at the bank for five years when the first of a series of three catastrophic events were set off, one behind the other, that changed the course of my life. These events contributed to stress-related illness and caused me to abandon my finance career, and they were the catalyst for a very turbulent time in our relationship. When I got to the end of this series of events I felt personally devastated, and I didn't know what to do or how to help myself change and heal the past.

Stormy Weather at Work

The first event occurred with my coworker, Roy, who was hit by a car on a beautiful, spring day as he was riding his bicycle to work. Roy ended up in a coma and his colleagues were distraught with worry that he was going to die. At this time I worked in a specialized lending group of eleven people, doing multimillion dollar loans for large corporate clients. Including Roy, three of us did similar work, and after Roy's accident I added half of his portfolio to my workload. He never came back to work and his position was never replaced.

Category Four Tropical Storm

In the fall of the same year, an even more traumatic incident occurred when my boss, Joe, melted down in rage. I had noticed that Joe had been acting strangely for a couple of months. He had started smoking again after sixteen years, and he was telling dirty jokes at work, which he had never done before. I started to keep my distance from him and only interacted with him on client matters.

In October, just before the Canadian Thanksgiving weekend, our vice president was in Toronto for the quarterly departmental meetings. I saw Joe speaking to Cheryl, one of the support staff, and sensed something was wrong. Cheryl was sitting down and Joe was standing bent over with both hands on the arms of her chair, glaring down at her. I walked over and asked him to ease up. He raised his head, turned on me, and started yelling, "Who do you think you are, interfering with me?"

I saw the anger in his eyes and heard the venom in his voice. He kept coming closer to me, crowding my body space. All I could think about was how I was going to get out of there. I slowly started to back away from him so that I could get to the front of the office where there were more people.

We had a few moments of calm before the real storm hit. Joe had gone out for coffee, and when he came back he walked up to my desk and asked me to come into his private office. I imagined myself being trapped behind closed doors with him and the alarm bells went off in my head. I told Joe that if he wanted to speak to me he could do it here in front of everyone; I had nothing to hide.

I could feel the fury and rage emanating from his body. His fists were shoved deep into his trouser pockets and they were rapidly pumping up and down. He spewed threats at me about having me fired when our vice president was back in the office. He went on and on and on, and all I could think about was what would happen if those fists came out of his pockets. I stood my ground, in high-heeled shoes and a turquoise blue business suit, and looked him directly in the eye. My coworkers all stood around us in a circle with incredulous looks on their faces, too stunned to take action and call the police. We were all hoping Joe would just run out of steam and eventually wind down without hurting me or anyone else. It was the scariest and blackest day in my whole work history.

Joe was given an office in a different building until an investigation could be held a month later. Even so, my coworkers and I allowed our imaginations to run wild, thinking that one day he would walk through the front door with a shotgun and kill us. Joe knew where I lived, and I feared for my safety and that of my family. Every day when I went to work, I carefully opened the door to the garage and looked around to make sure it was empty, that he wasn't hiding there, waiting for me. I threaded my keys through my fingers, forming "brass knuckles" to protect myself as I walked to my car. I lived in fear and anxiety for a whole year and it slowly wore me down. I became needier and less available in my relationship with Milo. I was constantly exhausted.

Things got worse before they got better. Joe had been removed from our workplace and it was a relief to have him gone, but now I had my job, his job, and half of Roy's job to do. I worked in a specialized department and it was impossible to find someone to come in and help us on a temporary basis. I had a strong sense of moral obligation to the company and to the clients to hold everything together and pretend as if it was business as usual. But it wasn't business as usual; I was crumbling.

More Thunderstorms

If all of this wasn't enough, one more catastrophe struck to add additional worry and burden to my life. My best friend at work was hit by a car on her way home from work one dark, rainy night, and now she was at home with a concussion and minor brain injuries. We didn't know how long it would be before she could return to work. I missed her. She had been my confidant at work, and now she was experiencing her own hell. I was numb from all of this worry and sadness. When would it end?

To sum it up, I was experiencing fear and anxiety, and at the same time I had acquired a crushing workload. I had no sense of my own physical and mental limitations and kept pushing myself to do more. As the stress mounted, I began to experience symptoms of mental illness. My memory started to shut down like a computer when the screen goes blank. People had conversations with me, and unless I needed the information immediately, I didn't remember the conversation. My boss asked me a question about something we had talked about the day before, and I couldn't even remember that we had had a discussion. Not being able to access my memory struck fear in my belly. What was happening to me? My memory and intelligence were my main assets — without them I would not be able to work. Thus another worry was added to the pile.

I had just received my Chartered Financial Analyst designation after three long years of grueling work, and now it was all wasted. I couldn't even remember a conversation. How was I going to remember all the financial details that were involved in making a multimillion dollar lending decision? Sadness and fear permeated my body, and I felt like I was walking around in a perpetual fog. I finally went to the doctor and yes, I was suffering from extreme stress. I had to accept that I was not invincible. I needed to take time off work to regain my mental health.

SELF-REFLECTION QUESTIONS

- How would you rate your level of stress?
- What is causing you stress?
- What are you doing to combat the stress?
- What do you notice about your energy levels?
- What do you notice about your mental processing abilities?

Steadying Our Relationship Boat

Relationships are affected by internal and external forces, and by the choices we make. It takes dedication and skill to shoot the boiling rapids of work, family, and community commitments. Our relationship boat had sustained some puncture wounds from having to maneuver through these treacherous waters. Unfortunately several things got in the way of me stopping to help repair our boat. The first was that I was in denial about how damaged our boat was; I couldn't imagine not being in relationship with Milo. Second, I was so busy trying to keep myself together emotionally that I did not notice the water our boat was carrying. Due to the drama and disappointment at work, I didn't have any personal resources left to help repair the relationship. Finally, I did not actually know how to be more intimate and loving, to even begin to repair the boat. We needed help, but rather than seeking it, we just tried to cope with the situation.

Milo was going through his own difficult times at work, and the ill effects of stress were taking a toll on him, too. I was tired and short-tempered and didn't have the energy to listen to his problems and complaints. I had listened to him complain about work for years, and I was fed up with it. It became a competition between our egos as to whose problems and feelings of overwhelm were greater. Needless to say, conflict erupted. Sadly, neither of us was available to be empathetic and understanding for the other. Our relationship entered a very difficult time.

We started to argue. We grew distant. We no longer gave each other foot rubs in the evening on the couch; I was too tired and just fell asleep. Our sex life declined sharply, as neither of us was feeling very loving toward the other person. We just could not find the loving spark that would bring us together. If we did have sex, it felt like we were coming from a dark, angry, frustrated place, where we both needed to release energy or explode.

The problems in our relationship came to a head in the summer of 1998, when I was trying to plan our holidays. Milo was not willing to be engaged in planning our holiday that year, and with everything else falling apart in my world, this was the last straw. In fact, Milo had been withdrawing from taking an active role in routine household decisions, as well. It was like he didn't care anymore and was happy to leave the running of the house to me. I was too overwhelmed to look after the house on my own, however. I became fed up with trying to force him to participate in decisions; if he wasn't going to participate, then I wasn't going to go on holidays with him. I was exhausted.

Fortunately, relief finally came at work. I scaled back to thirty-five hours a week and took responsibility for only one job at a time. The stress started to dissipate and I felt less and less like melting down. Milo eventually got involved in planning our holiday. We spent a lot of time that year camping in the wilderness, which brought peace to our souls. It was an opportunity for me to get clear about why I was sharing my life with Milo in the first place.

I came to realize that there were three main qualities in Milo that I really respected. The first was that he was a kind, gentle, and generous man. Second, he was intelligent and very good at his work. Third, he was physically active and liked outdoor activities. We had some long conversations about the qualities that we valued in each other. After the holidays he seemed to come out of his funk, and we worked on being more supportive of each other. Our relationship returned to calm waters. We began referring to those times as the dark days of our relationship.

SELF-REFLECTION QUESTIONS

- What do you really not want to face about your relationship?
- Where are you feeling like you just don't know what to do?
- What is happening outside your relationship that is not working for you?
- How are you responding to these situations?
- What could you do differently to change these situations?
- Who could help you make these changes?

Now imagine that you are your partner, and ask these same questions from your partner's perspective. It is important to understand what is occurring with our partners, as this allows us to have more empathy for them.

- What is happening outside your relationship that is not working for your partner?
- What is causing your partner stress outside of your relationship?
- How is your partner responding to these situations?
- What could you do to be more supportive?
- To whom could the two of you reach out for help?

Invite your partner to come and join you. We can't command our partners to join us in resolving a situation; we can only invite them. We can, however, take responsibility for resolving the issues that affect us directly.

Leaving the Bank

I was driving to work one beautiful sunny day, and the sun was shining on the snow-covered peaks of the North Shore Mountains, and I thought, "Oh, how beautiful. I am so happy." Then I realized that my happiness was only an idea, a concept. I *thought* that I *should* feel happy seeing this beautiful scene, but I really did not feel the joy in my body. I knew right then that if I didn't start doing something different I was going to become ill. I had worked for the bank for a few more years after the tropical storm named Joe, and I now realized that I was just not happy. My memory was not as good as before and I had been declined a promotion. I felt constant stress to keep up and perform at a senior level in my job. In my heart, I felt disappointed. I had not fully achieved my goals for my finance career: I had not made it to the level of vice president. I had sacrificed my health and the quality of my relationship for work, and now it all seemed for nothing.

There is a difference between making an intellectual decision that we are finished and ready to leave, and emotionally accepting that something is over. I felt sad and angry about leaving the bank. I had made a huge investment in my finance career, and now it was coming to an end. I felt elated as I left the job behind, looking forward to new adventures, and at the same time felt very sad. The universe had signaled that it was time to move on. When I accepted the truth of this, the stars aligned in my favor and the bank made my position redundant, which allowed me to move on and choose a new career. Still, it wasn't until many years later that I resolved the grief around the loss of this career.

A South Pacific Adventure

Before I could even begin to think about what I wanted next, I needed some time to decompress from the pressure and stress under which I had been working for the past four years. I love adventure and travel, and I asked Milo to choose any place in the world he would like to go, where he would be happy. It was our tenth anniversary of living together, and I wanted to go away on a belated honeymoon. We ended up traveling to the beautiful tropical islands of the Kingdom of Tonga in the South Pacific.

It was a dream holiday for me. When we arrived in Nuku'alofa, the capital of Tonga, we took a sailboat to the Fafa Island Resort. The resort occupied the whole island; it had ten grass huts inland from the ocean and another ten superior huts on the ocean. We stayed in the inland huts for the first week, and then returned for an additional four-day stay to celebrate our tenth anniversary in one of the huts on the ocean. It was beautiful and magical: lovely sand beaches, palm trees swaying in the breeze, and the blue water of the South Pacific stretching wherever we looked.

After breakfast we would slowly walk around the island looking for shells. When we got hot it was time to get out the snorkeling gear and snorkel around the small coral reef just off the island. Then it was time for lunch, followed by a snooze and reading time in the oversized hammocks strung up in between the trees. Some days we went on a snorkeling adventure for the day and came back just in time for a game of beach volleyball.

Then it was time for a quick swim to wash off the sand and a shower before dinner. We walked down fragrant, hibiscus-lined pathways as we made our way to dinner, which was served on the deck overlooking the ocean. It was magical.

We travelled to many different islands and resorts within the Kingdom of Tonga. Sometimes we had access to a kayak, and we'd kayak around whatever island we were staying on. One day we rented scooters for the day to explore the island. I had never been on a scooter, and as we were going down a mud road we came across a big pothole filled with water. Needless to say I wiped out on my scooter. I was covered from the waist down with red mud—yuck! Of course Milo laughed at my predicament, but no worries, there was a beach close by. I went for a swim and we washed the bike off.

I loved our adventure together, and a month of travelling was way too short for me, so I carried on to Vietnam for another month, while Milo went home and back to work. When I got back home it seemed like Milo was pleased to see me, and we returned to a comfortable way of life together. I was ready to begin the search for a new line of work and find a full-time job. These were the questions I asked myself as I set out on this new journey.

SELF-REFLECTION QUESTIONS

- What makes you feel happy?
- When do you have a sense of joy?
- What gets in the way of you being happy?
- What holds you back the most in your life?
- What made you happy when you were young?
- What were the major turning points in your life?
- What was happening at the time?
- How were you feeling at each turning point?
- What relationships are most fulfilling for you?

- What relationships don't serve you?
- What are you passionate about?
- What do you really want?

Internal White Waters

Milo and I had faced our tropical storm together and survived. Our kayak was a little damaged after the storm, but over time it seemed that we were able to patch everything up. Our trip to Tonga for our tenth anniversary seemed to smooth over the damage, and once again everything seemed to be good in our relationship. We continued to paddle smoothly down our relationship river while I sought a new career. However, external events such as my decision to become self-employed had stirred up the emotional turmoil and stress that I had experienced during the tropical storm. It appeared that the stress had not healed itself with time but lay dormant, waiting for a new opportunity to express itself. Once again, I knew I was in trouble and had to do something to combat the overwhelming fear. I searched for resources that would help me deal with my insecurities.

CHAPTER 4

New Tools for My Backpack

AT A TIME WHEN MILO and I seemed to be floating along very peacefully on the relationship river, I wanted space to explore more deeply my questions about happiness. I also needed to figure out how to combat the stress that was plaguing my body.

Exploring — Looking for Help

I asked Milo to pull our kayak out of the water and make camp along the river shore while I went off and explored the area. I found a path that led away from the river and joined a small dirt road that took me to the local village. As I spoke to the people in the village I found that the elders were teaching their people some very interesting things. Craving new learning and open to insights, I became really excited about what I was hearing. After a few days I went back to camp full of enthusiasm and excitement and told Milo everything. But he was not interested in visiting the village and all the people that I had met. When more gatherings occurred in the village, I went back on my own and listened to the elders share their knowledge.

Over the next eight years, I studied with experts in the fields of personal and human development. They became my life teachers, my elders. They opened up a whole new world for me, a way of thinking that I did not know even existed. As I moved from one teacher to the next, my learning changed and became deeper. This work became my salvation. From the brink of a severe stress breakdown, it supported me to become emotionally resourceful and find a true sense of happiness in my life.

Learning from Elders

It was by following my intuition that I came across my first workshop leader, T. Harv Eker. His name was presented to me by three different people, and I decided this was a sign. When I attended his introductory seminar, I knew there was something there for me. I remembered advice I had been given, to follow what called me, and this seemed to be the first stop.

Harv's programs focused a lot on our relationship with money. This is where I first got in contact with the shame that I felt about being poor as a teenager and not having clothing that was as nice as the kids that lived in town. It was in these workshops that I faced a lot of the fear, anger, and grief that surrounded the circumstances with my old boss, Joe. I was starting to see the world from a different perspective.

At one of Harv's events I heard Jack Canfield speak, the coauthor of the Chicken Soup for the Soul series. Jack's work attracted me: I needed to address my lack of self-esteem and confidence. As you have seen, I thought that part of my stress came from my belief that I was not good enough. I believed that other people were better and smarter than me, and that I needed to be an expert before I could bring value to people. Things started to change for me at my first workshop with Jack, in Las Vegas.

Each morning we gave each other hugs in silence for ten minutes. I had a cynical thought: Who gives hugs in the real world? Giving hugs is fine when we are at a workshop, but at home, who would I give hugs to other than family and a few close friends? No one. So I assigned myself a project, to give out one hundred hugs to people who were not part of the seminar. I started giving hugs and counting.

On my way home from the conference, I was sitting in the San Francisco airport and it occurred to me that if giving one hundred hugs was impressive, then imagine what might happen if I gave out one thousand hugs. Being a person who takes action, I went and bought a journal and documented my goal: "I will have hugged 1,001 people by December 31, 2004, at midnight." I started immediately with the pilot who was waiting to fly us to Vancouver. I asked him, "Have you had a hug today?" He looked at me with a smile and said, "What is this about?" I looked him in the eye and told him that I would like him to have a great flight, and then I gave him a hug. At that time I had no idea of all the profound learning that would occur, or that giving hugs would be the beginning of my tearing down the walls of Plexiglas that kept me feeling separate from others.

On August 15, 2004, when I left the seminar, I had given 111 hugs, and had 890 hugs to go. For the next three and half months I asked store clerks, waitresses, people in my Toastmasters club, my friends, and basically anybody else that I came across if they would like a hug. Every morning I gave Milo a hug before he went to work. Before that we had rarely hugged; we'd just say good-bye. Every day, in the journal that I had bought in San Francisco, I recorded my hugs.

At first I felt strange and embarrassed asking people if they would like a hug, especially the clerk in my grocery store, but I did it anyway. Eventually I started to become known as an outgoing person with lots of upbeat energy. There was so much positive self-expression bottled up in me that it came pouring out when I made it OK to express myself. The more hugs I gave, the more my sense of being separate from others began to melt away.

On December 31, 2004, at ten in the evening, I still had sixty-six hugs to go. I was sitting in a cabin in Whistler playing games with my friends after a day of skiing. I got up from the table, got dressed, and drove to town on a cold New Year's Eve; it must have been minus fifteen degrees Celsius outside. I felt alone and at the same time determined. Where could I find a lot of people to hug?

I went to the Second Cup coffee shop and approached an older man just inside the door. "Would you help me out and give me a hug? I have a goal of giving 1,001 hugs by midnight tonight."

"Sure," he said, and gave me a hug.

I went to each person in the coffee shop and did the same thing and got one more hug. There was a table of four people, and they asked me how many hugs I had left to go. I said fifty-two, and then they started to count down for me, with each successive hug I gave. Fifty-one, fifty ... until there were only two left to go. In a lull with no new customers, one of the baristas brought two girls out from behind the counter who had been too shy to receive a hug from me, and they were my one-thousandth and one-thousand-and-first hugs given. It was so fitting that the two people who helped me finish my goal were likely just like me, self-conscious and shy.

From what seemed like a silly idea, I gained a huge amount of learning. Because I decided to risk looking stupid, to take action and document what happened along the way, I challenged my limitations and reaped profound benefits. This adventure required me to trust my intuition and take action. I started to make heartfelt connections with people, even if only for a few moments. My request made lots of people laugh and feel good. I started to feel a sense of joy and happiness in my body. I learned that people are happy to help if we make it easy for them. I also learned that it is really important to get across the finish line. It builds confidence to finish more projects. I learned that when I start something, and complete it, the joy and fulfillment last a long time.

SELF-REFLECTION QUESTIONS

- How often do you ignore your intuition?
- When have you had a good idea and didn't take action?
- What opportunities might you be missing?

In the rest of this chapter you'll read about my personal development journey and about the tools I gathered along the way that helped me change my thinking and behaviors. There are a lot of tools available that can help us to change our lives. I am sharing the ones that I used and found most practical.

During my journey of self-knowledge, I stored my tools in what I affectionately called "my blue backpack." Having this backpack of tools at my disposal gave me a sense of comfort. I kept my tools in mind when I needed support in a challenging situation. The tools you'll read about in this chapter helped me to be more grounded and less likely to have my mind spin out of control into a prolonged emotional reaction. I often pull these self-awareness tools out of my backpack when I need to manage challenges in the moment. Many of them have now become so habitual and automatic that I don't even know that I am using them.

I acquired the initial tools for my blue backpack from Harv's and Jack's live events. I have also purchased CDs from other personal development leaders, and listened to them many times when in the car or going for a run. Hearing something once is great, but hearing it many times is far more powerful, as the ideas start to become second nature. These tools helped me build my self-confidence and look at the world from a different perspective. Constant practice was the biggest factor in my success. Going to workshops is great, but to really excel, we must practice.

I discovered that I could learn from many different people. It turned out that a teacher was anyone who imparted an idea to me or created an environment in which I could learn. It could be a workshop leader, another workshop participant, a mastermind partner, my golf coach, or anyone, even Milo. Teaching and learning don't have to take place in a classroom. The classroom is just the beginning. Then I needed to put my learning into action.

Practice

Practice, practice, practice. I can't say it often enough. The mind loves new information—we read it, think about it, and then store it away for when we need it. We go to a workshop, listen to the speaker, write notes, do some exercises, and store it away. For most of us, however, there is a large gap between reading or hearing information and then putting it into action in our lives. If we throw the information tools into our backpacks without taking them out and using them often, they will get rusty, and eventually we will throw them out thinking them useless.

On my journey I preferred to be the tortoise rather than the hare. I attended only two to three courses a year, and I took action on as many things as I could. Three things helped me put my learning into action. First, I made a list of the top three things that I had learned from each course and wanted to practice in my life. Second, I talked to people about what I had learned and how I could implement it. Sometimes I became a teacher for others, which helped solidify in my mind what I wanted to do myself. This required me to be vulnerable and share with others what was not working in my life. I was OK with that because it helped me become committed to making a change. The third thing I did was to join several mastermind groups over the years.

In a mastermind group, three to six people get together on a regular basis to share their objectives, report their progress, and talk about their challenges. Often a group forms when the leader of a workshop offers it as an opportunity to the people who attended. There are some basic principles to keep in mind for a successful group. The people in the group need to form a common objective for the group and to form agreements on the structure and frequency of the meetings. People need to make a commitment to show up. And there has to be a way to deal with people who aren't committed. If one person lacks commitment it will affect the whole group. When it is time for a group to disband, hold a closing meeting to reflect on the original objectives. Bring your group's time to completion by honoring accomplishments and expressing gratitude for your fellow group members.

In the remainder of this chapter, I share some of the key tools for growth and development that I stored in my backpack, ready for use on a regular basis.

Free Coaching

I have learned silence from the talkative, tolerance from the intolerant, and kindness from the unkind; yet strangely, I am ungrateful to these teachers. —Kahlil Gibran

As I immersed myself in personal development, I realized that some of my most profound learning came from people who pissed me off. I call this "free coaching," and I am grateful to these people for showing me what I needed to learn. Significant learning can be accomplished in any situation simply by being self-aware. By asking questions like "What role did I play in this?" and "What could I have done differently?" Answering these questions honestly helped me to become very self-observant. I learned to sit down and write out my thoughts in a journal. Just sitting down and writing whatever came into my mind was a wonderful way to gain knowledge about myself and my thinking patterns. In this way, I was slowly changing my thinking and my behaviors in my relationships. Are you looking for free coaching? Try your spouse or partner, your ex-partner, your children, your friends, your colleagues, and anyone else who drops into your life.

▶ **TOOL: SELF-OBSERVATION QUESTIONS**

- What role did I play in this situation?
- What could I have done differently?

TOOL: JOURNALING

There are lots of different ways to journal. It is very important to have a dedicated book of some kind. You can use any notebook with blank pages, or you can purchase a special journal that feels sacred to you. I always purchase attractive journals to use as a sacred place to explore my thoughts.

Ways to use your journal:
• When you read the questions posed in this book, write down your answers. This will help you discover your thinking at a deeper level.
• When you have a new learning or discovery, write it down.
• When something upsets you, write it down. Then explore the situation from different perspectives. You can do this by asking yourself provocative questions and then answering them. Provocative questions are questions that cause you to think, that challenge your ego's desire to be right. Look at the questions in this book for examples.
• When you notice your mind is mulling something over and over, write it down and explore it.

As I wrote this book it was fascinating to go back and read ten years' worth of journals. I had written about five key underlying behaviors that I wanted to change, and it was interesting to notice how long it took for each one of them to disappear.

Taming Mind Chatter

When I started my business, there was always a sense of anxiety that I wouldn't be OK. This was one of my first big challenges. I would sit at my home office desk and feel dread in my stomach, my body vibrating at a low hum. I was terrified that I wouldn't be able to earn enough money to look after myself. At night my mind kept chattering and chattering away, and I could feel the sickness in my stomach as I tried to go to sleep. If I woke up in the middle of the night, this mind chatter came back to plague me.

There is a saying that whatever we focus on, whether positive or negative, grows. Like worry. It was hard not to focus on the feeling of dread in my stomach, but I chose to focus on something else instead. I chose to focus on becoming happy. After all, that was the main intention behind everything I was doing and all the changes I was making. Doing Morning Pages helped me combat anxiety and negative mind chatter.

▶ **TOOL: MORNING PAGES**

Morning Pages is a journaling technique. Get up in the morning, set your pen to paper, and keep writing for approximately two pages or until there is nothing left to write. When you write, don't stop and think, just keep writing and dump the noise that is going on in your mind. With Morning Pages you are dumping mind chatter. The result is more mental clarity and freedom.

Who Am I?

Maybe we look to find a new direction because our relationships or jobs are ending, or maybe we have simply become aware that the time is right. When I came home from Tonga and Vietnam after leaving my job at the bank, I made a commitment to myself: I would find a way to travel more and have more adventures. But first I needed to find a new line of work. I had money in the bank from my severance package, so that summer I turned my full attention to finding out what I was passionate about. Every day in my home office I opened up a self-help book and did the exercises, trying to figure it out. I was responding to a call that everyone feels at one time or another. We all need to know who we are, what we want, and what we are passionate about — whether our focus is finding a new line of work or finding a new relationship. It is only when we know ourselves that we can find what we are looking for.

My self-development started with writing my eulogy: How did I want to be remembered? This is what I wrote:

> Jacque was a kind and giving person who generously shared her knowledge with others. Her home and a bountiful table were always extended to friends. An extremely high level of energy allowed her to undertake a broad range of activities, from cooking and gardening to skiing and golf. Her adventurous nature and determination propelled her forward to tackle the unknown. Jacque was quick to understand new concepts and embrace them. She had excellent intuition with regard to people, being able to talk to them and make an accurate assessment of the situation. She was loved by the people she worked with for being a self-starter and supporting them with coaching to overcome their challenges. Jacque was never afraid of a challenge and worked with enthusiasm and vigor to get the job done. Being mechanically adept, she was proud of being able to undertake many tasks traditionally done by men. This allowed her to be a driving force in her home, tackling renovations and creating a comfortable life for herself and her family.

▶ ## TOOL: WHO ARE YOU?

- How would you like to be remembered?
- What would people say about you?
- How do people feel about you?

Key Attributes

My next self-discovery step was to take an inventory of my top attributes. What did I already have going for me? I noted that I was action oriented, adventurous, a self-starter, and generous, among other things.

Action Oriented

Once I decided what I wanted, I always seemed to know what the appropriate actions were to get there. When it came to accomplishing a task, I instinctively knew how to get from A to B, and after that there was no stopping me. Once I developed clarity about what I wanted to achieve, I would feel the motivation and excitement in my body that propelled me to move ahead and take action. I never did anything slowly; as long as I was taking action, I was happy.

In eleventh grade, I decided that I wanted to go to the University of Winnipeg. I wanted to start taking my senior-year courses over the summer so that in the fall I would have only two high school courses left and could start my first year of university. To do this I had to finish eleventh grade two months early. I applied myself with dogged determination to finish all the extra work that my teachers gave me so that I could execute my plan. I was doing something no one else in my school was doing. Academically it was a great move for me. In my senior year I earned the best grades I ever had, and found out just how good it felt to study hard and succeed in school.

Adventurous

I am adventurous by nature. When I was twenty-four, I was ready to leave my job. Did I want a new job? Not really. Did I want to go back to school? No—I had just finished a two-year college degree, and going back to school didn't feel exciting. Did I want to travel? Now here was an idea, but where would I go? I decided on Europe because it seemed safe as I was traveling on my own. I determined how much money I needed to save and how quickly I could do that. I put all my belongings in storage. I headed off to Europe for four months, and ended up staying a whole year.

I started with a monthlong tour of Britain and then stayed with family friends in a beautiful little town in Holland. I loved this city. The streets were all done in cobblestones, and the buildings were all made out of stone, with house after house joined together in rows.

My next destinations were Austria and Switzerland. One day as I was writing in my journal, I met a Scotsman who was living with a Swiss girl. I took a risk staying at their place and we went out to a pub that night with him all dressed up in his kilt. Good fun, if a little shocking for the Swiss people. In Grindelwald, I could see snow up on the high alpine peaks, so I took a train to a small town nearby and walked from the town all the way up a path to the top of the mountain peak where I could see the snow. It was a brilliant fall day, and the hike took me about four hours. I was hungry, but I refused to stop for lunch until I reached the snow.

Over the next two months, I went to Italy, Greece, Egypt, France, Spain, Germany, and then back to London. Each country brought with it new challenges and delights. I saw lots of beautiful places, got myself out of a few tight spots with the help of other travelers, and even went to one country where I hadn't intended to go. Following an unexpected meeting with an acquaintance from my tiny hometown, I traveled with him and his friends to Egypt. I rode on a camel, hiked around the pyramids, and saw the Sphinx. Afterward I decided that I wasn't ready to go back to Winnipeg, so I returned to London and worked there for the next eight months. This is where I met some of my best lifelong friends.

Self-Starter

No one has ever had to give me direction and tell me what to do. I have always had lots of initiative to take on new tasks with an abundance of energy. I seem to have a very quick understanding of new concepts and a natural ability to apply them to apparently unrelated areas of life. I can take things that seem complicated and make them accessible for other people. When I left the bank, I decided that I wanted to become a really good golfer. I started taking weekly golf lessons. Soon I realized that what I was learning in golf also applied to what entrepreneurs need to do to be successful in business, so I developed a set of courses called Swing into Leadership, using golf as a metaphor for a number of concepts that are valuable in business and in life.

Generous

You've already heard my wagon wheel couch story, so you know how frugal I am by nature, but I'm also generous. When I got my first job at fifteen, I bought french fries for my high school friends. Even though their parents were better off than my parents, and having french fries was probably not a significant event for them, it was a big deal for me to be able to share what I had. Entertaining and feeding people always gave me joy. This continued as an adult, when Milo and I hosted many dinner parties and barbeques. I loved the planning and the preparing of food and then serving our guests, who were always in awe of the beautiful food presented. These dinner parties were a way for me to share my love. At the same time I received recognition and acknowledgement, and felt love in return.

My key attributes are:

- Action oriented
- Adventurous
- Decisive
- Driven
- Energetic
- Generous
- Learner
- Practical
- Self-starter

▶ **TOOL: KEY ATTRIBUTES**

Note the following things in a journal, starting when you were fifteen years old and then every five years thereafter:

- What was I doing that I really enjoyed?
- What successes was I having?
- What was I doing that made me different from others?
- What attracted people to me?
- What would my close friends say about me?

Notice any trends that occur over the different time periods as you go through your life.

Take at least two weeks to jot things down in your journal as you think about them. At the end of the journaling period, pull out the key activities or concepts that seem to repeat themselves. Notice what you love to do, how you naturally like to behave, and what significant qualities stand out. Make a note of these and notice how they are manifesting in your current life.

- Do your key attributes serve you?
- How could you use them even more effectively to have more of what you want in life?
- You could also do the assessment in StrengthsFinder 2.0 by Tom Rath.

What Are My Values?

When I first started to complete personal development exercises, I realized how important it was to uncover my values. Values are basic preferences, behaviors, or ways of being that we are naturally drawn to. When we orient ourselves around our values, we are more likely to experience fulfillment in our lives. There are many free values-based exercises available on the Internet. Some are focused on personal values, and others are focused on work. Complete some of these exercises and take note of the most common words that attract you.

As I completed these exercises, the following list of values emerged for me: excellence, generosity, happiness, learning, persistence, and responsibility. I started to use these values as my personal compass. By focusing on my values, I was able to align my actions with them, and this allowed me to behave in a way that was in integrity with who I wanted to be. I often hear someone say, "That person has no integrity." What is actually occurring is that the two people have different sets of values that are not in alignment. Each of us has a unique set of values that gives us our unique flavor, and your flavor will be very different from some other people.

I started to focus on being more in integrity with my own values to achieve a greater sense of satisfaction and well-being in my life. Let's look more deeply at two of my most important values, generosity and learning, and how learning to set appropriate boundaries complemented my values.

Generosity

When I was in graduate school studying economics, I used to drive my car to and from university. A woman in my class who did not have a car lived fairly close to me. When weekend events were planned, I would stop at her place and pick her up. I did this for the first year of grad school, until I noticed that she never offered me any money for gas. I was being generous by picking her up, but was I going overboard? I had to think about how much generosity I was going to extend. I started to feel like I was being used rather than appreciated. I decided I had extended enough generosity and stopped offering to go out of my way to give her a ride. As a result, in the second year of graduate school, she no longer chose to be my friend. It was a good lesson—I had learned my own boundary. Now I had a better sense of how much giving was enough and how much was too much. When we keep giving and giving without being conscious of our boundaries we can end up feeling used, and then we get angry with the other person. We are really angry with ourselves, however, for not honoring a reasonable boundary.

This example shows that values and boundaries are complementary. One works with the other to provide a sense of balance, which allows us to determine how to best express our values.

Learning

Another one of my core values is learning, and my parents were very strong about it, too. I can remember my father saying, "Get a good education and then ..." It was implied that with a good education, I would find a good job. I took my father's advice to heart, but I did not know when to say enough. I have a business degree and an undergraduate degree, a master's degree, a senior-level finance degree, a coaching degree, and then nine years of personal development learning on top of all that! Over the past few years I've started to become more discerning about what I truly want to learn. I ask myself, "What would really be of value for me to learn?"

As I increased my integrity with my values, life started to feel more rewarding and fulfilling for me. Once you have a sense of what your values are, look for ways to act in greater integrity with them. You may start using your values to guide your decisions and actions more often, you may work on learning to set boundaries regarding what is enough, or you may become more discerning about your actions.

▶ **TOOL: VALUES**

Complete one or more online personal values clarification exercises. Determine your top five personal values.

For each value, ask yourself:
- Where does this value show up in my life?
- What makes this value important to me?
- Who am I when I am living this value? How do I behave? What is my thinking? How do I feel?
- How can I create more integrity around this value?
- Where might I need to be more discerning with this value?
- What boundary might I need to set around this value?

What Are My Behavior Patterns?

Through self-exploration I uncovered changes that I wanted to make in my behavior. This required that I understand my current behaviors and also who I wanted to be. With consistent focus over time, I started to change how I was showing up in the world. T. Harv Ecker often said, "The way you do anything is the way you do everything." I wanted to find a new and more easeful way of doing things in this world.

I wanted to be more open with people and not be viewed as having a crusty outside exterior. People seemed to get caught on my sharp edges and then I had to repair the damage. Most of the time I didn't know why I was having this effect on people. I just knew I felt like I was walking on eggshells most of the time just trying to get things done. My intended behavior and how people perceived and responded to me were often two different things. At the bank sometimes I asked one of the support staff a question about why a mistake had been made, and they responded with defensiveness. I had a sense that they were afraid that I might blow up and bite their head off. Yet I didn't know what in me caused them to feel this way.

At the bank, when I got an innovative idea in my head for changes that would make things work better, I'd use all my willpower to push my ideas forward. Unfortunately, willpower often attracted willpower from the opposite direction. I once organized a meeting of my counterparts to examine our workflow and come up with a way to restructure and make it more efficient while serving our clients and the bank even better. We invited the manager from business services to join us in redesigning the structure. Unfortunately, she did not have the same perspective we did, and I ignored and discounted her perspective as being obstructionist. What we were proposing made logical sense to me. But my drive and persistence to push for what I believed to be "the right solution" resulted in the whole project bogging down and going nowhere. The manager dug in her heels and insisted that what we were proposing could not be done. After this experience

I didn't know what I could do to be more successful. I felt under-employed and underchallenged and I couldn't wait to get out of that position. When the opportunity presented itself, I jumped on it and moved to another department.

Can you sense my level of being disgruntled? I was not able to see situations for what they were. I was totally caught up in the drama and trying to force an outcome that I thought would be best for the clients and most efficient for the bank. My heart was in the right spot, but the way I was being in relationship with the business services manager was not going to get me to where I wanted to go. It's the same in our primary relationships: we need to step back and take a close look at ourselves before we blame our partners for everything. Self-awareness is a major key to success and to being able to start making life changes.

▶ **TOOL: A NEW WAY OF BEING**

What things are you doing in one area of your life that also show up in other areas? Start to notice your patterns and become curious about them.

- What do you notice about your behaviors at work?
- What do you notice about your behaviors at home?
- What do you notice about the way you treat people?
- When are people upset with you?
- What role did you play in their upset?
- What patterns or trends keep reoccurring?

Self-Appreciation

When I was getting divorced there was a huge amount of work to do to bring our relationship to a close. We needed to get the house ready for sale. I needed to find a new place to live. I still had my business to run. I had signed up for a new coaching course. I was on the executive board of our local Chamber of Commerce and chairing the committee for the annual golf tournament. I felt overwhelmed and underappreciated due to the number of commitments I had made. I was used to being a human doing machine, and I didn't give myself any recognition: I just kept doing and doing and doing.

Life is about enjoying the journey, whatever journey we are on. Stuck in a compulsive pattern of focusing on a task, completing it, and then immediately starting another task, I took absolutely no time to appreciate and feel the success of my accomplishments. I missed out on experiencing the beauty of my life. Instead I had the experience of not being appreciated and felt that life was hard. I used the following tools to become more self-aware and have greater appreciation for myself and my life.

TOOL: SELF-ACKNOWLEDGMENT

AND GRATITUDE

At the end of every day, write the following in your journal:

• What are three things I would like to acknowledge myself for?
• What are three things that I appreciate about myself?
• What are three things I am grateful for?

When you have completed your writing, notice the feeling in your body. Do you have a sense of well-being? Can you describe what emotion this is? Write this down too.

▶ **TOOL: APPRECIATION**

Because I was so busy doing, I had no sense of who I was "being" or how I felt at any given moment. If you are someone who gets caught up in the doingness of life, then do this exercise three times a day:

• Stop for a moment, ask yourself, "What am I enjoying right now?" and write down the answer.

▶ **TOOL: MIRROR EXERCISE**

At night before you go to bed, stand in front of the mirror and look yourself directly in your eyes. Tell yourself, "I love you." Tell yourself, "What I appreciate about you is …" Come up with three things every day, even if they are the same things as the day before. Do this for twenty-one days or longer, until you really sense the love you have for yourself.

Connection

All my self-awareness learning and practicing helped me feel connected to others. Connection is a major factor in having a sense of happiness in life. Most of my life I had felt separate from others and disconnected; even with lots of people around I still felt alone and lonely. I had always felt separate and isolated from my friends and my siblings. I never felt like they loved me. I always felt like I was in competition with others and was concerned that I didn't measure up.

When I was getting divorced, I still had lingering feelings of being alone and I desperately wanted to feel more connected with people, so I signed up for a second course with Jack Canfield. I knew the problem didn't rest with other people; it was with me. During the seminar I felt alone and uncomfortable, with no one to talk to when we were on break. Then one day others were in little groups talking, someone was playing the piano, I was standing alone—and for the first time I didn't feel alone. I closed my eyes, and I still felt connected to everyone. This was a huge breakthrough for me. My experiment with giving 1,001 hugs was slowly melting the iceberg of unhappiness in me, and I had my first glimpse of true happiness—what happiness from the inside could feel like.

I had always been a person who operated from a very logical, thinking perspective. I was not connected to my emotions; I had pushed them back behind a wall. On the last day of this seminar, Jack was playing the guitar at the front of the room and leading a meditation. All of a sudden I started to cry for no reason. I could feel something crumble inside of me. It felt like this huge wall inside my body was falling down, which allowed the unification of my emotions with my thinking mind. This wall had kept me separate and feeling isolated from others. I had a glimpse of what it felt like to be connected; now my work was to feel this way on a constant basis. (Fully dismantling this wall required me to let go of my emotional conditioning from childhood. Tools for letting go of emotional baggage can be found in chapters 12 and 13.)

My Backpack Is Full

It wasn't only my relationship with Milo that caused me to start seeking change; it was more a feeling that this was a crucial time for me to change.

When I started my new career in coaching in 2002, it opened up the door to a whole new world called personal development. I was forty-three years old and I had spent twenty-eight of those years in some kind of formal education, receiving several degrees from various educational institutions, and not once did anyone suggest that I might need to learn how to be happy.

Finding happiness was neither easy nor hard, but it was a journey, and it required me to be willing to explore many different aspects of my life. Milo wasn't ready to go on this journey with me. However, for a time he was willing to look after the campsite, ensure there was wood for a fire, water to drink, and food for our table. He encouraged me to go out and explore and learn, if that was what I wanted to do. I was very grateful for his support. I respected his desire not to participate and I hoped that I could share with him the tools that I was gathering in my travels.

As I travelled from village to village, listening to the elders of the personal development world share their wisdom, I started to get clarity about what I wanted more of in my life:

• To have love, joy, and abundance
• To posess ease, gentleness, calm, and patience
• To have access to humor
• To feel a deep connection with others
• To be more accepting
• To be more curious
• To become less attached to outcomes
• To let go of control
• To freely and easily feel emotions in the moment
• To trust myself in the moment; to be my own best friend
• To know that I am lovable, capable, whole, and magnificent

It took some time. I had never asked myself these questions before, and I didn't know what I really valued. I diligently wrote in my journal about my adventures and all the places I traveled, in what seemed like dark and foreign emotional lands. Venturing into these unknown places felt scary at times, like I was walking on a narrow ledge on a mountain slope where I might fall off if I made a misstep. But I kept my focus forward because in my heart I knew that I desperately wanted to feel the beauty of life, and to let go of all the emotions that scared me.

I also wanted to let go of a whole collection of baggage that did not serve me:

- Feeling I was alone in the world, and not connected to others
- Having explosive emotional outbursts, especially anger
- Feeling constantly annoyed and frustrated
- Carrying around deep sadness
- Being afraid of failure
- Feeling "not good enough"
- Having the attitude that I know more than others
- Having the attitude that I am always right

I was determined to have a happier life. By 2005, three years later, I had made significant progress and was a happier person. Even though I wasn't unhappy any longer, I knew there was more to learn. Every year I set out on two or three journeys to see what else might be out there in unexplored territories of personal growth. The beautiful new backpack I had purchased at the start of my journey became heavy with all the new tools I had gathered along the way. As challenges presented themselves, I could now reach into my backpack and pull out a tool that would help me respond to the situation in a more centered and resourceful manner.

I was starting to have fun and feel a sense of satisfaction and even joy. I felt like I had arrived at my destination; I knew how to behave in a way that made me happy. Many of my clients said I was the happiest person they knew. My relationship with Milo was good. I had become very resourceful with my backpack of tools: when we encountered a problem in our relationship, I pulled out the tools to fix the situation. We lived together easily, did fun things together, didn't have many disagreements, and had a reasonably good sex life. What more was there to a relationship? I was about to find out.

CHAPTER 5

Shock and Awe

THE STORM CLOUDS IN my relationship had been building for a few years, but I had refused to look up into the sky to see what was brewing. I didn't really want to know. The river Milo and I were travelling down was reasonably interesting; we had lots of fun and good times together. Being with Milo was like the best of both worlds for me; being single and being married at the same time. I could go and do whatever I wanted to do on my own, and I had my partner and best buddy to do things with too. Our relationship had a consistent routine, which felt very comfortable for me. Perhaps this is why I felt that our relationship was on smooth waters.

However, I had become aware that something was missing in our relationship; I just didn't want to bring it into my conscious mind. So rather than face the truth, I became very good at keeping the waters of our relationship smooth and calm. When we were in danger of rocking our boat with a disagreement, I pulled a personal development tool out of my backpack and adjusted my behavior, keeping our boat stable. As long as things were peaceful it never occurred to me that something serious might be wrong with the relationship. I had grown up in a household where there was lots of shouting, and I thought conflict was an indication of problems in a relationship. Milo and I didn't seem to have any conflict.

I knew our relationship was not perfect, but then, I thought, whose relationship is? Isn't relationship about loving your partner unconditionally and accepting him for who he is? That was exactly what I was doing, and I had become very good at doing it.

My deepest desire was that Milo would communicate with me. I yearned for intellectual conversations and it seemed like he was just not interested, so I decided to just accept that he was not going to satisfy my desire for more in-depth connection. I satisfied my desire for connection by engaging in conversations with my friends. It never occurred to me that Milo might be seeking this connection elsewhere. I stopped hoping that Milo might change and settled for Milo's and my relationship being "good enough." If Milo had not taken the step to end it, I would still be there, working to keep the relationship intact, to keep us going in circles, neither of us fully living our dreams.

Three's a Crowd

It didn't completely surprise me when I came home from one of my multiday expeditions one day to find a woman sitting with Milo. Deep down inside some place I knew our relationship was in trouble. Since my mom passed away, we seemed to have no reason to be together. We no longer had a family. Had I created the situation in which Milo could leave me? Was I setting him up to be the bad guy? I didn't have the strength to leave our relationship and be the bad person myself. I was in denial and making the best of things, toughing it out so to speak. Being tough was something that I learned very early in life and had become good at.

Here is how I helped to facilitate the end. I invited an acquaintance of mine from my Toastmasters club, Claire, to join us to play golf. She quickly became a regular. She also became Milo's regular partner when I was away on weekend personal development programs. Then she started to come up to the cabin with us at Whistler, and before I knew it she was a regular at the cabin.

Milo started to ensure that she would travel up to Whistler with us; he would go out of his way to accommodate her. Being naïve through this whole process, I told her to go ahead and be friends with Milo, that he needed more friends. I trusted Milo 100 percent to be faithful. I was wrong.

In February we were on a ski trip out of town. I woke up in the middle of the night, and Milo was not in bed. I walked downstairs and saw Milo and Claire caressing each other on the couch. I was so angry and shaking so hard I could not sleep; I got up at three a.m. and watched a movie. It amazed me that he went back to bed and had no problem sleeping. Maybe this was not the first time they had been together.

Later that month at a four-day workshop I heard a key message: "If your man does not want to be with you, then set him free. Men need to have freedom." I remember going for a walk with Milo after the workshop and giving him this message. If he didn't want to be with me, then he should go. I just couldn't imagine that he would leave me. I had grown and changed and was coming into my own as a woman and a human being. I was softening. I no longer needed to control everything. I was becoming vibrant, outgoing, and happy. Milo was still a quiet man who wanted to be in his own safe world.

But there was obviously something Milo was looking for in life that he was not finding in our relationship. He fell madly in love with Claire. Milo shared with me that he had never felt happy and that our relationship was not providing him with happiness. He told me that his connection with Claire felt much more like he was at home, that he had finally found someone he could relate to. They both had the same offbeat sense of humor and a certain cynicism about life. They both liked the same music and the same sports activities. They resonated with each other, he said. Milo said that getting together with Claire might be his only chance to find happiness. He told me, "I can make Claire happy; she needs me. You don't need me anymore."

What was he talking about I didn't need him anymore? How was I going to live without him? I felt like he had just taken the paddle and hit me in the head. I felt the worst devastation in my life, even worse than when my mother died. All of a sudden we were in very fast-flowing water, about to go over the edge of a waterfall that would capsize our kayak and end our journey on this relationship river.

However it happens, the end of a love relationship hurts. It hurts whether we have been living together for a short time or for a long time, if we are ending a marriage or a partnership. All our hopes and dreams of what could have been are suddenly gone. When it happened to me I had to face my fears squarely — and everything else I didn't want to face. Being in relationship had given me a false sense of safety from all the unknowns in my world. Now it felt as though my small boat was being plunged into ice-cold rapids. I had to paddle hard for shore, using all the strength I had, or be pulled under by the current of overwhelming emotions.

Paddling Alone

When I reflected back on our relationship over the years, I felt like I was doing all the paddling when it came to organizing our life and making fun things happen. I usually organized all the group activities, everything that we would need for sailing, and the cycling trips and skiing trips with friends. I poured over the forestry maps to determine where we would go for summer camping holidays. I booked tee times at golf courses and accommodations for when we weren't camping. In running the house I made 95 percent of the decisions unilaterally, except major purchases.

Not only was I working full time, I was also taking responsibility for almost everything that occurred in our joint life. Milo was a master at being able to relax on weekends and read books. I always seemed to be working. I was working in my gardens; I was working cooking food on weekends so there would be healthy food in the freezer for us to eat during the week. It felt like I was on a treadmill. Have you felt this way? When I was working in my finance job, I was on a bus into the city by six a.m. and often did not get home until seven p.m. I had dinner and fell into bed shortly thereafter. On weekends it felt like my second job was to look after the home and us.

To Milo's credit he did participate in the domestic duties. He was great at cleaning up the kitchen and doing the dishes after my cooking sprees. We cooperated when it came to laundry and yard work, and Milo was great at keeping things fixed up. For the little everyday things in life, Milo participated in steering our boat and helped to keep it in the middle of the river.

When it came to making any real change or doing things that would have supported us to get ahead financially, however, Milo's answer was always no. When I suggested that we look at buying a rental house and fixing it up, the answer was no. When my mom passed away, and I suggested that we take in a renter to earn some additional money, the answer was no. It felt like Milo did not want to do anything extra to support our joint relationship to be more financially successful. He just did not want to expend the energy.

It became apparent to me that I had never trusted a man to make major decisions for me. I had never surrendered to the idea of letting a man look after me. I didn't leave room. In order to feel safe, I needed to look after myself. I was a very competent and independent woman, and my ego took full control of what was happening. On an energetic level I didn't trust a man to look after me — then who do you think I attracted into my life? Men for whom I was the driving force. Men who could trust me to look after them.

SELF-REFLECTION QUESTIONS

- If you are the one paddling the boat, what keeps you paddling all by yourself?
- What have you done to ask your partner to join you in doing more paddling?
- What is it about you that got you started paddling the boat all by yourself?

Driving Myself to Avoid Feeling

Perhaps it is unfair of me to blame Milo for sending our kayak over such a steep waterfall. It might be useful to take a look at some of my other behaviors that were useful, but maybe just a little, well, overboard. My pragmatic and frugal behavior was clearly demonstrated in my relationship with food preparation. At the grocery store I was impulsive; if any canned goods that I regularly bought were on sale, I would stock up. Looking at my pantry, you might wonder if the closest grocery story was one hundred miles away, rather than ten blocks.

My pattern was that on Saturdays, I would sit down with a coffee and my cookbooks at six a.m. in the morning and start looking at all the delicious recipes. Before I knew it I'd have four or five different dishes on my list of things to make. I'd cook all day; most of the time two recipes were in progress at the same time. By the end of the day, it would look like a bomb had gone off in the kitchen, and I'd be absolutely exhausted, hardly able to stand. Luckily Milo would come in and save the kitchen, scrubbing the pots and stove to return the kitchen to its normal calm state until the next cooking marathon. I would be exhausted, but so proud and pleased to be able to pack fifteen or twenty meals away in the deep freeze before I went to bed. Of course I had my practical reasons: my food was healthier, tastier, and way cheaper than buying it in the store. But what was the cost of my time and the impact on our relationship of this driven behavior?

The most insane event that I recall happened one Saturday in the summer. Milo and I went out to pick strawberries. On the way home we bought some raspberries and gooseberries, even though I had gooseberries and black currants in the freezer at home. Are you beginning to see how things can get out of control? The next day I started to make jam early in the morning. Six a.m., I was up and at it with my coffee, putting the first of the fruit in a huge pot. As soon as the pot was empty, in went more fruit, more sugar, lots of stirring, and another pot was on its way. We covered the dining room table with thick towels and set the jam out there to cool. As the day progressed, the table became more laden with all the varieties of jam — strawberry, raspberry, gooseberry, rhubarb, apricot. By the time the last jar was sealed and on the table I was once again exhausted from cooking over the hot stove all day, in the heat of summer, but we had ninety-six jars of jam on the table. Who in their right mind makes ninety-six jars of jam?

I gardened in the same way. I loved my gardens. I would get up at six a.m. on a Saturday morning, make coffee, and then head outside to my garden. I had a small English-style flower garden in the backyard, and relatively large flower gardens that I had built in the front yard. Along one side of the yard I had originally built two rose gardens by digging and lifting out the sod for two four-by-eight-foot gardens, which I later expanded into a ten-by-forty-foot strip that ran the length of the driveway. Over time I continued to convert more and more of the front yard into gardens. Of course, it didn't occur to me that I could have had a smaller garden. I did everything with a vengeance, and the yard would look great, but by the end of the day I would be so tired and physically exhausted, I could hardly walk. I would beg Milo to come out and help me clean up and put my tools away.

Looking back now it all seems a little crazy. Why did I bury myself in all of that work? What stopped me from knowing when enough was enough? Why did I have to build gardens so big that I would have to either hire help or spend at least one day every week working in them? I just didn't seem to know when to stop. The answer now seems quite simple; there was something that I was avoiding feeling. Whether it was cooking, gardening, or even sports, I was always on the go. Something was missing in my life and I was desperately trying to create it. Working that hard became an addiction. I was pouring love into my gardens and receiving a sense of love from the beauty I was creating. The beauty of my gardens was nourishing my heart. I didn't realize I was missing this nourishment in my relationship with Milo. I was so deeply buried in constant activity that even if Milo had been offering love, I might easily have missed it. Lack of intimacy had become a dynamic system and a vicious circle. I felt unloved, so

I worked myself to exhaustion, which left me no energy to cultivate an intimate relationship with my partner. And my partner
seemed unaware of the need to cultivate a more intimate relationship with me.

We used sports as another way of hiding from greater intimacy. Even though Milo and I had a lot of fun golfing and skiing together, these activities did not help us come together and
have a more intimate relationship. Sporting activities were a place
for us to hang out and spend quality time together, but we never
took the next step to deepen our feelings for each other and become more intimate. After a day of skiing or golf we often felt
very tired, with sore muscles or exposure to the sun, and at night
we fell into bed exhausted. Looking back, the sports seemed to
be another way for me to be busy and for both of us to avoid the
truth. Is there something you and your partner do that is fun, but
doesn't enhance the depth of your relationship?

SELF-REFLECTION QUESTIONS

- What behaviors do you have that create a barrier in
  your relationship?
- What activities do you become consumed in that crowd
  out your relationship?
- What do you do that gets in the way of you having energy to be intimate with your partner?
- Is it your partner who is hiding by being busy? Have
  you tried to get your partner's attention?

Trapped by "I Should"

I always had this notion that I *should* make a contribution to the community. For example, that I should be on a volunteer board and give back to the community in that way. Over a period of about seven years I sat on three different boards and spent countless hours assisting organizations to move their agendas forward. At the Chamber of Commerce board, not only did I hold a board position for two years, but I also chaired the events committee and designed new programs and activities. I had a love-hate relationship with the time I spent doing this. I loved the idea that I was giving to a bigger cause, and at the same time I invested a huge amount of personal time and didn't really enjoy it.

After six or seven years of volunteer work I realized that this was not my preferred way of making a contribution to the world. One of my key talents is my ability to take action, and this ability was slowed down considerably when I worked in a group and consensus was required. I felt a lot of frustration, which of course I took home to my relationship, because nothing happens in isolation.

One of my coaching clients, Linda, has two young children. She is very committed to the health and vibrancy of her local elementary school and her neighborhood. She told me there was a constant battle going on within herself about how much time she donated to the community and how it affected her time with her family and her work. This internal battle left her feeling like she never had enough time. She was doing a great deal of work, and creating stress and exhaustion for herself, but she didn't feel proud of what she had accomplished. You can imagine how little energy Linda had left to nurture an intimate relationship with her partner.

Think about the things you feel compelled to do — community giving, spending time with your extended family, or anything else — and notice if your mind is saying "I should." When you do things from the place of "I should," you are not living in alignment with your heart. This drains energy from you and from

your relationship. Even though the cause appears to be important, make sure you know your true priorities. This will help you
realize when enough is enough. When time is limited, if you say
yes to one thing, you are saying no to something else.

SELF-REFLECTION QUESTIONS

- What did you last say yes to? What were you saying
  no to?
- Where do you impose shoulds on yourself?
- Think about the different activities you're involved in.
  How do they enhance your life and your relationship?
- How do these activities detract from your relationship?
- What choices could you make to nurture the health of
  your relationship and make it a priority in your life?

Floating in Circles

Given the way I had avoided taking a hard look at myself and my
relationship, it was no surprise that Milo's wanting to leave was
a huge shock. This couldn't be happening to me! I thought. I lay
in bed and cried myself to sleep. How would I ever survive this? I
felt like my heart was going to explode, and I felt numb from the
crying. I was in absolute overwhelm. It was all way more than I
could cope with. I felt like I was going to die.

After Milo announced that he was leaving, I went to a workshop called Sex, Passion & Enlightenment, and he spent the weekend with Claire. It was a bit of irony, my attending a workshop to
learn how to bring more passion and spark into my relationship
while my husband was with another woman creating that spark!

Milo did not have the kind of weekend that he expected, how-ever. It was his first weekend of freedom with Claire, and he had spent it crying about the ending of our relationship. When they went for a motorcycle ride and stopped off at a gift store, he saw bottles of herb vinegars and oils, all sorts of things that I would have liked. "Jacque would love this," he thought.

Milo told me that all he could think about was my pain. The hurt he was causing me was more than he could accept being responsible for. Did he really want to leave or should he stay? He just didn't know the answer. I told him I loved him and would love him forever no matter what happened. I considered our home a safe place for him to stay and figure out what it was he really wanted.

I didn't want to be alone; I didn't want him to go. Would it be possible to reverse everything that happened, I wondered. Maybe now that it was out in the open and we had crossed this thresh-old, he would be willing to do some work to become happier. I could feel the power of determination course through my body. I felt that all of this was fixable, if only Milo was willing. It seemed obvious to me that his unhappiness didn't really have anything to do with our relationship. The question was, did Milo really want to leave me?

Within two weeks I started to feel angry. It seemed that Milo was staying with me purely because he was afraid to leave and be alone. His job was in Vancouver, and Claire lived a two-hour ferry ride away, so if he left me he'd have to find his own place to live. Moving out on his own would be a big decision for him. What if he was making a mistake? Was it better to be with me, a woman he no longer loved, than to be alone? Had he really stopped lov-ing me or was something else going on?

I had gained a level of emotional freedom, and Milo felt I no longer needed him. Claire gave him purpose—he could help make her feel better. With her there was new love, excitement, passion, and endless possibility. He thought he had finally found his opportunity for real happiness, his last chance. But he didn't like being the bad guy. I had never done anything to hurt him, and now he felt like he was destroying me. How could he do that? He was not an evil, uncaring man.

Sometimes I felt like it would be easier if he left; then I wouldn't have to see him every day. But he didn't talk about leaving or make any move to leave. He got up, went to work, and came home, and we continued to exist in a somewhat normal routine. I couldn't imagine what it would be like to not see him every day, to not have him in the house. I had spent eighteen years with Milo. The longest I had ever been apart from him was the month that I traveled in Vietnam after we celebrated our tenth anniversary, and even then I had looked for an email from him at least every second day.

My mind and emotional body were going through a wrestling match. My mind understood that Milo had disengaged and no longer loved me, but my emotional body just wouldn't let go. It couldn't fathom the possibility that he didn't love me. A deep feeling of love and empathy pierced my heart. I could feel his pain, and I felt such tenderness and concern for him. I understood that he was a very confused man and was just trying his best to be happy. Deep down I knew the only thing that would save our relationship was if Milo developed the ability to love himself and become happy. I held on to this hope for a while and then finally had to let it go.

SELF-REFLECTION QUESTIONS

- What emotions or situations are you denying?
- What feels too difficult to face?
- What are you hoping will happen?
- What are you afraid will happen?

Paddling through Heavy Fog

I had been in denial about the difficulties in our relationship for a long time before the end. One factor in my denial was a very deep fear of being alone. I had been afraid to lose my mother because then I would be alone, but I had lost her anyway. Losing Milo too was more than my emotional circuits could handle. How could I survive without him?

As I progressed through the separation process I began to understand why this loss was so terrifying for me. Several significant events had occurred when I was young that caused me to accumulate a significant amount of emotional baggage, and the emotional energy stored in my emotional baggage provided the fuel for my overwhelming fears.

It was this emotional baggage I was trying to cover up with all my cooking and gardening and other compulsive behaviors. Emotional conditioning led me to behave like a child constantly wanting to get my needs met first. I had started my journey into adulthood during my search for happiness, and divorce propelled me along on this journey even faster. In *Spiritual Warfare* Jed McKenna says that for anyone who behaves like a "Human Child," other than a child, the most important topic of interest for us should be to free ourselves from the emotional shackles that cripple our spirit, so we can resume our "right and proper life." This was my goal.

All the tools in my backpack helped me use the emotional trauma of divorce to free myself from the emotional baggage that I was hauling along in our kayak as Milo and I made our relationship journey down the river. I wasn't aware that I had brought all this baggage along on the trip, but then most of us aren't. It is true that I had contributed my fair share to the demise of our relationship over the years, and I was attempting to do something about it. Taking responsibility for my own part in the failure of this relationship has assisted me to move significantly forward in my quest to be a Human Adult, to use Jed McKenna's term, rather than a Child. And a Human Adult was what I needed to be as I dealt with all the emotions that arose.

SELF-REFLECTION QUESTIONS

- What do you know is going on in your relationship that you don't want to believe?
- What are you afraid to find out?
- What is creating the fear in you?
- How have you contributed to this situation occurring?
- What has your intuition been telling you that you haven't been willing to listen to?
- How have you set up the betrayal, so you wouldn't have to take responsibility?
- What potential opportunity is this situation creating for you?

CHAPTER 6

Capsized in the Current

WHETHER THE DECISION TO END the relationship is ours, our partners', or mutual, the emotions that go along with divorce can be overwhelming. The time and sequence in which we experience these feelings is different for each one of us. If one partner has been thinking of leaving the relationship for some time, this partner will likely have a head start on detaching from it. In some cases, as with Milo, a new relationship may have already begun. Others of us just realize clearly, "I've made a mistake and I need to get out." However the divorce or separation comes about, it is essential to become free of the emotional trauma that goes along with it. What we don't work through and resolve today will become more smelly laundry that we end up stuffing away in our emotional baggage to be carried forward with us into the future and into our next relationships.

I came to realize that I had allowed Milo to systematically withdraw his love from me. I didn't love myself enough to tell him this wasn't OK, nor did I know how to show him more love. I just kept accepting the way it was and settling for less and less love, until there was finally no love coming from Milo. I wasn't willing to take a stand for myself; in fact, I waited until Milo's deception was too much for him to take.

It hurt to be rejected by someone that I loved so deeply, but as time went by it was far from devastating. Instead, I felt more connected with myself and my needs. It would have been really nice to be held through this difficult time, to be told that everything would be OK. So I looked around. Who could fill this need for me? I realized I could connect with people who cared — a true friend is always ready with a loving hug. I also told myself that everything would be OK, and it was true. Because I knew that no matter what happened, I would meet my challenges with integrity. I stopped avoiding the emotions that go along with living. I stopped hiding from my life.

SELF-REFLECTION QUESTIONS

- What are the major emotions you are dealing with right now?
- Exercise: Write a short piece about each emotion that you are feeling.
- I feel sad because ...
- I feel afraid because ...
- I feel angry because ...
- I feel ashamed because ...
- I feel guilty because ...
- I feel sorry because ...
- I feel _____ because ...

Sadness

I felt deep grief about the decision to end our relationship; it was hard for me to take it all in. I was exhausted and didn't want to get out of bed in the morning. I would go to my office and work for a few hours, but quite frankly, I didn't feel like it, and my mind was not focused on my business. The only thing I could think about was the rejection that I felt. By eleven in the morning I would be exhausted and all I wanted to do was go back to bed for a nap. I could nap for hours; it was sheer willpower that got me out of bed and moving. I was drowning in sadness. If I just lay in bed, I thought, maybe all of this would go away, maybe it wouldn't be true.

As much as possible, be present to your sadness in the moment; it is a very real feeling. Due to the magnitude of emotional energy, we may experience overwhelming physical sensations as well as intense thoughts. Our bodies may want to shut down so we don't have to feel the sadness. The more we can be present to the sadness we feel, the better. Part 2 of this book will show you in detail a process that will help you to be really present to your physical sensations. In the meantime, get in touch with your sadness. It is an indication of what you loved about your relationship. When you focus your mind on what you loved about your relationship, you get in touch with what is actually important to you, and this is very good insight for the future.

When Milo and I first started living together I was a control freak. After several years of personal development work I was able to let go of a lot of my need for control. Not everything had to be my way! I could finally listen to Milo and hear his requests. I had finally become happy enough that I had stopped making negative comments and being so judgmental. I became aware that there were many perspectives on the way things could be done and that my way was not the only correct way. Why would he leave me when I was finally becoming an easier person to live with? It just didn't make sense.

Maybe it was because he really liked me the way I was, a rather difficult person to live with. Then at least he had an excuse for feeling the way he did and he didn't have to look at himself. The more I shifted my behavior, the less blame he could put on me for the way he felt. Plus I started reflecting things back to him. For example, I expressed that when we are judgmental of others, the person we are really judgmental about is ourselves. I was holding up a mirror for Milo to look at his own behavior, and I believe he wanted to avoid this at all costs. He would rather leave me than consider the role he was playing in his own unhappiness.

I felt sad that he did not value our relationship enough to do this, but then, I couldn't force him to do anything that he didn't want to. This is another truth, we can't force others to change, we can only change ourselves.

SELF-REFLECTION QUESTIONS

- What did you love about your relationship that you are feeling sad about?
- If you were to look at your partner through the eyes of empathy, where could you open your heart to understanding your partner's humanness?

Be Kind to Yourself

Being in denial and feeling sadness are natural parts of grief. We are grieving the death of a relationship and everything that we loved about it. As part of the grieving process it is natural to feel exhausted and to have a lack of focus. We may experience trouble sleeping or eating and have wild mood swings, or we may enter into depression. This is all natural. During the grieving period it is important to be kind and gentle with ourselves and to look after our health. We may have a tendency to avoid what we are feeling and thus become susceptible to addictions, such as using drugs, drinking too much alcohol, chain smoking, or losing ourselves in sexual relationships. Addictive substances numb us out and help to make the pain go away. I was very proud that I made it through this time period without abusing alcohol, which had been my numbing-out drug of choice in the past. I was very careful and limited myself to no more than two glasses of wine at a time and no more than three days a week. It is important that we experience the grief that we are feeling. There is important information in these feelings.

SELF-REFLECTION QUESTIONS

- What habits do you need to pay particular attention to?
- How could you be more kind to yourself?

Loss and Letting Go

The end of a relationship is like an empty campsite, which once had been full of the hustle and bustle of life as people prepared their meals, or filled with the companionable quiet of people relaxing. In the evenings the campers sat quietly around a crackling campfire, wood smoke permeating the air. The stars above were so close that you could touch them in the night sky. Everything seemed peaceful and right with the world. But now all the campers are gone, the fires are burnt out, and the forest trees and animals once again reign quietly serene. At the end of a wonderful holiday I always feel a bit sad looking around the campsite — what I had looked forward to so much is now over.

As I look back on my relationship with Milo, it feels much like this empty campsite. Everything I loved and valued is gone, what I had looked forward to and dreamed of is over, a quiet peacefulness has taken its place, but I still feel sad. There had been something very comforting about the consistency and predictability we shared. Besides the loss of my partner, I also grieved the loss of my house and my beloved garden, and the friends and activities that Milo and I had shared.

SELF-REFLECTION QUESTIONS

- What have you lost with the ending of this relationship?
- What will you miss?
- What about this relationship are you relieved that you will no longer be experiencing?

My Home

My home was gone, sold to strangers, just days before my fiftieth birthday. This was the first home I had ever owned, and I had treasured it. Together Milo, Mom, and I had become a family in this house. It had been a coming of age for me; I was no longer a student living like a gypsy. I had a job, a man who loved me, and my own home. I had reached adulthood.

It wasn't the house itself that was so important, it was all the memories. We'd had many great dinner parties in this house entertaining our friends. Mom and I spent hundreds of hours together in the kitchen cooking food and talking about the week's events. This had been a place where love and friendship blossomed. Even though Mom wasn't alive anymore, I still felt her presence in the house with me.

To add insult to injury, I had to give up all my family's antique furniture. No one in my family needed it, and I had no room for an antique dining room set in my four-hundred-square-foot studio. In a panic to get the furniture moved out of the house on time, I borrowed an old half-ton truck and unceremoniously dropped it all off at the auction house. I felt sad to let everything go, there were years of precious history in that furniture, but I just couldn't keep it. Letting go of the furniture was a mini disaster in the midst of a much larger catastrophe.

My Gardens

With the house, I also lost my gardens. From the moment we pur-chased the property I started working outside on the yard. I had worked hard to build the gardens that bore so much beauty every year, and now they were gone. I divided the roots of my favorite perennials and took my babies with me, transplanting them into a friend's garden. I worked in a frenzy to move as many plants as possible before we needed to be out of the house. I even trans-planted some of the flowers to the gardens in the yard of Milo's rental house. I couldn't let go, it was so painful.

Then one day, nine months later at the beginning of spring, I drove by my old house to see what flowers would be peeking their heads through the ground. Bad mistake. All the gardens I had built were gone, paved over by grass. All the flowering shrubs I had planted had been ripped out. When I saw this it broke my heart. What I had built with tender loving care was de-stroyed. Knowing that I could build new gardens again in the future didn't lessen the pain of seeing what I had built disappear.

Grief is not rational. As much as people tell us to focus on the positive and that everything will be fine in the future, we still need to deal with the irrationality of grief. Grief is caused by our energetic attachments to things or to people. We have made up stories in our minds and given significant meaning to our rela-tionships with these things and people. We may try to manage our grief by denying it or pushing it away. We may try to pave over our grief the way the new owners of my house laid sod on top of my garden. Instead of living in denial and hoping that time would take care of it, I intentionally felt into the emotional energy of my grief and this brought the emotional feelings to completion. Chapter 13 of this book explains how to do this. When the emo-tional feelings were complete I could then remember and feel all the love and was no longer swamped by sadness. I was free.

Favorite Activities

Milo and I had many activities together, and I felt I was losing not only him but all of my favorite pastimes. Both of us loved to be outside and in the woods; in camping we both experienced a sense of tranquility. It refilled my spiritual teacup and soothed my soul. Being the only people at a wilderness campsite for several days with the towering evergreen trees brought a special kind of connection with nature. I experienced a deep and profound sense of peace. At the end of a day of solitude we'd turn off the lantern and watch the flickering flames of the firelight; the darkness would wrap around me like a blanket keeping me safe.

Milo added his own spark and specialness to the night. He'd bring some magnesium turnings from his chemistry lab and put them into the bottom of a tin can, then put it in the fire. The magnesium would turn white hot as it burned extra bright in the bottom of the can, acting like an incredibly bright spotlight. It was our own special set of fireworks to end another blissful day in nature. As the fire burned down we'd watch the stars until I couldn't keep my eyes open, and then I'd crawl into the tent for the healing powers of Mother Nature's love as I slept on the ground.

Who would I go camping with now? Who would put up the tarps in case it rained? After all those years, I still hadn't learned how to tie even a bowline knot! Who would go into the forest with me to look for fallen trees or dig through the slash from a logging site for pieces of wood for our campfire? We had purchased an inflatable kayak to go paddling on the lakes we camped beside, and now I had no one to go with. I couldn't think of anyone who would be a good companion in the woods. When would I get an opportunity to camp again? My heart ached with this thought.

Friends

I was also dealing with the loss of our friends. Who would I go skiing with? We had skied with the same two couples for twelve years, and other than our little group I didn't know anyone who skied. We knew their kids who had grown up and were now getting married and having their own children. I felt connected to their lives. Not only would I no longer go skiing, I would probably lose contact with this group of people as we went our separate directions.

When relationships end, friendships also may come to an end. People that a couple has spent a lot of time with may choose one partner over the other, feeling that it's no longer possible to be friends with both. Friends may become emotionally involved in the ending of the relationship and take sides. Friendships may just slide away from us when we are single, as people who are in couple relationships tend to socialize with other couples. When Milo and I were together I would often phone couples who were our friends and make arrangements to get together for dinner. When I became single I stopped phoning people to come over for dinner, and virtually no one called me. Yet when I called to find out what they were doing and invited myself over, I was always welcome.

Dynamics change with friends when we are single instead of part of a couple. This is a natural change; we can take it personally and make up a story that our friends don't care about us anymore, or we can pick up the phone and call them. If they truly don't want to be friends anymore, they will make excuses or we will feel unwelcome energy when we arrive at their house. But every time I have invited myself over, I have been welcomed with open arms. My hosts even told me they were grateful that I called!

Family and Special Occasions

I love Christmas and all the traditions: putting up Christmas lights, decorating the house and the Christmas tree. Milo and I almost always spent Christmas with Mom and Milo's two sisters who lived in Vancouver. It became our tradition. When I was growing up on the farm, my parents were quite poor, and I never had many Christmas presents under the tree. But with Milo and his family there were tons of presents. As an adult I was having the Christmas that I had always wanted as a child. Milo was generous and always bought me really nice presents; his sisters had great taste and always gave me wonderful gifts. Some of my most adored jewelry had been given to me by his sisters. We had wonderful Christmas dinners of turkey, stuffing, and yam soufflé. I missed this family tradition.

When my relationship with Milo ended, I was no longer in contact with his sisters as much; now it required a conscious decision and effort. Our friendship seemed to just slip away.

A Heavy Heart

My heart felt heavy and sad as I looked around the campsite of my life and saw everything gone: home, gardens, friendships, special occasions, skiing, and most of all, camping. Tears rolled down my checks as I thought of everything I had lost. Nothing would be the same again, no matter what happened in the future.

We create meaning in our lives through all the things we own, the activities we participate in, and the traditions we develop. We use these things to identify who we are. Without your partner who are you? Without your job who are you? Without your children who are you? We are mothers and fathers, wives and husbands, teachers and executives. These labels are not who we truly are inside, but they serve to give us some meaning in life and help us feel grounded and safe.

When something is suddenly taken away, the mind does not have time to adjust to the new situation. The mind is a meaning-making machine, and it is very tenacious about the stories it creates. I had created a story around my gardens, that I would never have another garden in my life. At a certain point I realized this wasn't true. I like gardening, and if I want a garden again I will build one. The attachment we have to things and activities is a signal of what it is we love and fear letting go of. We feel secure when we have familiar experiences, sometimes even when the experiences are not pleasant. We may stay in a relationship for a long time after it stops feeling good because we don't want to lose the sense of safety we feel in what is familiar.

SELF-REFLECTION QUESTIONS

- What things will you miss most in your relationship?
- What activities are you afraid you will have to give up?
- What friends do you want to ensure you remain in contact with?
- What traditions will you have to recreate?
- What is most important to you about each of these?
- What does it mean to you to give them up?
- How could you replace them in the future?
- What new opportunities does this create?

Hurt

Milo once said he had never really loved me, and this gnawed away at my mind. How could I have lived with someone for eighteen years who claimed he had never really loved me anyhow, but had just been going through the motions? It hurt that he did not value the time we had lived together. Milo said he cherished our relationship less because I pursued him. Deep down I still wanted to believe that Milo cherished me. Milo had held me every night in his arms; I thought this was how he showed his love. It now felt like one great big lie. I expected honesty and love and what I got was years of lies. This felt like the biggest rejection I had ever had to face.

I don't think Milo really meant that he had never loved me; I think it was his way of trying to shirk responsibility for the hurt he was causing me. In his mind, if he really didn't love me, then it would make his deception and affair more palatable to his own conscience. When we cheat on our partners we are really cheating ourselves. If we value honesty and commitment, then when we cheat we lose integrity.

I believe Milo felt love neither for himself nor me. We can't love someone else when we have lost the feeling of love for ourselves. When we are in this dark place and we are desperately looking for love, we make up a story that justifies an affair. Maybe we don't love our partners anyway, or maybe the story is that they don't love us. This hurts both those who have an affair and their partners. The degree to which our lives work is dependent upon our integrity and our ability to live up to our commitments. Being out of integrity causes suffering. When we are in integrity we will attract more of what we want into our lives.

Milo's affair added to my sadness and anger. The sadness came from a place I held sacred inside of me, and from a judgment of myself. When I was in my twenties, I had cheated on my partner at the time. I was in a very sad and dark place, desperately looking for love and not finding it in my partner, so I cheated. I have had to live with this breach of my own values. When I thought about Milo cheating, it brought a lump up into my throat. I thought about forgiveness and bringing love into my heart, both for me, the young woman who hurt so much many years ago, and for Milo, who had made the same mistake. Intellectually I knew Milo's affair was a manifestation of his unhappiness just as mine had been in the past.

SELF-REFLECTION QUESTIONS

- What things have occurred in your relationship that are hurtful?
- What has happened that breaches a bond that you held sacred?
- Have you ever done something similar?
- If you were to look at your partner with empathy, where could you open your heart to forgiveness?

Anger and Betrayal

When I heard Milo say, "I want to leave and be with Claire," I wanted to smash her to bits for wrecking my life, but oddly I was not angry with him. I have had fleeting moments of being very angry with Milo, like when I found out he had lied to me about not seeing her while he was trying to figure out what to do about our relationship. It was easier to project my anger onto to Claire rather than Milo, someone I still loved. My anger with Milo was more at a low simmer in my body, underneath the surface. It was a constant hum of white noise that my mind could block out.

I projected my volatile anger onto Claire and let my thoughts stray into the territory of blame. It was so easy to get on an endless loop of thoughts like "How could someone I included in our life and group of friends betray me?" This thinking only caused me suffering. I knew that I needed to make the effort to shift my thinking away from this place or I'd drive myself crazy. I needed to let it go.

Years ago I had learned three simple questions from Hale Dwoskin, and they came in very handy now. I asked myself, "Could I let this go?" "Would I let this go?" and "When?" To the first and second questions I answered, "Yes" and "No" but the third question I answered, "Now." Contemplating these questions allowed me to unhook my obsessive thinking, which was adding fuel to my feelings of anger and betrayal and hence increasing my suffering.

When we love someone we usually trust that person fully, and that is a very good thing for the relationship. Mistrust attracts conflict and discord into our relationships; trust is where we want to be coming from. When we find out that a betrayal has occurred, we have to understand that the person is not really betraying us, they are betraying themselves. They are living in a world of lies, their lies. The place for us to focus our mind is on love and forgiveness. It is a time to open our hearts to loving ourselves and also to loving our partners for the pain they are suffering, even if they are not present to it. When we fill our hearts with love it is we who feel the love. When we forgive our partners in this moment we also forgive ourselves for all the little betrayals that we have committed over time.

▶ TOOL: AFFIRMATION

State this affirmation repeatedly: "Love and forgiveness are inside of me." You can do this at night as a way of falling asleep, or when you are driving in your car, or when you go for a walk.

▶ TOOL: FILLING YOUR HEART WITH LOVE

Close your eyes and imagine your heart filling with love and expanding as you breathe in. When you breathe out, imagine sending this love out into the universe to the people you love and to those who need healing.

Finally, the only thing I could do was have empathy for both Milo and myself. I had been practicing living from a place of love for the past couple of years. As I moved forward with the divorce I tried to hold love in my heart for Milo, even though what he had done was not lovable. As for Claire, one piece of advice saved me from experiencing long-term anger toward her. One of my teachers had said that anger is within you, and if you hold anger toward someone, the only person that anger is going to hurt is you. Claire would not experience any of the anger I was feeling. I was the one who experienced the anger in my body. I knew this was not in my best interest. So I let it go.

Judgment has a mirror effect. When we judge another as being wrong, we really need to take a look at ourselves. What are we doing currently or what have we done in the past that had a similar essence? When I asked this question of myself around Milo's infidelity, I did not look too good. What I had done in a previous relationship, being unfaithful before having the courage to admit that the relationship wasn't working, was awfully similar to what I was judging Milo for. I could easily have rationalized away what I had done. It was only one weekend, I was really unhappy, I was very young. Initially I felt anger toward Milo, but when I looked inside, I could see that I was angry with myself for compromising my own values of honesty and faithfulness. I needed to forgive myself for the mistake I had made thirty years ago, just as I needed to forgive Milo for his behavior in this situation.

I also needed to forgive Claire. If she was anything like me thirty years ago, then I needed to have empathy for the lonely woman who was having an affair with the husband of a friend. She must not have had much self-respect to get involved with a married man and betray a friendship. When we can hold true compassion in our hearts for people who betray their own integrity, we know that we are well on the way to healing our feelings of anger and betrayal.

SELF-REFLECTION QUESTIONS

• What is it that you feel angry about?
• How do you feel betrayed?
• What is your judgment about this situation and the behavior of the people involved?
• When have you betrayed yourself or someone else?
• What do you need to forgive yourself for?
• How could you extend forgiveness to others?
• How would this benefit you?

Fear

When a relationship ends we can be bombarded by many fears. If we depended upon our partners to look after many aspects of our lives, it can be daunting to take on responsibility for these things. It is especially difficult if our partners had stopped paying the bills or if there is a huge amount of debt that now needs to be paid off. Now we need to figure out how to generate an income and pay off the debt.

In a women's divorce group I attended, people shared comments about how fear affected their situation. "When I was going through it, it could be so overwhelming that I was immobilized." "I was a stay-at-home mom and had to go back to work. That's when it really hit me that everything depended on me." It is frightening when we have to deal with the unknown and learn how to do things that were previously done for us. Fear arises when we feel like we are not in control of what is happening in our lives. Ultimately fear comes from emotional conditioning and the doom-and-gloom stories our minds tell us. Our thoughts provoke reactions that lead to worry and anxiety.

Financial Fears

With courage we can overcome big obstacles, including financial challenges. My friend Cindy said, "I'm still working on improving my credit and there are still wounds to heal, but I'm much better than I was when I was with my husband. He took a lot, and I've found I'm stronger than I thought I was. I survived and it's getting better and better."

Even though I am very accomplished at managing a household and I didn't have to deal with debt, I still experienced fear. For me, like many others, the biggest fears I faced were where to live and how to have enough money to support myself. Having enough money was both a real practical concern and a fear stemming from family conditioning. Let's look at how fear about money can play out at two different levels. Then you can take a look at your fears and sort out what is real from the story that you are telling yourself.

Let's deal with the practical side first. I had been self-employed for seven years, doing leadership coaching with clients. Running my own business was a whole different adventure from having a corporate job where the paycheck was deposited in my bank account every two weeks. My income depended on doing a great job for my clients, and it also depended on attracting new clients in the future. During my divorce, however, I felt depressed, and I had no enthusiasm to do any business development work. Each month that I sat in the doldrums my client base shrank. I was down to only 25 percent of what I could handle. At the same time, I started looking for a condominium to purchase. But if I spent my money on a condominium, then I might not have enough cash to support myself. I decided to be conservative and not to purchase a place.

Many people find themselves in financially crippling situations of huge debt and very little income. One partner may have abused the family finances, leaving the other partner somewhat helpless. It takes courage and determination to face these challenges. We have to approach these situations one day at a time and handle them piece by piece. We can't allow our fear to over-whelm us. You can use the tools in this book to help you deal with your fears from a place of strength.

Fear also arises from the stories that we make up in our heads. I had been afraid of not having enough money to live on ever since I graduated from university and started working at the bank. When we purchased our house, I was afraid we would not have enough money to make the mortgage payments. Even when my income increased to six figures, I still lay awake at night and worried about whether we would have enough money. Now I wondered, without the security of Milo's income, would I be able to make it? Would I be safe when we sold the house and I had to be on my own? What would happen when I got old? Who would look after me, and would I have enough money to pay them? Some days I felt completely overwhelmed by the fear of getting old and not having enough money to look after myself. This fear obviously didn't have anything to do with the present moment—it was way off in the future—but nonetheless I felt the fear as if it were occurring in real time.

The following is a list of fears that many people have when going through divorce. The list comes from the book *Rebuilding: When Your Relationship Ends,* by Bruce Fisher, EdD.

- Fear of the unknown
- Fear of the decisions you have to make
- Fear about money
- Fear of being a single parent
- Fear of losing your kids
- Fear of not having someone to talk to who will understand
- Fear of going to court
- Fear of your anger and your partner being angry at you
- Fear of being alone and living alone
- Fear of being hurt even more than you have been hurt
- Fear of change

SELF-REFLECTION QUESTIONS

What are your fears? Make a list of your fears and answer this set of questions for each:

• What makes you afraid of this?
• What is the worst thing that could happen?
• What is your desired outcome?
• How would you like to feel?
• What are all the different possibilities that would give you your desired outcome?
• What is your first step?
• Who could you talk to about this?
• Who could help you?
• What is the first thing you would like to say when you ask for help?

When we make decisions from a calm and centered place rather than a reactive place, we can make appropriate decisions that leave us in the best possible position. If we make decisions from a reactive place, we can get ourselves into trouble. To make decisions from a centered place, we need to know what we fear, and what stories we are making up that don't serve us. Later in this book, in chapter 13, I will show you how to feel into fear and resolve the underlying emotional conditioning that provides the energy to keep these fears alive in your body. When the energy from the fear is resolved, the negative stories will also start to disappear.

Worry

Worry comes from being focused on negative events that might occur in the future. I found that worry went hand in hand with fear and was one of the biggest wastes of my personal energy, adding stress to my life and my relationships. My lifelong worries compounded the new fears and concerns that came with divorce.

Many of my worries were impossible to explain. These fears were irrational from a logical perspective, nonetheless they existed in my body as a physical sensation of anxiety. I had a fear of starving, for one, and I would stockpile large quantities of food when it was on sale and store it in my pantry or freezer. There was always food in my house, and the refrigerator never got close to empty. I was almost obsessive-compulsive when it came to purchasing food on sale. It wasn't only a fear of starving, there was also a deep fear of not having enough money.

Do you ever worry about what people will think of you? So did I. I was always self-conscious about how much I weighed. As a child I was taller than the other kids, and I experienced myself as being bigger too. By the time I was in high school I was no longer taller, I was just heavier. I felt self-conscious about this extra weight but I lacked the ability to do anything about it—due to my fear of starving! Like lots of people I went on diets and would lose weight, then before very long the weight would slowly creep back up. My weight seemed to be in inverse proportion to my level of self-esteem. When I started to feel better about myself, I lost weight, and when an emotional upset occurred, the weight came right back like an old friend. I didn't know how to defuse all the unhappy emotional energy that was bombarding my body, so I comforted myself with food and then felt self-conscious about what others thought. It was a vicious cycle that started to unwind when I was able to release my emotional conditioning.

All of this worry was due to my own lack of self-esteem, my own inability to love myself. I was transmitting this sort of energy out into the universe. In alignment with the law of attraction, I was bringing to myself what I was sending out. I attracted a man who was very intelligent, but unfortunately he had the same lack of self-esteem. Together we created a safe environment in which we could both survive. All this insecurity resulted in anxiety and stress, and to make myself feel good I treated myself to lots of great meals and wine. Do you think this helped to make me a slim person? Of course not. It added to my excess weight and continued to feed my lack of self-esteem. The vicious cycle continued.

Fear, worry, and lack of self-esteem don't suddenly present themselves when we get divorced; they have long been part of our relationships and have kept us from having more fulfilling lives. When we get divorced, however, all the energy that fuels these emotions becomes fully activated within our bodies, and it will swamp us if we don't find ways to keep it under control. We must look at the reality of the situation rather than the story we have been in the habit of telling. We can shift our attention to focus on what we want to have happen rather than what we don't want to happen.

SELF-REFLECTION QUESTIONS

- What are you worried about?
- What is the truth of the situation right now?
- If your worry were to come true, what would be your first step?
- What would you like to have happen?

Loneliness

Humans have an unquenchable impulse toward a meaningful existence and a valued place in the social order. According to Quartz and Sejnowski in *Liars, Lovers, and Heroes*, loneliness brings vulnerability and the need to identify with something larger than our private existence. Divorce does not create loneliness, but it certainly triggers the fear of being alone. I've battled loneliness all my life. My sense of loneliness came from feeling separate from others. I didn't feel connected. I grew up in a family of adults and I learned how to act like an adult at a very early age, which created a sense of being "different" from most other kids. Even though I behaved in a very mature way, on the inside I was insecure and always looking for approval.

In my mid-twenties I hooked up with a group of other Canadians on a work-abroad program in London. For the first time in my life I had good friends. Returning to Canada to complete my undergraduate degree, I was lonely once again. Then in graduate school I became the party organizer as a way to avoid being alone. When Milo and I got together, I was the one who rented the cabin and did the organizing for ski trips or cycling trips. I always had people over for dinner and barbeques. It probably looked as though I had a great love of people. I did, but I was also carefully avoiding being alone.

For people who feel they are constantly swimming upstream against loneliness, divorce can be especially traumatic. People react differently to being plunged back into the cold waters of being alone after having been in a relationship. There are the "turtles" who hide within a shell of dejection, peering out every so often to see what's out there. There are the "barnacles" who glue themselves to others — to anyone — so that they always have a sense of contact. And then there are the "beavers" who keep busy with projects and frenetic activity, to escape the feelings of loneliness. I was both a barnacle and a beaver. I organized it so that I was either always with people or I was very busy, or both at once!

Those of us who have had a history of not wanting to be alone may find that divorce is not the time to unpack our fear of loneliness. Instead this is a good time to reach out to friends and community and seek out connection. As you reach out, be mindful not to depend upon one or two people for all your support, instead spread yourself around a bit. You may want to find a divorce support group in your area, where you can receive support and also give support to others. This could also be a good time to get involved in a new activity you have always wanted to do.

When the time is right you will be able to work on resolving the underlying fear of being alone. When you resolve this fear you'll find there is a certain peacefulness that comes with solitude. Being alone can be wonderfully rejuvenating rather than frightening. Everyone needs a balance of silence and solitude, community and connection.

SELF-REFLECTION QUESTIONS

- What do you really enjoy doing?
- Are you doing these activities?
- Who do you really enjoy being with?
- Are you spending time with these people?
- Do you feel compelled to enter another love relationship?
- What is compelling you? Is it fear of loneliness, or a healthy desire for companionship? Is it a little of both?
- What is something beautiful and joyful you've experienced in solitude?

Guilt

One of the things I loved about Milo was that he was a nice man, kind and considerate. When I first started dating him I realized that I too would like to show people more kindness. I tended to be very tough and much more focused on myself, mostly out of a fear of being hurt. Milo was gentler, and seemed always to be trying to do the right thing and please others.

During the time when Milo and I were sorting out the end of our relationship, we discussed guilt. Milo told me things that astounded me. For instance, he was convinced that if he did not have feelings of guilt, he would not know the difference between right and wrong. He was plagued by a constant fear of not doing the right thing. This boggled my mind. For eighteen years I had lived with this man who in my perception was extremely kind — and suddenly I find out that he behaved in this way only out of fear of the black demons of guilt that went along with doing something wrong. Love and empathy welled up in my heart for Milo. How he must have suffered throughout his life, constantly fearful of making a mistake and being punished!

Many of us are plagued by feelings of guilt. We have been conditioned to feel guilty by general rules of society, by our parents, by our church, and by our own need for acceptance. As children we were constantly bombarded by rules for right and wrong. Don't hit others, don't yell, don't be rude. Children should be seen and not heard. Don't display affection in public. And many, many, more. When we broke these rules, our parents punished us, our teachers punished us, or God would punish us. As a result of this emotional conditioning, we internalized our guilt as self-punishment.

Guilt is an emotion associated with having done something wrong. It is the result of a betrayal committed against someone else or oneself. We assess our own actions, and if we have not lived up to our standards, we decide we have done something wrong and punish ourselves. We become our own judge and jury. The unfortunate thing is that many times we aren't even aware we are punishing ourselves. This internal punishment can result in stress, depression, suffering, and physical disease. I am very grateful for having received this very simple but very good advice: "Never waste time feeling guilty. If you did something you don't want to repeat, start anew. Period."

The challenge for us as adults is to define our own set of values, as discussed in chapter 4, and to practice living by these values. Our values are like a flashlight that helps us find our way through the dark places in this complicated wilderness called life. When we commit to a practice of living by our values, we come into integrity with ourselves. A practice is something we work at doing on a consistent basis. This is the opposite of guilt, which is the state in which you are constantly trying to avoid doing the "wrong" things.

SELF-REFLECTION QUESTIONS

- What do you believe you did wrong in your relationship?
- What underlying value of yours did you breach?
- What could you have done differently?
- What can you do to forgive yourself?
- What forgiveness do you need from another person?

Exercise: Write a letter to the person you would like forgiveness from. Explain how you were feeling and what was happening for you. Then write a paragraph, or more, as if you were that person forgiving you and expressing his or her understanding. Now write a paragraph, or more, from your own perspective, forgiving yourself for whatever it is you regret doing.

Stress and Depression

All the emotions that bombard us when our relationships end (especially if we punish ourselves with guilt) show up in the form of added stress and potential depression. We make it worse when we get caught in the trap of our own stories and create more suffering for ourselves. We must be vigilant in maintaining our mental and physical health to get us through the emotional trauma.

Milo clearly entered into a period of depression—he had no appetite; he was listless and disconnected. Within weeks he looked like a mere shell of himself. I worried that he would decline into a serious stress-related illness. I lived in denial that our relationship was over and in fear that Milo would become really sick and incapacitated. I had my own overwhelming emotional challenges, caught as I was in the grip of rejection and sadness, and I too felt mildly depressed. I just wanted to avoid what was going on and stay in bed and sleep. This desire to sleep and avoid reality was so enticing that I had to force myself to get out of bed each day.

A vicious cycle takes place when we feel we can't cope with all the overwhelming emotions, and instead of being present to the feelings, we attempt to avoid them. This avoidance can drop us down into the black hole of depression, a place our bodies and minds go to avoid reality. Depression is more than simple sadness or upset due to the ups and downs of everyday life. Depression engulfs daily life, interfering with our ability to work, eat, sleep, and have fun. It is often accompanied by negative thoughts and pessimistic feelings of helplessness, hopelessness, and worthlessness. These are symptoms of depression:[1]

- You have trouble falling asleep or have restless sleep.
- You sleep too much, more than ten hours per day.
- You feel sad.
- You regularly eat more (or less) food than usual.
- You regularly eat more (or less) often than usual.
- You have lost or gained more than two pounds over the last two weeks.
- You find it hard to focus and make decisions.
- You put blame on yourself more than usual.
- You are less interested than usual in people and activities.
- You get tired more easily than usual.
- You feel more sluggish than usual.
- You feel more agitated and fidgety than usual.
- You feel that life is empty and wonder if it is worth living.

If you answered yes to four or more of these statements, you may want to take action to change your feelings. If you answered yes to the last statement, then please seek immediate medical help. It is estimated that 15 percent [2] of the American population will experience depression in their lifetime, more than will experience heart disease and cancer. The important thing is deciding to do something about depression. Standard forms of treating the symptoms of depression include psychotherapy, counseling, and drug therapy provided by a medical doctor. Another way is to use natural herbal remedies to improve mood and nervous functioning and boost the body's sense of well-being. Find a naturopath for professional guidance. You can also address the underlying cause of depression, which is linked to one's own sense of wholeness, well-being, and purpose in life.

I did several things to work through my depression. First, I always set an alarm clock and made myself get out of bed each morning, then I allowed myself thirty-minute naps during the day if I felt I needed them. I went outside and exercised, going for a run or a walk every day. I found something positive to focus on. For me that was working on my business. I went to a naturopath for supplements to offset the amount of cortisol my body was producing from stress. I worked on feeling into all the emotional trauma and upset that I was experiencing. I started to drop off my emotional baggage, which reduced the feelings of overwhelm. Finally I made a decision to let Milo go. If he did not want to be with me, why would I want to hang on to him?

Suffering

It is important to understand that we can cause a great deal of our own suffering and pain if we are not willing to let go of our partners, and also if we are unwilling or unable to work through our emotional reactions. Suffering can show up as illness, or as depression. We will find ourselves bringing this additional emotional baggage into our next relationships, and it may make us less attractive to potential partners.

Henry's situation was a classic example of how things can go very wrong for a person who is not willing to let go of the relationship. His wife, Marilyn, decided within a few months of marriage that she could not live with him and wanted a divorce. For Henry, marriage was a commitment for life. He couldn't understand what he had done wrong, and he kept asking himself, "Why would she do something like this?" He was unable to get an answer to this question and he was unwilling to let the question go. He participated in a year of therapy, and his attachment to being married remained. He was unable to sleep and spent many nights crying on his living room couch. He took up smoking cigarettes to ease the stress; and ended up smoking at least two packs a day. Clients at his hair salon slowly started to disappear; they could no longer bear to hear his sad story. He got caught in a horrible downward spiral that he had to work his way out of. Most of Henry's friends had disappeared, so he had to establish new friendships and connections. Fortunately he still had the support of a few good friends and he was able to claw his way back to health.

Keeping Your Head Above Water

This book is designed to help you work through the challenges you are facing as you enter into your divorce. This book is full of resources to help you overcome suffering and the underlying causes of depression, which are linked to your own sense of feeling whole and complete and having a purpose in life.

In addition to the tools shared in this and previous chapters, I will introduce you to several techniques to *feel into* all the emotional energy you are being bombarded with. When I combined these techniques with the tools I had learned in the world of personal development, my progress toward a state of joyfulness skyrocketed. These tools and techniques will allow you to combat depression and move through divorce faster and with a greater sense of ease. You may find that you are more emotion-ally resourceful than you dreamed. In time, you may even realize that you feel better than ever before. The trick is to use the tools and practice the techniques until they become an automatic habit. This makes it possible to manage emotions in the moment and permanently resolve them in the long term.

The standard advice when working with relationship chal-lenges is to gain an intellectual understanding of the situation and then manage your feelings and responses based on this un-derstanding. This is a very valid approach. What I bring you, however, is new — a fast way to drop off your emotional baggage and deal with your emotions. If you practice both at the same time — that is, both understanding intellectually and dropping your emotional baggage — you will become significantly more emotionally resourceful. A whole new set of options open up. Let's go see what's possible.

PART
TWO

HEADING OUT ON MY OWN

CHAPTER 7

Separate Ways

MILO'S ANNOUNCEMENT THAT HE wanted to leave our relationship was pivotal for my personal development. I had already done a significant amount of work to make positive changes in myself—I was no longer Bulldozer Beatrice, but well on my way to becoming Vibrant Virginia: a bubbly, happy, outgoing woman who felt like the real me. I was satisfied with my life. My relationship with Milo wasn't perfect, but I thought it was good enough. The important part was that I was finally happy with who I was—quite a different person from the woman Milo had hooked up with eighteen years earlier.

Principles for Living

As I explored the world of personal development, I discovered whole villages filled with fascinating and helpful ideas. In each village, I met an elder who presented some new gift or concept for me to practice, and that helped me change my thinking and the way I perceived the world. These concepts have become a set of principles to live by that I incorporated into my life. A personal development journey requires not only that we make a commitment to learning, but that we use—that we actually apply—whatever we have learned. Only then can we achieve the intentions we have set for ourselves. I wouldn't have been able to change my long-held behaviors without this commitment. I had to rethink everything I had learned from my parents and society about "the way life is."

When I changed my thinking, I experienced a dramatic shift in perspective. A whole new reality took shape in my life.

When Milo said he wanted to leave it was a shock, to be sure. But because I had been hanging out with wise elders in the villages of personal growth, I was able to draw on the key principles I had learned, to consciously decide how I wanted our relationship to come to a close. I formed an intention that our relationship would end with grace and ease — or at least as much grace and ease as I could muster while being emotionally devastated. And that was how it happened. I gathered all the vital principles I had learned, and used them to support myself through the emotionally difficult, sometimes even hellish transition. Hopefully these same principles will make your journey through divorce a little easier and serve you well in future life.

Living Consciously

The philosophical conversation about the nature of consciousness has a very long history. There is no common agreement about what consciousness is, or how it works. For our purposes, to be conscious means that we are in an alert, cognitive state, aware of ourselves and the situation. There is a higher consciousness that goes beyond what sustains you physically and encompasses all levels of your being — spiritual, mental, emotional, and physical. I have experienced firsthand that the more aware I am of my thoughts, my feelings, and my spiritual essence, the greater my sense of well-being and self-esteem.

When we take the idea of conscious awareness and extend it into our relationships, it provides an opportunity to be third-party observers of ourselves. When you look back over your relationship, what were your thoughts about it? How were you actually feeling about your relationship? What was your connection to your partner when you met? If you noticed things that you didn't like about your partner, how were these things similar to things within yourself? If you stop and take some time to really look at yourself and your partner, all of a sudden you'll see a whole new picture. You'll see how your partner and you are very much alike in essence. The emotional challenges your partner faces are likely to be closely related to your own challenges in some way.

▶ **PRINCIPLE: MIRROR EFFECT**

Others are simply mirrors of ourselves. What we see in others is true about us. As the saying goes, "It takes one to know one."

Many psychological and relationship counselors view relationships as a place to solve problems of childhood emotional conditioning, such as anger, self-esteem, sexuality, masculinity, and femininity. As adults we make decisions consciously or unconsciously to make sense of and heal what occurred in our early childhood years. When we enter into relationship we often attract partners who have similar family of origin conditioning. This is one of the reasons that we feel so comfortable together. As Daphne Kingma states in her book *Coming Apart*, love brings mystery and romance, but the deeper truth is that we enter into relationships for very specific reasons, whether we are aware of them or not. When we are able to see these reasons and observe our behavior within our relationships, we are being conscious. This knowledge and information provides us with the raw material for transforming our lives and completing the process of growing up to leave our childhood insecurities and fears behind.

For example, when Milo and I first got together we talked a lot about our work environments, mostly complaining about what was wrong at work rather than talking about the great things that were happening. We both had all sorts of judgments about other people and what they were doing. Because their behavior didn't make sense to us, we felt frustrated with our work situations. The bottom line is that both Milo and I were critical and judgmental people, and we were complainers. We were sending out the same kind of energy into the world and hence we attracted each other.

SELF-REFLECTION QUESTIONS

- When you look back over your relationship, what are your thoughts about it?
- How were you actually feeling about your relationship?
- What made you feel connected to your partner?
- What challenges did your partner have?
- How were these challenges similar to yours?
- What behaviors did your partner have?
- How were these behaviors similar to yours?

Freedom of Choice

Once we are conscious of what's occurring around us, then everything in life is a choice. In the early days of my introduction to spiritual development, I was sitting in a seminar room listening to a wise teacher named Anjali speak. The words and concepts she was using were so unfamiliar to me that I hardly understood what she was trying to communicate. Slowly a great big "aha" started to form in my mind: At any moment I have the freedom to choose how I want to feel, how I want to think, and whether I want to respond or react to a situation. I have the freedom to choose at any moment what my behavior is. To choose I need to be conscious, and the more conscious I am the more refined my choices can be.

▶ **PRINCIPLE: FREEDOM OF CHOICE**

- We can choose in any moment who we want to be.
- We can choose to respond to situations instead of re-acting to them.
- Other people's actions have nothing to do with us.

Choosing my actions meant I was no longer a victim of my emotional reactions. I had the ability to be self-aware and to choose my behaviors rather than allow my emotions to control me. Before learning this I was stuck in the limiting belief that I couldn't do anything about my behavior. The principle of free choice allowed me to live into my own personal power. By choosing, I could have a more positive impact on my relationships with people.

There is an important distinction between the words *react* and *respond*. If I go to the doctor and get medication for an infection, and I break out in a rash due to the medication, I say "I have reacted poorly" to it. However if I take the medication and my infection clears up, I say "I have responded well." The same distinction is true when talking about emotional responses. In the beginning I had an explosive emotional reaction to Milo's announcement to leave. I was overwhelmed by sadness. Over the long term however, I chose to respond from a place of love and understanding. I believe a key to my ultimate happiness was my ability to be conscious and respond appropriately to each situation as it occurred. Responding appropriately meant choosing to behave in a way that had the greatest positive impact. When I responded appropriately to situations, I was more likely to stay out of conflict and thus to find an appropriate resolution. Being resourceful enough to make conscious choices meant I actually got to choose how I wanted to be. When I was angry with someone, I could choose to not be angry. To make this choice, I needed to be conscious of my environment and of myself, particularly of my thinking. I noticed that my mind would make up a story about the situation I was angry about. It would keep going over and over the story, twisting it this way and that way, providing additional fuel to the emotional fire. These stories did not serve me as I endeavored to respond instead of react.

To illustrate, a friend asked one time if she could sleep at my place after going to a party. I said sure, just let me know when you will be arriving. When I didn't hear from her, my mind started to make up a story about how inconsiderate she was and how she was taking advantage of my hospitality. When I recognized what my mind was doing, I stopped and asked myself, "What exactly is it I am angry about?" Why do I care if she doesn't call me and can't get into my apartment? Later I found out my friend's cell phone had died. Someone else at the party had offered her a place to stay. Everything worked out fine. By changing my thinking, I let go of the anger and saved myself a lot of unnecessary irritation.

When we have an expectation that something will happen, and then it doesn't, we tend to make up stories about the situation. The degree to which we are attached to the situation will determine our level of emotional intensity. My emotional intensity increases if I have any sense of guilt or rejection around the situation.

The world is uncertain and all sorts of things can happen that get in the way of a set of actions taking place, or that cause a different set of actions to occur. Why take it personally and get upset? What someone else chooses to do really has nothing to do with me anyway; they are just doing whatever it is they do. They are being who they are being, either by conscious choice or more likely by default. Their actions have nothing to do with me and everything to do with them. I don't want to take *everything* personally, so there's really no point in taking *anything* personally. Having this understanding about other people's behavior and about how my mind works made it easier for me to start exercising choice over my thinking and my emotions.

SELF-REFLECTION QUESTIONS

- What are the stories that your mind is telling you?
- How do these stories make you feel?
- What is another story that you could tell?
- How does this new story make you feel?
- What would happen if you chose a different story?
- Notice: What gets in the way of you choosing your thinking?
- Notice: What gets in the way of you choosing how you want to feel?

Constant Learning

My divorce was a very expensive endeavor, both financially and emotionally. It occurred to me that if I was going to get divorced and lose half of my joint net worth, then I had better learn as much as I could from the situation. I chose to apply to my real life all the learning I had done in seminar rooms over seven years. This was going to be my PhD in Personal Development! It was fine to learn in the classroom, but the real test was how I applied what I had learned. Especially now, when I felt like the world was crashing down around my ears. In *Spiritual Warfare*, Jed McKenna points out that the classroom can be a seductive place of constant learning, but at some point you have to step into your life and learn in the field.

▶ ### PRINCIPLE: EVERYTHING IS A
LEARNING OPPORTUNITY

• Look for the learning in everything.

You may think that divorce is simply about ending a relationship that has not worked out. I've seen comments on Facebook like "Let's get out of this relationship so I can start living my life" and "Thank goodness I am out of that relationship!" Ending a relationship may bring smooth waters and an easy closure or a violent storm of bitterness and conflict. We must pass through these events whether we like it or not. However strange it may sound, divorce provides an amazing classroom and a great opportunity to learn. It requires us to open up to see the truth of our relationship. It gives us the opportunity to choose to learn everything we can about ourselves and who we are (or were) in our relationships. As Milo and I started to go our separate ways, I started to look at myself and how I had contributed to our relationship coming to an end.

You may have dreaded divorce, or you may have looked forward to it. Either way, it is an opportunity to reflect on the quality of the relationship you are leaving, what you enjoyed about it, and what wasn't working. Relationships, at their best, can be great learning opportunities where we work with our partners to grow and develop a life that inspires and supports both of us. If we are closed to learning and self-reflection, we may resist making any sort of change whatsoever. This resistance to change makes the process of divorce feel much more difficult as we attempt to live in denial rather than facing (and if possible, embracing) the situation as it is. If you're open to learning, the difficult feelings around your divorce can be turned into a great adventure that will result in huge personal benefits, no matter what the outcome.

As you bring understanding, healing, and the resolution of emotional energy from your emotional baggage, you have an opportunity to choose to be different going forward. You have the possibility of a more rewarding life. You don't need to be a slave, hauling around emotional baggage from childhood conditioning. You don't need to add emotional trauma from divorce to the baggage and carry around an even heavier weight. If you don't resolve this energy you are likely to attract essentially the same partner again. But it doesn't have to be. Embrace learning, even from divorce, and gain mental longevity, a strong positive sense of self-worth, and the possibility of an amazing relationship in the future.

Although I spent twenty-nine years obtaining formal education, it didn't help me find happiness. That didn't happen until I started delving into personal development. I have benefited immensely from my decision to use my divorce as an opportunity for deep personal learning. I am profoundly grateful for being able to resolve much of the emotional conditioning that I was hauling around. Resolving this emotional energy has opened up the possibility for me to live my dream life and find a deeper level of happiness and meaning. What would you like for yourself?

SELF-REFLECTION QUESTIONS

- What are your beliefs about learning?
- How open are you to learning?
- What might be possible if you opened yourself up to learning?
- What would get in the way of using your divorce as an opportunity for learning?
- What is the first thing you learned from your divorce?

PRINCIPLE: PRACTICE SELF-OBSERVATION

- Be willing to constantly look inside yourself and make an honest observation of how you are being in the moment.

Who I Was—The Story of Bulldozer Beatrice

At a workshop I attended we were invited to give ourselves a pen name, write a short one-act play about how we showed up in the world, and then act it out. I chose the name Bulldozer Beatrice. She was a powerhouse of energy who moved forward at lightning speed on a straight line from A to B. She paid no attention to those she rolled over on her journey to her destination—not because she was mean, but because she was oblivious. When Beatrice got an idea, she couldn't help but take action. People often felt like they needed to move aside or get bulldozed by Beatrice.

Beatrice could be an amazing asset. It was great if you were one of Beatrice's friends. Beatrice could throw a dinner party for twenty people in a flash. She rented cabins for downhill skiing and cycling trips. Knowing Beatrice was like having your own private events coordinator.

Beatrice's energy could be overwhelming, however, especially if you didn't know her well. You'd approach with caution: she just might bowl you over. Until conflict erupted, Beatrice wouldn't even know that she had stepped on you and she could never figure out why you would stand in her way. She always saw her cause as "right" and in the interest of all. Beatrice often didn't understand the objections of people into whom she had run headfirst.

Beatrice just wanted to be accepted, liked, and loved. She desperately wanted to be on the inside of the in crowd's circle, but didn't know how. Beatrice was dynamic, smart, and funny; she was athletic and competitive and had a wonderful heart. Despite the hard outer shell that Beatrice displayed, she was a marshmallow on the inside, soft and sweet. But something was missing. Deep sadness and loneliness filled her chest as she felt so alone and separate. She wondered if anyone would ever really love her.

Who I Became — The Story of Vibrant Virginia

Vibrant Virginia is a woman wearing a bright yellow sweater. Her gait is lively and she bounces along the street purposefully headed to her destination. Virginia has a sunny smile on her face and when asked how she is doing she always responds quickly. "Excellent!" Virginia prides herself on being very aware of situations and other people. She can see when people are caught in their stories, and she is patient and empathetic. Virginia feels good being able to serve others.

Virginia can even listen to Milo's stories about work and not give him any advice or feel frustrated. She has finally understood that Milo just needs to talk and that he is unlikely to change. So she chooses to love him for who he is.

At social events Virginia can be the life of the party. She is always sure to greet people with a smile and give everyone she knows a big hug. She is oh so much more comfortable than she used to be, no longer plagued by insecurity. She is so pleased with her newfound happiness that sometimes she can be a little too exuberant for people who are more reserved. She moves at a fast pace that can feel like a bit of a whirlwind, but everyone seems to appreciate her and enjoy her company. Her clients have been known to say that she is the happiest person they know.

Both Beatrice and Virginia are full of big energy. Virginia is a big, bold, happy version of Beatrice. She feels more secure and can let go of wanting to control everything, so others feel more at ease around her. I have come a long way from Beatrice to Virginia. Life is easier for me, more fun, and much more enjoyable. As Virginia I am constantly stretching, growing, and learning and I am proud of my progress. I'm curious about what is possible for me and I constantly set new intentions for what might be possible.

SELF-REFLECTION QUESTIONS

- What one-act play would you write about yourself?
- What pen name would you give yourself?
- How do you feel about this person?

If you decide to write your one-act play, think about acting it out for a couple of people. You may decide to open your heart and fully love the beautiful person in your play.

Who Do I Want to Be?

Who do I want to be? This was a very big question for me. If I didn't want to behave like Bulldozer Beatrice anymore, then how did I want to behave? I understood that this would influence my success in life. When I first learned this concept I didn't know how to be any different, so I decided to accept myself just the way I was. I knew that I could choose to be different, however, and I became very curious and aware of my behavior.

▶ **PRINCIPLE: CHOOSE WHO YOU WANT TO BE**

- Actively choose who you want to be.

As I observed myself over the course of a year, I noticed that I was always in action — any action would do. I didn't know who I was when I was quiet and still. I never sat down long enough to find out. I set myself the goal to take action from a calm place rather than a frantic one. I wanted to accomplish tasks by being methodical and in a place of enjoyment. I did not want to keep tackling projects like there was no tomorrow. I realized that all my frantic activity and rushing around was allowing me to avoid being present to my feelings. And I never felt a sense of accomplishment or success; I just pushed on to the next task. To address my behavior I developed a practice to stop and notice, several times a day, what I was enjoying about what I was doing.

I noticed that when I couldn't be in control, I felt anxious and worried. I felt that if I controlled the outcome of events it would give me a sense of security and everything would be OK. I was also afraid of being left out, not being included. I often took the position of leader within a group, which gave me a sense of being in control and also guaranteed that I would be in the center of the activity and not left out.

The combination of my need to be in control and my drive to get things done resulted in people perceiving me as a very assertive person and, if emotionally provoked, aggressive. This behavior did not win me an abundance of friends and business associates. I had a small solid core of friends who could see my wonderful qualities through my rough exterior, but many people chose never to get close to me. There was something about Bulldozer Beatrice that was not too attractive! This aspect of my personality caused me to feel separate and lonely, lacking the joy, love and abundance that I wanted to feel. I wanted to experience life with a sense of gratitude in my heart, and all I could feel was a sense of competition.

Coaching helped me release the energy from my emotional conditioning that was a barrier to my realizing my intentions. I worked on becoming a gentler, softer person, moving more slowly and being more present to what was occurring in the moment. I became more centered, more aware of what was happening outside of me as well as how I was feeling. The gentler I became, the more my rough edges started to disappear, and I could feel the quality of my relationships deepen.

SELF-REFLECTION QUESTIONS

- What have you noticed about your own behaviors?
- How do you feel about yourself?
- What is it about the way you are being that doesn't serve you?
- What is it that you enjoy?
- Who are you being when you create this enjoyment?
- How would you like to be?

Living from Love

One of the most profound things I did to change who I was being was to choose to live from a place of love. Satyen Raja, one of the elders I studied with, suggested we take a look at our lives and ask ourselves the question, "Am I living my life fully?" For me the question expanded: Was I willing to live in a way that would bring a sense of ecstasy into my life? This meant no longer settling for a way of life that simply felt good, with no major problems. I was being challenged to step up and into the life that I was meant to be living, to live my life with a sense of passion, purpose, and love. Settling for good enough, or OK, was selling myself short. When I did so, I was not fully living the life God intended for me. To live life fully I needed to be willing to step into my greatness.

To make this shift I had to understand what it meant to open my heart to love and live from that place. To open my heart to love meant being able to choose to feel the sensation of love in my heart any time I wanted to. It became a practice. When I was sitting across from someone, I put my attention on him or her, purposefully opened up my heart, and radiated love. I did this simply by becoming aware of my heart in my chest and expanding it with a sense of love. Another way I practiced was to take a deep breath, filling my chest and belly with air, and imagine that I was bringing love into my body. Then when I exhaled I sent the sensation of love out into the world with my breath. I started to become aware that I could feel the sensation of love whenever I wanted. The feeling of love was something that resided inside of me; it didn't come from outside. I started to experience myself as *being* love.

▶ PRINCIPLE: LIVE FROM A PLACE OF LOVE

- Love yourself first.
- Love others even when they are not lovable.
- Practice being love in everything you do.

My next step in the practice of living love was to extend this love to myself. When I looked in the mirror I saw myself as a short, stocky woman. Nothing special. Intellectually I understood that this wasn't true, that I am special and each one of us is special. To internalize the sense of being special I needed to experience it.

As I was working with this intention I met a woman at a workshop who told me what a beautiful, dynamic, and amazing woman I was. I was perplexed. I wondered how she could know this about me—she had just met me. But this was her experience of me. It was certainly not the woman I called Bulldozer Beatrice! That night as I was dancing with the group, I had an out-of-body experience where I saw myself the way she saw me. It was like I was standing outside of my body and for the first time in my life observing myself as a vibrant, dynamic, sexy woman. Seeing and experiencing myself this way allowed me to hold the experience in my body. I decided on a practice to permanently change my image of myself. Every morning for the next three months I stated this affirmation: "I am a sexy, dynamic, and vibrant woman." While I repeated the affirmation I did deep belly breathing. It wasn't long before I regularly started to see myself this way, and my positive view of myself has been increasing ever since.

After opening up to loving myself, the next step was to open up to loving others just the way they were. Could I love others even when their behavior was not that lovable? This was the biggest challenge of all. I faced this challenge with Milo as our relationship was coming to an end. His cheating on me was not very lovable. But could I still love him? The answer was yes. I had loved him for eighteen years and I have not stopped loving him.

Some time after leaving Milo, I dated a man who had a fourteen-year-old daughter. Some of her behaviors were not very lovable, so my practice was to keep my heart open and love her anyway. Now whenever I observe someone having what looks to me like bad behavior, my challenge is to hold my heart open and be curious about what is actually going on rather than being judgmental.

For most of us our core reason for seeking a committed relationship is to love and be loved. We may confuse love with getting our emotional needs met through our partners, and when this does not happen we may feel like something is missing from our relationships. In his book *The Five Love Languages*, Gary Chapman wrote about expressing love through giving gifts, spending quality time together, and offering acts of kindness, touch, and words of affirmation. People may focus on needing these outer expressions of love for their relationships to feel complete. What each person needs to feel loved is highly unique and individual and largely depends on emotional conditioning. Most of us are aware of only a fraction of our emotional needs. Most of the ways we might feel loved are below the surface like an iceberg, waiting to be discovered and experienced. One of the primary values of a committed life partnership is the ongoing process of getting to know ourselves and our partners at ever-deepening levels, building mutual trust, and growing our capacities for connection, for emotional intimacy, and for giving and receiving love.

Expressions of love based on actions and words only scratch the surface. We each have the potential for love to permeate our way of being. Because we are all connected energetically, we are all one. By loving myself and others I automatically extend love out into the world. Expressing love through who I am influences the way I do everything—the way I do laundry, the way I make meals, the way I clean the house. All the tasks that I do every day can be done with a sense of love in my heart.

When I practiced *being love* every day I started to experience the world differently. A new kind of joy and self-satisfaction stirred within me. I started to feel proud of how I was showing up in the world and how I was treating people. I began to treat myself as though I were precious, I felt more self-esteem and a deeper sense of happiness. Ultimately, no one else can make you happy. But I was making myself happy, and others around me experienced my open heart and love. The practice of being love has become a new way that I walk through the world.

▶ **PRINCIPLE: HAPPINESS COMES FROM INSIDE**

- True everlasting happiness comes from inside of you.
- No one can make you happy.
- You can only make yourself happy.

SELF-REFLECTION QUESTIONS

- What would be possible if you felt more love in your life?
- How could you live in a way that brings more love into your life?
- What could you do to show yourself more love?
- Who causes your heart to close?
- How could you open your heart to that person?

Key Principles for Divorce

For a number of years I had been working on who I was being in life in general. When Milo announced that he wanted to go his own way, I was put to the test: Who would I be in adversity? Could I open my heart and live from a place of love in the midst of emotional trauma? This may seem like an odd question to ask while facing the challenges of divorce. However, I think it was one of the most important questions I asked myself. Living from a place of love was a key principle as I worked toward bringing my relationship to a close with grace. Holding love in my heart enabled me to feel love in addition to all the raw hurt and devastation. This sense of love helped me make daily choices that were beneficial to my well-being, choices as basic as getting out of bed in the morning when it felt too difficult to move. Practicing being love led to several other core principles, including those of ease and grace and being open to help.

Ease and Grace

Several months after Milo's infidelity it became apparent to me that he was not committed to our relationship, but just did not have the strength to make the final decision to go in a separate direction. We were floating in circles, both of us afraid to make the final decision. Tom, one of the elders I was studying with at the time, gave me a profound insight. He said, "Milo has clearly indicated his preference for another woman and to leave the relationship. Why are you not willing to let go?"

This statement shocked me into reality. Why would I want to stay with someone who no longer wanted to be with me? I had been afraid to face the truth that the relationship was over. Once I stopped resisting this truth, I was able to choose a new way of being to assist me in bringing the relationship to an end.

This shift in my thinking helped me begin to resolve my emotional attachments to Milo and to our life together. I didn't want our divorce to be difficult. I didn't want conflict. It was time to move on to the next step no matter how unsettling it felt. I knew the experience of ending our relationship would affect how I was going to feel in the future. I wanted to feel a sense of grace as I released Milo from this relationship and set him free to move forward in the direction he had chosen.

I also wanted to be proud of myself and my behavior as the relationship came to a close, and not bitter and angry. I knew people who had been divorced for several years and were still very angry with their former spouses. I didn't want to fall into the same trap. I knew that whatever energy I carried around in my body would attract similar energy from others. I wanted to be able to go through my divorce in a way that was emotionally healthy for both of us.

It is almost impossible to get through divorce without some level of disagreement; it is the degree of conflict that remains to be determined. We all have different perspectives, and when emotions run high these become most apparent. Our attitudes, fears, and emotional responses are like dry kindling that can turn any small bonfire into a raging forest fire out of control. When we are in a precarious emotional state, lashing out in anger can be very easy. As we lash out from this place of hurt and anger we throw more fuel on the fire. Before we know it our former partners are throwing fuel on the fire too and together we have a raging bonfire.

Even though conflict may be inevitable, we do have a choice about how we respond to a former partner. If we *respond* instead of *reacting*, the process will be easier and healthier for both of us. If we are caught in the midst of emotional reactions, on the other hand, everything is much more difficult. When we enter into conflict and bitterness, we run the risk of carrying around long-term anger. I met one woman, Nancy, who had never escaped from the reactive mode. She was still angry with her ex-husband although she had left him nine years ago. She still blamed him for everything that had gone wrong in their marriage.

To stay out of conflict I consciously took responsibility for my role in our troubles. I kept asking myself questions like "What is my role in this? How did I create this?" By asking these questions I was making a conscious choice to look at myself first rather than blame Milo. I recognized that most of what Milo was doing had nothing to do with me, even though it felt like it did. It is so important to learn not to take personally what our former partners are doing. Whatever drama they are choosing to play out is all about them.

I tried to understand why Milo was doing what he was doing, and quite simply the problem was that he was deeply unhappy. He was trying to solve his own unhappiness. When I recognized this, I could say to myself, "What is happening has nothing to do with me." I made a conscious choice not to battle back from a place of anger, throwing fuel onto the fire, and escalating the conflict.

► **PRINCIPLE: CLOSE YOUR RELATIONSHIP**

WITH EASE AND GRACE

• Choose your intention for how you would like to bring your relationship to a close.

I am not suggesting for a moment that you give in to all your partner's demands just to avoid a conflict. Each of you will have your own perspective as to what you want when the relationship comes to an end. You need to negotiate how you want to divide your assets and the way you want to share the parenting of your children. Even in situations where conflict exists, you have the ability to make a conscious choice as to who you are being and the way you want to behave in these negotiations, regardless of how your partner behaves. If even one of you is coming from a place of full conscious choice about who you are being, negotiation will be easier. Even better, when you practice being who you ideally want to be, in this difficult situation, you will build your capacity to be this way in all your future relationships.

In her book *For Better: The Science of a Good Marriage,* Tara Parker-Pope cites a number of scientific studies showing that couples who live in loving, passionate, long-term relationships have better health. Other studies indicate that arguments result in increased stress and a depressed immune system, both of which are linked with a range of health problems. When there is a high level of hostility in our relationships, our cells are not as effective at healing themselves. Parker-Pope says that when we once again become single we should be especially vigilant about our health, in areas such as stress management, diet, and exercise. There is a huge health benefit to bringing your relationship to a close from a place of ease and grace rather than from a place of anger or conflict.

SELF-REFLECTION QUESTIONS

- What intention would you like to have as you deal with your relationship challenges?
- How would you behave if you were living up to your intention?
- How would you behave if you weren't living up to your intention?

- What would get in the way of your behaving the way you want to?
- What would be the benefit of living up to your intention?

Be Open to Help

Are you open to help? This may seem like a silly question, but many people are not open to receiving help and hence they don't ask for help. Lots of people are more open to helping others than to receiving help themselves, and this is a challenge when going through divorce. Though you might not expect it, help is available all the time from all sorts of different sources. If you are closed to receiving help, you won't recognize all the sources that are available. To gauge whether you are open or closed, notice how many times you say, "No, I can do that myself," when people offer help. If you keep saying no, it is an indication that you are closed to receiving help.

PRINCIPLE: BE OPEN TO HELP

- Ask specifically for the help you need.
- Don't be attached to receiving what you ask for.
- Seek help from many sources.

Most of my life I tried to do everything myself. Perhaps I thought if I couldn't do things on my own and needed to ask for help I was a failure. Eventually I learned that successful people ask for help all the time and are open to being helped. Being open to help is very important in all aspects of life and it is especially important when going through divorce. When Milo first told me that he wanted to leave, I drew very heavily on the support of several of my closest friends. I went for walks on the beach or in the woods with them. I talked about my feelings, what I was thinking, and what I might do to work through the situation. I stayed over at friends' houses when it felt too overwhelming to be alone.

Friends are a very important source of help. Sometimes my friends offered help, but most of the time I needed to ask for it. Friends may not know what we need, therefore we need to be ready to ask. When I was in the thick of selling the house, packing, and finding a new place to live, I asked for the help of my friends. They provided moral support and my first two places to live. I realized later that I could have asked my friends for more help in packing and moving instead of trying to do it all on my own. Moving out of the house turned out to be one of the hardest things that I have ever done.

Choose friends who are good listeners to share your thinking with. I was very fortunate to have one friend who really listened to me and heard what I had to say. I felt most supported when she asked me questions about what I really wanted. She didn't try to tell me what she thought I should do. By talking with her I was able to work through much of my own thinking and access the knowledge inside of me. We all hold the knowledge of what is right for us inside ourselves. Although it is often hidden behind emotional reactions, intuition can show us the truth of a situation. When we access our deeper wisdom, we know what the correct course of action is for us.

I was leery of friends who focused on offering sympathy, however, because their advice often came from their own emotional reactions. Acting on the suggestions of these friends would have meant taking action based on their emotional reactions rather than mine. Use your friends as a sounding board for your thinking, and at the same time be careful of taking action based on their advice. Make sure that the advice is not coming from your friend's emotional reaction, and that it is appropriate for you. It is a good practice to wait before acting on advice.

One key to overcoming my challenging situation was being

open and vulnerable with people about what was happening. Emotional trauma impacts the rest of our lives. When I was open, people provided me with lots of support. In reaching out to others, though, one of the pitfalls to avoid is coming from a place of negativity, blame, or bitterness. Our supporters get tired of listening when we are constantly playing the victim role. Over time people find this toxic. If you notice certain individuals limit their time with you, check in: Are you complaining? Also watch out for friends who would love to jump on the negativity bandwagon with you, as this sort of commiseration will not serve you in moving forward and getting past conflict.

Professional support can be very helpful. As a professional has no vested interest in the outcome, he or she is there to support you 100 percent. Community organizations and churches often provide divorce support groups. Many people who have a background in counseling or psychotherapy specialize in relationship and divorce counseling. Coaches also provide support for relationship challenges. Not all counselors and coaches are the same, so choose someone you feel comfortable with and with whom you can develop a good connection. Notice if their advice is a good fit for you.

You can expect to develop clarity and insight about your situation through a counseling or coaching relationship. From this place of clarity you will have a better foundation for making decisions. When we are ending a relationship we have many decisions to make that will affect our lives emotionally and financially. We may be caught in the grip of emotional turmoil, which is one of the worst places to be when we have to make decisions. The more grounded and centered we are, the better our decisions will be, which is especially important when we consider shared responsibility for the welfare of children. Professionals can help us gain insight into our situations and resolve the emotional turmoil we encounter. This is what one of my coaching clients, who worked with me after separating from his wife, said:

> This has been a year of many great experiences. I
> have a better relationship with my father than I have

ever had, and I now feel like I am in control in a way that I have never been before. For many months it was painful, and now at the end of a year it is wonderful to no longer feel the emotional pain. From the work we have done I know in the future, whether with my current wife or with a new person, I will be able to be more tuned in to the relationship.

SELF-REFLECTION QUESTIONS

- What kind of help do you want?
- Who are three people you could ask?
- What would stop you from asking?
- What is the possible benefit of asking?
- When will you ask these people for help?

Going Our Own Ways

Milo and I had reached the point from which our paths would diverge. We were each going to go our own way. It was a sad and difficult time for both of us. I made a choice to be very conscious about how we were relating to each other and how we treated each other. I was aware that I had the freedom to choose my behavior as I set out on my new path. I could decide to use the divorce as a source of learning and growth, or I could resist. In the midst of my pain I tapped into my own personal power and made a decision about who I wanted to be as I went through this experience. I wanted to be proud of myself. I didn't want to feel guilty in the future about anything that I did, and I certainly didn't want to ruin my health — it wasn't worth it. From this place of power I drew on the lovely Vibrant Virginia and said, "Sister, let's go and make the best of this. Who would you really like to be?" Virginia realized that it might be good to practice being a little softer and gentler, and divorce gave her lots of opportunity.

You got married because you loved someone, and now I am suggesting that as you get divorced you also stand in the place of love. If we can be in the place of love as we separate from a partner, then we can stand in the place of love any time we choose. Standing in this place of love helps us to choose a worthy intention that will guide us. My intention was ease and grace. Having a clear intention can keep us from slogging it out in the realms of anger and conflict. The business of bringing a relationship to a close needs to happen. We do have a choice, however, over how we respond or react to our partners' proposals. We can stand in a centered and grounded place as we negotiate—or we can create an angry battlefield of carnage. It all depends upon who we want to be as we go our own way.

This is a difficult time, and it is difficult to keep our hearts open to love. That is why it must become a practice, just like going to the gym. It is important that we connect with the familiar faces of our friends. We may have to help them to help us, to ask for what we need—this is a great life skill.

As you practice the principles in this chapter, you will be using your divorce to start your own personal exploration. If you answer the questions in this book and undertake these principles, I guarantee you will gain great insight into yourself. Although it may be hard, step boldly onto this new path. You can do it.

CHAPTER 8

Looking Back up the River

THE TOOLS AND PRINCIPLES THAT I gained from my time with the elders served as a life vest and prevented me from drowning when our kayak turned over. I was able to swim strongly for shore and pull myself out of the cold waters of Milo's announcement. As I sat dripping wet on the shore and looking back at our overturned boat, I wondered what had happened. Could it have been prevented? I hadn't even seen it coming. If I was going to forge on into future relationships, what could I learn from the ending of this one?

I made a fire, sat on the riverbank, and reflected on the river of our relationship. Soon enough I would need to get moving and find safety with other people, but for the moment I sensed that it would serve me well to sit still and take time to delve into the problems that I had encountered in marriage.

We all have hopes and dreams for our relationships, and yet sometimes something goes wrong and our dreams come to an end. Some marriages are an endless source of conflict, and it is not surprising when they come to an end; others, like mine, end all of a sudden without any apparent reason. What causes conflict in a marriage? What can cause our boats to capsize?

Why Do Marriages End?

Marriages end for many different reasons. Understanding why your own marriage is coming to a conclusion will provide useful information about how to keep from making the same mistake again in the future. What could we resolve or be aware of to ensure a better outcome next time? The reasons for a breakup point to underlying conflicts and conditioning. There is lots of evidence to suggest that we attract specific people into our lives in order to learn certain life lessons. Until we learn these lessons, we will likely attract similar circumstances again.

Many couples get married without identifying any common objectives for the relationship. Maybe they don't have anything to work toward, or maybe they can't agree upon what they really want. Problems occur in marriages around money, family, sex, addictions, and housework. These problems can be accentuated where there is poor communication, fear of conflict, or inability to express feelings.

The cause of a breakup are like boulders in the river of the relationship that we either steer around or crash into. Unfortunately these same boulders seem to reappear over and over again — until we become highly competent at navigating around them, or until we remove them from the river. By the time you finish this book you will recognize that your relationship offers you several choices:

- Do nothing and hope it all works out.
- Manage what is occurring in your relationship and try to steer around the boulders.
- Resolve the underlying emotional issues in your relationship so that some of the boulders disappear.
- Get out of your kayak, leave the river, and hope the next river doesn't have any boulders.

My suggestion is to first remove the boulders, and then decide if you would like to stay on the river.

Life provides many sources of boulders. Once you know what they are, you can become much more adept at steering around them or even eliminating them.

No Map

A fundamental problem for Milo and me was that we had no map
or vision of what we wanted to create together with our union. It
was as though we had come together to be safe and beyond that
we had no purpose. We had no picture of what the river looked
like or where we would really like to go on this river system. Milo
never wanted to talk about the future or have anything to do with
establishing joint goals. In the early years, he was convinced that
he would not live long enough to even reach retirement, which
surprised me. I suggested he save some money anyhow, just in
case, which he did. I often talked about having a house on the
ocean, and one day, driving back from a ski trip in Whistler, I
designed the house in my mind and described it to him. He said
it sounded fine. That was our joint visioning exercise! This lack of
desire to plan together was an indication of a lack of connection
in our relationship. When our partners don't communicate, it is
hard to know what their truth is.

In reality Milo and I wanted very different things in life. As
I contemplated my future without him, I realized that life for
me is an adventure. I am never happier than when heading out,
whether to Europe or on a skiing or camping trip. Milo and I had
great outdoor adventures for our holidays and I loved every one
of them, pouring rain or not. Apart from the camping trips, however, Milo liked to stay around home and have a quiet life; he did
not want to go on adventures.

It turned out that our relationship was not an adventure, nor
did it have a clear purpose. Instead, we were rudderless. We fell
into the routine of everyday living and looking after my mother,
and settled for that as a purpose. Maybe if we'd had children, it
would have been different; the children would have given us purpose, at least for a while. Then the children would have moved
out and we would have been faced with the challenge of finding
a new purpose.

Even when we do have a map of where we are going in our
relationships, our maps will need constant revision and updat-

ing as life changes. This requires a commitment to communicate. Without a purpose we may start to wonder why we are on this river anyhow. Maybe there is a more exciting river to explore.

SELF-REFLECTION QUESTIONS

- What vision did you and your partner have for your relationship?
- What was your relationship really about?
- What would you have liked the purpose of your relationship to be?

Money

How money is handled in a relationship encompasses several areas. We can look at how we spend money, the amount of debt we are willing to carry, and the degree to which each of us will focus our time and energy on earning money. Dealing with money requires that we communicate clearly about our values around money. When we don't communicate, or if we have significantly different values, we can end up in a situation like Terry found herself in with her husband, John.

Before marrying John, Terry had been used to managing her own money, and she had never had financial problems. But John was always focused on how there was never enough money. So it amazed Terry that John wasn't better at managing his money, given his focus on there being a lack of it. "You would think that if there wasn't enough money, a person would be more judicious with it, but whatever money came in got spent." This was not the way Terry handled money. She always ensured that there was a little put away for a rainy day.

The week Terry moved out, she felt something opening up, as though there were more money in her bank account. Energetically, she had broken away from the scarcity pattern. She realized that she could make her financial life work, despite the revelation of $30,000 in credit card debt that John had accumulated.

In *For Better*, Tara Parker-Pope points out that financial issues rank as one of the top reasons cited for divorce. Although earning power dynamics have changed over time—one in three women now earns more than her husband—money is still the number one source of conflict in marriages. Partners who have different values, goals, priorities, and habits around money and debt are likely to argue. Part of building a life together is creating a common vision for the financial relationship, and this requires in depth conversations about money.

The following five questions can indicate how likely it is that you will encounter conflict around money in your relationship. Think about these five questions carefully and answer each one yes or no:

- My partner spends money judiciously.
- We save enough money.
- We are in alignment about significant purchases.
- We manage debt appropriately.
- My partner doesn't have a need to control the money.

How many did you answer no to? If you answered no to even one, then understand that financial issues could be taking a toll on your relationship.

Problems around money come in many different shades: One partner has an addiction problem—alcohol, drugs, gambling—which is being enabled by the major income earner's financial support. Or, the partner who is responsible for managing the combined money is not making the car payments or paying the bills, and now there is an unknown amount of accumulated debt. Or, one partner is spending huge amounts of money, and running up the credit cards so high that it is almost impossible to pay them off.

These kinds of situations are signals that all is not right in the relationship. Someone is not taking responsibility for the joint relationship, and the other has given up his or her power, having blind trust that their partner is acting appropriately. When it comes to money, we all need to be self-responsible and aware. Trust your partner, just don't be blind: you never know when it will be vitally important that you know what is happening to the money in your relationship.

Conflict around money often arises due to family conditioning. We may use money as a means to feel happy and secure, we may shun money because we think it is bad, or we may want to completely avoid the role it plays in our lives. Each of these typical attitudes toward handling money carries a potential for conflict.

There are several ways to alleviate some of the conflict around money. One is to resolve our underlying emotional conditioning around money, as this drives our behavior patterns. Another is to find some simple financial solutions, either to keep track of where we spend money or to allocate money for specific purposes. A great resource for understanding where we spend money is *The Adventures of Alice in Moneyland,* by A Woman Named Pepe. Having honest conversations with our partners about the five questions posed earlier in this section is another way to alleviate conflict. Talk about each other's values with regard to money. Have a conversation that places the way each of you handle money within the context of the map you developed for your relationship together. Handling money is all about finding a balance between pursuing long-term objectives, having a sense of security, and enjoying life.

When we have a vision for our lives, and know what objectives we and our partners have for marriage, it is much easier to establish a set of agreements about money. Those of us with significant debt may want to seek the advice of a financial counselor on the best way to manage our money and repay the debt as quickly as possible.

SELF-REFLECTION QUESTIONS

• When it comes to money, what is your greatest concern?
• What are your strengths in handling money?
• What would you like to be different about the way you
  handle money?

Money and Divorce

It is important that neither partner totally abdicates responsibility for money management. Not paying attention to how money is being handled in our partnerships is like sitting in our boats going around in circles and looking at the beautiful trees, pretending everything is fine. We must know how money is being spent and what our accumulated assets and debt levels are. If we are naïve about money, it is very easy for people to take advantage of us, as Terry discovered when she learned of her partner's credit card debt. Be alert in case something unexpected happens and you have to take steps to protect yourself. Divorce can bring out ugliness and greed around money, and partners can do some pretty awful things to each other as they leave the relationship.

Tammy bears witness: "I took care of our bills. However, my husband was the primary breadwinner. I had given up my career to follow his dreams. I was a stay-at-home wife until I filed for divorce. Before that I had been unemployed for three years, which has made it nearly impossible to find any work. My ex has managed to leave me penniless because he was able to hire a very good lawyer, and I could not afford to fight."

Money can be a lofty bank on the river that holds us in our marriages, and it can also be one of the ugliest battlegrounds. When we are in a place of fear we often go into fight-or-flight mode, and unfortunately, when it comes to money many people enter into fight mode. For both married and common law relationships, the legal system regulates what will happen to joint assets. (The laws differ by type of relationship and by state or province.) However, the legal system does not care whether you personally maintain any of your assets or not; it just cares that society as a whole is not disrupted. Fighting your way up the riverbank of finance to kick dirt in the other person's face will probably cost thousands of dollars in legal bills, plus significant emotional turmoil. As Tammy found out, whoever controls the most money has access to the best legal support.

Milo and I were fortunate: We gave each other a helping hand up the financial riverbank. We worked together to see if one of us wanted and could afford to keep the house. At the end of the day, both of us decided to let the house go. Together we came to the conclusion that how we split the assets was not going to make a major difference in either of our lives. Why fight about it? We simply paid the debts and split the money in half. Because we had never gotten married, we created our own separation agreement, signed it, had it witnessed, and put it away for safekeeping.

We have a number of options for how we go about splitting up the assets in our relationships, and it is largely up to us and our partners to determine the ease with which this will take place. Do you want to fight or do you want to negotiate? Do you want to get even or do you want a peaceful parting that is also equitable? You can find lawyers who will fight to maximize your interest, and lawyers who will do their best to obtain a fair and reasonable settlement. Instead of a lawyer, you can work with a mediator who will negotiate on your behalf to arrange a settlement. You can negotiate your own settlement, as Milo and I did, and then get legal support to register your settlement. It all depends upon how collaborative you want to be.

You would be well-advised to take some professional advice. When children are involved, and especially when one of the partners has stayed home to look after them, it will be necessary to have professional help to negotiate a fair and equitable allocation of income and assets.

Be aware that the divorce proceedings will be a reflection of your emotional state. The more emotionally resourceful you are, the easier the process will be.

SELF-REFLECTION QUESTIONS

- What fears could you resolve before even starting the financial negotiations?
- If you were to have your way, what would be your ideal way to negotiate a settlement?
- What is your financial situation right now?
- What would be a reasonable settlement if you took the position that it was no one's fault that the marriage was coming to an end?
- What professional resources are available in your community to assist you?

Family

Family relationships can cause stress when partners do not set clear boundaries or share mutual perspectives on family. Conflict may arise if parents or siblings don't like our partners and then interfere in the relationship. Or perhaps a family member is constantly asking for help in terms of time or financial resources. Our partners may view these requests as taking resources away from our own immediate family. A power struggle can ensue when partners then attempt to get their way and control the situation.

Many different underlying dynamics may be occurring where someone in the extended family is asking for help. Those asked for help may feel guilty about not helping, perhaps because they are trying to make up for a past situation or make themselves feel worthy. The partners may be jealous of the attention given to family members, or may feel there is a scarcity of love or money and that what is being given to the extended family will not be available for them. All of these dynamics set up a lose-lose situation for the couple. John Gottman states in *The Seven Principles for Making Marriage Work* that we need to create a sense of "we-ness" with our partner, showing them that our primary allegiance is to them.

Modern-day couples have high expectations around emotional support, friendship, and quality time together, and when a new baby arrives on the scene it can create stress in the marriage. Children require time and money, create a lot more housework, and change the dynamic in a couple's romantic life. They become the center of attention, needing nurturing and cutting into the quality time the couple previously spent together. Wanting to spend a significant amount of time with their children, parents may shortchange themselves of adult-oriented activities. In *For Better*, Tara Parker-Pope reports that many studies indicate parents have more arguments, and that marital happiness and relationship quality declines with the arrival of children. It is not surprising, given the demands of parenthood, that parents suffer a higher incidence of depression than do nonparents. Depression places further strain on a relationship.

If you have children and are struggling in your relationship, know that you are not alone. Research suggests that you need to make time for more than parenting. Parents who are devoted to their children will make it a priority to also have time for each other. Studies indicate children from happier families achieve higher academic grades and are more socially adjusted. Therefore looking after the quality of your marriage will also assist you in looking after the welfare of your children. Even though having children presents difficulties, on a life-happiness scale couples with children are just as happy as couples without children. The question is, are you willing to invest the effort required to keep your intimate relationship filled with love when children arrive on the scene?

SELF-REFLECTION QUESTIONS

- What role does family conflict play in your marriage?
- Where could you be more understanding of your partner's need to support his or her family?
- Is your relationship truly suffering because your partner supports his or her family?
- What conversation do you need to have with your partner?
- What is happening in your parenting that you could let go of to make more time available for yourself?
- Where could you make more time for your partner?

Housework

How many people really love to do housework? It's no surprise that housework can be a significant cause of marital conflict. Fair allocation of work is the major issue, especially when both partners are working outside of the home and children are involved. Even though so many women have paid employment, they still do most of the housework. When women get married they spend 70 percent more time on housework than they did when they were single, and men spend 12 percent less time.[2] Many women won't ask for help, believing their partners should just offer, should just know what to do. Women can also be very particular as to how the work is done and tend to micromanage their partners. This can be a way for a woman to feel more powerful. Men, meanwhile, have a tendency to assume that housework is a feminine role, so when they do housework they may feel they are helping their partners out instead of taking responsibility for a shared need.

There are long-term historical gender roles in the area of

housework, and these result in deeply ingrained attitudes and behaviors. Ladies, we can either assert that we are right based on our views of women's liberation, or we can get help to come up with a win-win strategy. My first suggestion is to let go of the attitude that men should know what to do. Ask for help on a specific task, thank your partner for helping. Make it a game — use it as an opportunity to feel gratitude and an opportunity for your partner to feel acknowledged. Most men want their partners to be happy and like to be acknowledged for what they do. We are all looking for acknowledgment and recognition.

Men tend to do one thing at a time. When they have completed a task, it leaves their mind and they move on to the next one. Men need to be acknowledged specifically for what they have done, and to be most effective it needs to be shortly after the task is completed. Women's brains are different in that the connection between the right and left hemispheres is larger. This allows for a greater flow of information and greater ability to multitask. Brain science is showing us that men and women work differently, and so learning to respect each other is hugely important.

Many women don't like to ask for help; we often do things ourselves rather than ask. Even though the universe is full of help, most of us are trying to be tough and do everything on our own. This is a difficult way to live. Practice asking for help. When we open ourselves up to receiving help, more help is offered. Then we can be grateful for the help we receive. Don't take anything for granted.

Any of us can benefit from giving up control over how the housework is done. Our partners may have different standards than we do — their standards may be lower or higher, but most likely will not be exactly the same. Our lives would be a lot easier if we stopped trying to control how things are done and allowed our partners to do things their own way.

In general, men need to make a bigger contribution to housework, especially when their partners are working outside of the home. Even a modest shift in the distribution of household labor will make a significant difference in a relationship. However, the path to shifting household chores will require giving up control, asking for help, and respecting ingrained historical conditioning.

SELF-REFLECTION QUESTIONS

- What is your attitude about your partner's role in housework?
- What is your partner not doing to your satisfaction?
- What is your partner doing really well?
- How good are you at asking for help?
- How good are you at showing gratitude and providing specific acknowledgement for helping?
- Where do you need to let go of control?
- Where could you make a bigger contribution to housework?
- Where could you raise your standards to be in greater alignment with your partner's desires?

Sex

Differences in sexual desires can be a ripe source of marital conflict. Conflict can occur when there are differences regarding the frequency of sex, the degree of intimacy, and the degree of adventure each person might like. Studies indicate that sexual activity in a relationship declines over time unless a couple makes a conscious decision to have an active intimate sexual relationship. Tara Parker-Pope reports that the average adult has sex 58 times a year, or about once a week with a few extra days of bliss mixed in. The average sexual encounter lasts about thirty minutes. Younger people have more sex than older people. The average for married people under thirty is 112 times a year, and for those between fifty and fifty-nine, 54 times a year. The frequency of sex also declines the longer a couple is married. After the first year of marriage the frequency drops about 50 percent, and it continues to decline slowly each year thereafter.

Men and women report significant differences in their desire to have sex and in their definitions of a satisfying sexual relationship. Parker-Pope provides some interesting statistics on women's and men's differing levels of sexual desire. Sixty percent of women at the age of thirty want regular sex at the beginning of a relationship, and only 20 percent of women have the same wish at age fifty. So ladies, if your desire for sex is declining, you are not alone. Men's sexual desire, however, does not tend to decline as much with age: between 60 and 80 percent of men of all ages want regular sex. Women are usually looking for something different from their sexual relationships than men. They look for tenderness and caring, while tenderness is a low priority for men.

Frequency of sexual intimacy is an indication of the level of passion within the relationship. Couples that have sex more often generally have happier relationships. What contributes to a high-quality and active sex life? Remaining healthy as we age is a key factor. As people age, our health tends to decline, hampering our ability and desire to have sex.

If our sex lives are not what we would like, what can we do about it? First and foremost we need to be able to communicate with our partners. We need to find out if they would be willing to have more sex and what is getting in the way. Lack of communication can contribute to the demise of a relationship.

For example, Robert and his wife had sex only a couple of times a year for almost ten years. Robert continued to have a strong desire for a sexual relationship, but his wife had reached a place in her life where she no longer wanted to participate in a sexual relationship. Eventually their relationship came to a breaking point due to their significantly different levels of desire.

These patterns can be changed. A couple should first seek medical help, in the form of allopathic medicine, naturopathic medicine, or wellness counseling. A low sex drive can be associated with low testosterone, erectile dysfunction, menopause, depression, or side effects of medications. Also as we enter our late forties, hormonal changes can affect our desire to have sexual relations.

Menopause in women is much better understood today than it used to be; however, male menopause still does not have a high profile. In *Male Menopause*, Jed Diamond states that men go through hormonal and physiological changes too, and that men and women have much in common with regard to the effects of menopause. "The most fearful change for a man involves his sexuality," Diamond says. As they age, men often feel a loss of power, purpose and passion, and with this loss they can feel as though it is the beginning of the end for them.

Women may also feel a sense of loss as their childbearing years come to an end, or they may be dealing with significant fluctuations in sleep and mood as hormonal levels change. This is a time of significant transformation. We need to have empathy for our partners and the changes that are occurring within them. Given our longer lifespans, at menopause we are really just at the beginning of the next third of our lives.

Our sexuality may also be affected by emotional trauma from earlier periods in life, which may suppress our desire to be sexually active. My clients have used the Emotional Hot Button Removal techniques I teach in chapter 13 of this book and in my coaching to resolve emotional energy that was resulting in erectile dysfunction. The Emotional Hot Button Removal techniques may also be used to resolve the underlying causes of depression. These techniques enable us to let go of the emotional energy that we hold in our bodies from old traumas. When we let go of our emotional energy, it allows us more freedom to rekindle a sense of desire for our partners.

Some couples can simply make a conscious decision to have more sex. When we become sexually active again, even after a long time, our bodies flood with certain chemicals, and within minutes sex feels natural again. This doesn't work for everyone, though — some people find their stomachs knotting up with anxiety at the thought of forcing the issue. But the Emotional Hot Button Removal techniques can be used to resolve emotional reactions to the thought of having sex. Sitting down and talking to our partners specifically about our sexual desires can go a long way in bringing us closer together and alleviating the sexual desert that we may be lost in.

Resolving sexual inactivity can be worth it. Sexual intimacy can bridge a lot of relationship gaps that talking simply won't solve. People who have strong passionate relationships are happier and physically healthier than people who don't. For the sake of your relationship, your children, and your health, it is worthwhile to face the challenges of the bedroom. What you don't face now, you will likely have to face in the future if you choose to enter into a new relationship.

SELF-REFLECTION QUESTIONS

- How strong is your desire to have sexual relations with your partner?
- What is getting in the way of having more sex with your partner?
- What would improve the quality of sex in your relationship?
- What conversation do you need to have with your partner about sex?
- What stops you from talking to your partner about sex?

Addictions

People engage in all sorts of activities so they can disappear and avoid difficulties they don't want to face on the home front. We immerse ourselves in work, athletics, alcohol, drugs, and any number of hobbies that allow us to become fully absorbed and take our minds off our problems.

Some people immerse themselves so fully in their careers that they have little time for family. They get up early in the morning, go to work, come home for a short time to play with the children before going to bed. The next day they plug back into their computers and smartphones and re-immerse themselves in work. These people have made up a story that they need to work this much to get ahead and be successful. If you are a workaholic ask yourself, What defines success? Is it money or wealth? Is it your title and power at work? Or it is the quality of your relationships, specifically the quality of your relationship with your family? When it comes to career and work versus family, we all need to make a conscious choice about what is most important.

Often people avoid relationship problems by immersing themselves in some kind of activity. People jump into an inordinate amount of training to participate in extreme sports such as marathons and triathlons. Hobbies can be a great way to carve out some time for yourself, or they can be a place to hide from your family. For example, Greg liked to race cars. He spent every night after dinner in the garage working on his car, and on weekends he was at the racetrack. Racing became a way for him to avoid dealing with the lack of sexual intimacy in his marriage. I myself used cooking and gardening to avoid what I didn't want to face in my relationship. I didn't even realize what I was doing.

To distance themselves from the emotional wasteland of their relationships, some people take refuge in alcohol, marijuana, or harder drugs. All these alter our reality, and for a short time we forget our problems. However our problems will still be there right in front of us when we straighten out. Regardless of the method we use to escape, we are abandoning our families and avoiding our issues in favor of some other activity that seems much more attractive.

In my ten years of experience as a coach, I have consistently found that people avoid facing challenges. Most of us will avoid any type of conflict in favor of settling for the current situation. We may not like what is going on in our relationships, but we are frightened at the thought of venturing out into the white water of the rapids and tackling our problems. The possibility of over-turning the relationship boat is more than many of us are willing to risk. Fear of the relationship ending and having to deal with the emotional trauma that comes with divorce is enough to keep most of us safely circling in an eddy rather than daring to venture out into the center of the river. Unfortunately, circling in the eddy only presents an illusion of safety. What we are avoiding will eventually come to a breaking point when one partner or the other decides, even subconsciously, that a change needs to occur. We always have a choice: face the situation now and try to solve it, or wait until things fall apart and are no longer repairable.

SELF-REFLECTION QUESTIONS

- What role do addictions play in your relationship?
- If it is your addiction, what is it that you don't want to feel?
- What are you trying to ignore?
- If it is your partner's addiction, would they be willing to seek help?
- If it is you, are you willing to seek help?

Commitment in Action

It is a major decision to get married and we make a significant commitment to our partners to live our life together. I am not sure that we realize how big of a commitment we need to make to ensure that our relationship remains vibrant. Plus I don't think that most of us have the tools or the knowledge to work our way through the challenges I have just listed. To have a thriving relationship, our commitment needs to be more than staying together. We need to accept that we may need help to learn how to stoke the fires of our relationship to keep it burning hot and bright. Then we need to be committed to doing the work. Partners come together from a place of love, beginning with a strong chemical attraction. As this chemical attraction matures, our love needs to evolve too, into a place of deep connection and commitment at the intellectual and emotional levels. Today more than ever we have very high expectations that our partners will fulfill most of our needs and be the central figures in our lives. For these expectations to be fulfilled we need to be willing to learn and grow and communicate. We need to be open to listening to our partner and hearing their concerns and coming to some agreement about how we want to live together. We need to be open to making changes to improve how we show up in our relationship. We may need to examine our thinking and beliefs about money or housework or the way we spend time with our partner. Then we have to be willing to practice taking new actions to support the relationship. Being committed is about being committed to more than ourselves; it is about doing our best to maintain a healthy vibrant relationship.

I have had two significant committed relationships: one with Gary, and the second with Milo, from the age of thirty-one to forty-nine. Gary and I got married when I was twenty-two. Milo and I started living together when I was thirty-one; we never did get married. Yet in many ways I was much more committed to my relationship with Milo than I was with Gary, even though Milo and I didn't get married.

I met Gary when I was sixteen and he was twenty-three. At twenty-one, I had been going out with Gary for six years and I was running out of reasons not to get married. My attitude did not bode well for this commitment. We got married the following October. I was twenty-two.

From the very beginning our relationship was in trouble. I

took over total responsibility for our domestic life, organizing the wedding, finding us a house to rent; all he had to do was move in. I worked full-time, cooked all the meals and cleaned on weekends. I was a powerhouse and I did it all, mostly because I wanted to be loved. Being a powerhouse did not leave much room for Gary to show up in the relationship.

It wasn't very long before our relationship started to break down. The two of us had the same childhood conditioning: the man was the head of the house. But I didn't like the way my father dominated my mother. I was outspoken and I would not be told what to do! Sparks flew, arguments exploded, doors slammed, and I realized that I had made a grave mistake.

In hindsight I understand that Gary was just trying to exert himself as a man, and that back then I had no idea how to relax, be feminine, and give him room. I had no idea about masculine and feminine energy or that I might let him take the lead.

I met Milo ten years later, in 1991, and we moved in together about six months after we met. I was thirty-one, I had finished my graduate degree, and I was ready for a permanent relationship. Milo seemed ready for a permanent relationship, but he was not willing to get married. Milo had two major decisions to make. The first was about my career. Was he committed enough to our relationship that it would make sense for me to stay in Vancouver even if I were offered a job elsewhere? He said yes. Then, after we'd been living together for eighteen months, was he willing to purchase a house together and have my mom come and live with us. Again his answer was yes. That was the last "yes" I got out of him.

When it came to marriage, Milo would not even talk about it. He was willing to have a boat on the relationship river, but he was never willing to claim that boat as his pride and joy. I had wanted to get married, so I poured my heart and soul into our relationship boat to make it an ideal place that we could call home.

When the little voice in my head said that people who love each other get married, I asked myself what was important to me about being married. I could not come up with a good reason to be married, other than this was the way I thought life should be.

From a practical perspective I couldn't see that life would be any different if we were married; it didn't seem like we would love each other any more. Was I willing to force the issue? The answer was no. I knew it would be the end of our relationship, which was much more satisfying and a lot more fun than the relationship I'd had with Gary. Being married to Gary showed me that marriage didn't guarantee that a relationship would work.

In fact, I was mortified that Gary and I had sunk our marriage kayak in less than a year. I was ashamed and embarrassed about my failed marriage and I stuffed those feelings away under a layer of independence and thick skin. I was willing to overlook Milo's aversion to marriage due to my own previous failure. I had already crashed one boat and he hadn't crashed any, so maybe he was right, and we didn't need to be married to be committed.

Solid Banks for Your Commitment River

In any relationship there is some stormy weather, and if the riverbanks are low, it is very easy for our boats to run aground. People with strong religious beliefs may find that the banks of their relationship river seem steeper with formal marriage, which may make them feel more secure when things start to get stormy. When storm clouds build, many people turn to God for emotional and spiritual support and for guidance on what action to take. Prayer can, among other things, provide a valuable cooling-off period to help us avoid an impulsive reaction.

Parents may find their values around raising children provide a powerful reason to commit to their relationship. Sam, who could not have children, wanted children so badly that he accepted that his wife had cheated on him in return for their two children.

Fear of failure can provide another bank for a relationship river. Leaving a marriage can feel like a huge failure, as it did for me with my first marriage. Traditional conditioning for men is that they should provide for and protect their families, so when the family unit breaks up, they may feel like they are failing to carry through on their commitments.

Fear of being alone can keep us committed to a relationship. When our kayaks have been floating around in a nice calm eddy, going in circles, we may not want to leave its safety. We don't know what will happen, and we find it is safer to say, "My relationship isn't that bad." This keeps us floating around in circles being unhappy or unfulfilled.

So, what is commitment in a relationship? Is it about getting married? Is it about staying in a relationship for the rest of our lives? Is it about having a fulfilling, loving relationship for as long as we can? Is it about proactively working on our relationships to make them the best we can? Marriage and fear can create steep riverbanks to hold a relationship together, but do not necessarily mean that a relationship is thriving. For those of us with high expectations of maintaining a loving relationship, it takes commitment from both partners to proactively work to keep the love blossoming and the relationship healthy.

In both of my relationships, first with Gary and then with Milo, I felt like I was out there doing all the paddling myself. Due to my spiritual growth, I had chosen to live from a place of love every day, to treat people with love and understanding. That place of love became a riverbank that held me in relationship with Milo. I was able to accept him and love him for who he was, even though there were things that I wished were different.

Relationships are an amazing opportunity to learn about ourselves and our lives, if we are open to it. But are both people in the relationship committed enough to grow and learn? The banks of our relationship rivers can help keep us in our boats while we do the learning. It turned out I had a lot to learn and resolve in my life. Although Milo didn't want to learn, he provided me with a safe, stable environment from which I could do my learning.

SELF-REFLECTION QUESTIONS

- How important was it to you to get married?
- What does marriage mean to you?
- What are you committed to in your marriage?
- How committed are you to taking action to have your marriage work?
- What are you willing to do that might make that possible?

Communication

Milo and I did not communicate well. In fact we had very little communication, especially as time went on. In the early years of our relationship, Milo told me lots of stories. He was a voracious reader and would tell me about what he had read, carefully and slowly explaining the scientific concepts that were unfamiliar to me. I remember sitting on a beach at the edge of lake with him one very clear summer evening. We looked up at the stars and he started to explain the concept of mass drivers, which came from a science fiction book. Mass drivers are linear accelerators that lift mass up into orbit, like a spaceship that carries coal but does not need a rocket or engine attached to it. As I sat there and imagined what he was describing, I felt excited and connected to him. I loved that he shared his passion for science and knowledge with me. Sadly, I don't remember when he stopped telling me these stories.

When it came to his disillusionment and disappointment at work, however, Milo constantly complained. In the early years I listened and even sympathized. After a few years I started making suggestions, and then I just stopped listening. It was the death knell of our communication. Milo could not understand why I lacked compassion, and I couldn't understand why he didn't see that he was a habitual complainer. For several years we hardly discussed his work. It wasn't until I started coaching and doing personal development work that I gained the resourcefulness to be able to listen to him again. By that time, he felt shut down and wasn't willing to talk about work very much.

Milo was never good at communicating his feelings or the things that were important to him. He used to say, "I am the strong, silent type, like a cowboy." Many men are like Milo in that they prefer to solve their problems in a very solitary manner. Unfortunately when Milo completed his problem solving, he was still not willing to enter into conversation. As a result I never knew what was going on with him, what was important to him, or what concerned him.

Since many men share this problem-solving style, it can be valuable for their partners to accept it as a way of being. Our partners' choice to work things out internally is not about us. It may feel like they are pulling away from us, but we need to let them have their space. I would have preferred it if Milo had communicated with me. It would have taken a conscious effort on his part, but it would have fostered more closeness in our relationship. Not all men are like Milo; some are quite willing to communicate what is on their mind. It depends upon their personalities and their emotional conditioning. Women are the same. Some can be very vocal in sharing what is on their mind, and others not so much.

Lack of communication can fester for a long time before problems come to the surface. Lynn Toler, host of the television show *Divorce Court,* has seen a trend in which women all of a sudden abandon their partners for no apparent reason. Lynn calls it "The False OK." They tell the very same lie for years on end: they say, "OK," when they don't mean it. They tell their partners, "Everything's fine," even when it's not. "Keeping the peace" is what they call it. These women have not been speaking their truth, perhaps because they want to avoid conflict or because they don't feel heard. Then one day they have had enough and leave, and their partners are shocked.

Suzette's number one complaint about her husband, Brandon, was that he just did not seem to be engaged and participating in the relationship, caring about what happens. When I met with them as a couple, it turned out that Brandon said yes to whatever request Suzette made, whether or not he intended to fulfill it. Brandon was terrified of conflict. Every time he thought of saying no and facing Suzette's unhappiness, he felt a stabbing pain in his chest. Due to his past emotional conditioning, conflict caused an immediate emotional reaction. It was not surprising that Brandon avoided saying no. This could have been the downfall of their relationship. Fortunately when they resolved the underlying emotional conditioning, a whole new world of communication opened up for them.

In her book *For Better,* Tara Parker-Pope cites several studies that indicate it is not what we argue about but how we argue that predicts whether a marriage will stay together. Conflict can in fact be good for a marriage. It can enable a couple to work out their differences and come to a place of mutual understanding. Our ability to state what we want is important even if it is a complaint.

Criticism

A complaint sounds like this: "I wish we had sex more often."

Criticism sounds like this: "You never want to have sex. You're always too tired. What's happened to you?"

Criticism is a personal attack. It is even worse if we use body language that shows contempt, such as rolling our eyes. Opening a discussion with criticism, contempt, or sarcasm is a sign of serious trouble in a relationship. In *The Seven Principles for Making Marriage Work,* John Gottman states that criticism occurs when our partners are non-responsive to our requests or they have a sense of self-doubt due to childhood conditioning. Having good communication in your relationship requires a commitment to have conversations about what is important, a willingness to let go of past conditioning in order to learn better communication skills.

SELF-REFLECTION QUESTIONS

- What worked in your communication with your partner?
- What were you not saying and sharing with your partner?
- How good were you at listening to your partner and hearing what he or she had to say?
- How willing was your partner to communicate?
- Did you raise complaints with your partner, or were you critical of your partner?
- Was your conflict respectful or did it include contempt?

Sometimes We Just Make a Mistake

Embarrassment is a powerful emotion that keeps us from acting on our inner knowledge. Sarah told me that the day she moved in with her boyfriend, she knew she was making a big mistake. "However, I did not want to admit it, so I justified my actions to others. I wondered if maybe I was overreacting to the situation. Looking back, I recognize that the man I moved in with continually manipulated me and led me to believe that our problems were my fault. He knew how to push my buttons and create doubt in my mind."

Sarah entered into a relationship with the wrong person and justified it because his similarity to her father's behavior resonated with her. This sort of thing happens to many of us, and we realize too late that it was a big mistake. My first husband wasn't a bad man; I just had a lot of growing up to do before getting married.

SELF-REFLECTION QUESTIONS

- What was your intuition showing you to be true about your relationship?
- What were you choosing to ignore about the truth of your relationship?
- What were you afraid of?

It Is What It Is

When we look back over our relationships, we may find areas where we were incompatible and unable to develop a solid foundation. We may have always had conflict in certain areas, such as money or housework. Perhaps one of us was no longer interested in a sexual relationship. We may have hooked up with someone who had the worst qualities of one of our parents, but we didn't recognize it because being with this person felt so comfortable.

Milo and I were at odds about how we would participate in our journey down the relationship river. I wanted him to be more engaged and more connected. I wanted to have a map for our relationship, and for us to be able to communicate about what was important.

CHAPTER 9

Do I Enter the Jungle?

AFTER FIVE MONTHS OF SITTING in limbo, it became apparent to me that Milo was not going to make the final decision. I'd have to do it. What was it that I wanted in relationship anyhow? If this was all going to come to an end, then how could I ensure that my next relationship would be more successful? Couples research showed me that some level of relationship stress is inevitable in even the happiest of marriages, but that we can understand disagreement as a signal to fix something. Yet, my own emotions, along with all of my questions about relationships and what I wanted in the future, looked like a vast jungle of trees and vines. It was time to use the machete of contemplation to learn more about the jungle of intimate relationship.

Paddling the Relationship Boat: The Feminine Role

Many women have received strong conditioning from parents and society about getting an education and being independent. Independence can have unintended negative effects on our relationships, however. Esther said, "When I was a teenager, my mom would always tell me how important it was to go to college, so I could have a career and not be financially dependent on someone else. I thank her because I have always been able to support myself and my family." However, "Mom was so adamant about my having a career that I thought a career and a serious relationship were incompatible."

I could see that some other women were more feminine, more girly than me. Was I doing something to drive Milo away? Was there something for me to understand about being feminine that I had missed in my education? With these questions in mind I read *Dish: Midlife Women Tell the Truth about Work, Relationships, and the Rest of Life,* by Barbara Moses, and concluded I didn't have the unhappiness that many other women suffered from unfulfilled expectations. Milo and I were best friends and great companions. As I exposed myself to more teachers on my great journey of life exploration, I realized I had missed learning about femininity. In school I had totally discounted all the girly things my female peers were doing. I thought they were silly. Instead I focused on being very athletic and able to compete with the boys. I had always thought the way to succeed was to show the boys and men that I could hold my own with them. I had no idea that this way of thinking would not serve me well in my relationship with my husband. But after all, if I could do everything that he could do, why did I need him?

The Greek goddess archetypes demonstrate that women have different natural modalities available to them. There are women who have a natural affinity for the outdoors and nature, women who are more attracted to education and business, women who naturally desire to raise children and be nurturers at home, women who are great supporters of their partners' careers, and women who are naturally sexy lovers. We may possess many of these archetypes over our lifetimes, or we may experience only a couple of them. I have been the outdoorswoman and the businesswoman. Now I am developing the lover archetype.

Due to our work in a male-dominated culture, women have become more homogeneous. Working both outside of the house and inside the home, as the main caregivers of the family, women have very little time and energy for being beautiful, romantic, and sexy. We take on the roles of mother and businesswoman, while missing the lover archetype.

In fact, many of us have placed so little value on our beauty and femininity that we have missed cultivating it despite being bombarded by advertising telling us that we need to be slim and without wrinkles. Femininity is not just looks, however; it is how we behave within our relationships. To keep our relationships hot and sexy we need to cultivate feminine behavior. It is not enough to know how to look beautiful if the clothes and makeup are being applied only to the outside. Inner beauty must be tended to for it to grow and blossom. We want to bring all of our femininity to our relationships, regardless of what physical size or shape we are or what the advertisements tell us about beauty.

Our feminine beauty is meant to serve ourselves, our partners, and ultimately our relationships. Most women want to be in a romantic intimate relationship. If we want our partners to stand in their masculine space we must give them room by standing in our feminine space. Polarity is what creates romantic sparks in a relationship, and polarity only exists when we bring opposites together.

Romantic relationships also depend upon how connected we feel within ourselves. Do you love yourself? When you look in the mirror do you see a beautiful, sexy woman? Can you list your good qualities and are you proud of them? When you feel all of this and then dress up the outside, with beautiful makeup, clothes that suit your body shape, nice shoes, and a great haircut, you present the best of yourself. It is important to cultivate both inner and outer beauty. If you practice the tools and techniques described in this book, you will be working on your inner beauty.

Some women find that dressing up on the outside is very natural, while others may never have paid much attention to how they look. I had been working hard on my inner beauty but had no idea how to dress up the outside. Friends and books can give us ideas on selecting a wardrobe, using colors, and choosing hairstyles, or we can hire an image consultant. As soon as we have the intention to change, resources appear.

I was a tomboy growing up and had ignored most of the information on cultivating beauty. When I decided to revamp my outside I did it for me; it was a way of treating myself as something precious. I wanted to feel like a sexy, dynamic woman. Now, feeling beautiful lifts my spirits and helps me appreciate myself. When I am getting dressed up and applying fresh makeup, I am thinking of my partner and how enjoyable our evening together will be. When I have this focus, I am creating the reality that I want to occur.

SELF-REFLECTION QUESTIONS

Women:
• What could you do to enhance your femininity?
• How would you like to feel as a feminine woman?
• Who could you ask for help?

Men:
• What could you do to provide more support for your partner's feminine nature?
• Where could you be less critical of the differences between you?

Paddling the Relationship Boat: The Masculine Role

On my first holiday as a single woman, I went white-water kayaking in Belize. For four days, I sat in the front of the boat with the lead guide. By the second day of the trip I became aware that for the most part Pedro did not need my help to paddle the kayak. I could just sit back and relax. This made me feel unsettled. I wanted to paddle and show him how good I was, but he would tell me, "Don't paddle." I realized that the lesson for me was to stop trying to interfere in what was his domain. He was there to look after me. My role was to sit back, be the princess, and allow him to take care of me. I have received this same feedback from men who are strong in their masculine energy: "Stop trying to do everything." I am learning how to allow a man to take care of me; I don't have to be responsible for everything.

Some men have more feminine traits, and some women have more masculine traits. In general, however, men are more interested in practical subjects, whereas women are more interested in building relationships. Men work through problems systematically, one item at a time, and women work in flow, often moving between two or three tasks at a time. Men deal with problems in a solitary way; they like to go away and think about things on their own and then come back with a solution. Women may perceive this way of problem solving as pulling away, but we just need to have patience and give men space. Men generally express their anger physically while women express it verbally.

Men are goal oriented, and it is important for them to have a purpose in life. Men have traditionally been responsible for looking after their partner and family. Men who are in their full power have a clear purpose in life. They know what it is they are passionate about and what draws them to give all of themselves. Men are happiest when they have this knowledge and are doing work that is meaningful to them and their community.

Social structures have evolved over time, but men are still most fulfilled when they are able to look after their partners. In one workshop, the women had the opportunity to interview the men and find out what it was they really wanted in their relationships. These answers came from a group of men involved in personal development work and ranging in age from thirty to sixty-five years old. Their answers indicated that men want women to show their love in a positive way rather than being needy and complaining when something isn't working. Men do not like to be controlled or manipulated; they want the freedom to be themselves. They want women to surrender and trust that they will provide, protect, and take care of us. They want us to inspire and empower them to be their best. They want women to take impeccable care of themselves physically, mentally, and emotionally. They want us to be joyful, playful, and willing to let go of our preferences in the interest of harmony. Basically men want to lead and be respected and trusted as leaders of the family.

When women started to enter the workplace in significant numbers after the 1960s, they started to teach men how to treat them as independent people. Many niceties between men and women were no longer considered necessary. We no longer needed men to carry the grocery bags; we were strong enough to carry our own bags. We no longer needed men to be the family source of income; we could earn our own money. It was no longer important that men get dressed up for a date and come pick us up at the door. We could just meet them at a restaurant after work. This cultural change has taught men that it is no longer appropriate to be chivalrous. In our society, women have taken away the traditional masculine role of providing and protecting. We have attempted to reshape men into being more caring and emotionally intelligent, which is not a natural role for most of them.

Is it any wonder that women feel like we have taken on the burdens of life and men are just going along for the ride? Yet men are trying to fulfill their historical place in the family and are bewildered by all of the new expectations. Men and women paddling down the river of a relationship are both trying to steer the kayak, and they are often working against each other. On the white-water kayaking trip I mentioned earlier, I observed that the couples where both people were trying to steer the boat ended up flipping their boats more often than anyone else. What was true on the river is just as true in relationship. Couples who are not working together often cause their trip down the river to be more difficult than necessary.

SELF-REFLECTION QUESTIONS

Women:
- What do you notice is different about the way you and your partner do things?
- How could you allow your partner more room to express masculine energy?
- Where could you be less critical?
- Where could you let go of the paddle?

Men:
- Where do you need to pick up the paddle and start steering the boat?
- What do you need to do to be more in your power?
- What could you do to bring more chivalry into your relationship?
- How could you remind your partner of what role you want to hold in the relationship?

Different Kinds of Relationships

Robert Masters has worked as a psychotherapist and teacher since 1977. In his book *Transformation through Intimacy,* he outlines four stages of relationships. We can use a variety of signs and behaviors to recognize the stage in which we are operating. As our relationships grow, we continue to include the earlier stages, although how we relate to these stages becomes more mature. I used this model to look at my relationship with Milo and understand the dynamic that was occurring between us—both to understand the past and to choose where I would like to be in the future.

Stage One

Stage one is a me-centered relationship run by the ego. The ego of one partner usually dominates that of the other partner. In this stage each person is focused on "What is in it for me?" There is usually an uneasy coalition of some sort, with very little intimacy. The relationship is usually held together through a power dynamic rooted in fear and obedience, with the man often holding most of the power. Betrayal in the relationship is common, whether through sexual or emotional affairs or pornography.

When one or both partners are emotionally reactive, conflict usually erupts when each partner wants to be right. Being right is much more important than being happy or actually caring about the other. The dominant partner often blames the less dominant partner. The weaker partner usually backs down and feels like a victim, internalizing his or her emotional feelings and withdrawing from passion. The weaker partner may express hurt and frustration by complaining to a friend, but will rarely take action due to fear of losing the dominant partner, whom they have come to rely upon. In this type of relationship, the less dominant person may not speak his or her own truth due to fear of change and loss. At this stage the relationship often becomes lifeless and void of any passion or love. One partner may be giving the "false OK" until one day he or she just decides to leave.

Stage Two

The we-centered codependent relationship described by stage two is where equality is highly valued and differences may get flattened out. The couple acts as one and cultivates a guarded separation from whatever exists outside. Partners negotiate over what would best serve the relationship, diplomatically defusing whatever might threaten it. Both partners generally show a great deal of tolerance. The betrayal that occurs is that the potential of each individual is devalued in favor of the safety and comfort provided by the relationship. In we-centered relationships the ego is well and alive, although it is suppressed so as not to rock the boat. We-centered couples withhold speaking their truth and avoid facing their differences for fear of the relationship changing in a negative way. It is better to keep quiet than to challenge what is not working. The couple misses out on the opportunity to use reactivity and conflict as a means to growth. They are willing to settle for good enough.

Stage Three

In stage three, a we-centered co-independent relationship, both partners make it a priority to maintain their individuality while still working together in partnership. They negotiate over differences and take more personal risks. Autonomy, although much more adult than in me-centered relationships, is often given too much weight. More maturity and a deeper sense of connection are present. However, when emotional reactivity occurs, partners often withdraw from each other and behave the opposite from the way their emotional reactivity is pointing. Conflict is avoided to preserve the illusion of a safe, skirmish-free relationship.

Stage Four

The being-centered relationship of stage four contains all the qualities of the previous three stages. The difference is that the couple does not act out the qualities of the other stages; they relate to those qualities instead. The relationship is rooted in shared love, power, depth, and presence. This stage is characterized by ever-deepening passion where the couple can explore places and patterns in themselves that they would otherwise avoid. The relationship becomes a place where both people can work through their childhood conditioning in a loving and supported way. Being-centered couples are rarely reactive;

instead they cut through the reactivity to explore its underlying cause. Once they can see through their reactivity, they have an opportunity to respond to the situation at hand.

In the first two stages of relationship, couples often stay together more for security and comfort than for real intimacy. Masters points out that there is often an implicit agreement not to rock the boat while they're trying to find some happiness floating around in the eddy of their relationship. Poor communication, emotional immaturity, endless arguments, cruel put-downs and mismatched desires are some of the things that clutter up what he calls "me- and we-centered relationships." In stage four, the relationship is a sacred container that the couple is deeply committed to nurturing and protecting. It is this type of relationship in which we find greater freedom, joy, and happiness.

Milo and I functioned primarily at stage three. We maintained our individuality, and yet we worked in harmony with each other. Milo avoided conflict, and as a result our relationship functioned with a high degree of harmony, but a low level of intimacy. In this way our relationship was more like stage two, because we did not share what was important to us. Early on in our relationship, we operated in stage one, with me being the dominant partner. We always maintained kindness toward each other, no matter what. Milo was a kind man and one of my intentions was to be more like him, so I worked on being kinder too. The more personal development work I did, the higher the stage at which I was able to operate. However we never made it to stage four.

SELF-REFLECTION QUESTIONS

- What stage is your relationship operating at?
- What stage are you operating at in your relationship?
- What could you do differently to operate at a higher stage?

The Purpose of Relationship

Masters states that if we want to live a deeper life, get into an intimate relationship: it will expose everything we do not want to expose about ourselves. By "intimate," Masters means there is relational closeness between the couple. Intimate relationship has the ability to transform difficulties into opportunities. To achieve this we need to be resourceful enough to operate at a stage three relationship with the intention to evolve into a stage four relationship. At stage four, we can support each other to work through our emotional conditioning and reactivity. Offering loving support, we can help each other see when we are reacting. We can assist each other to transform what is wrong into the loving compost from which a deep intimate connection can grow and blossom.

Relationships are a place for us to heal the wounds of the past, especially our childhood emotional conditioning. Within the depth of an intimate relationship, we can help each other transcend our past hurts and regain a sense of wholeness and completeness. We can leave behind the illusion of separateness and move into our full power, truly living the purpose of our lives.

This chapter so far has looked at the macro aspects of a relationship: how masculine and feminine roles are different in relationship, and how they need to be different to keep a relationship vibrant. We have also been considering the functional stages of relationship. Next we will focus on the micro level, discovering who we want to be in a relationship, and what we are looking for from our partners. All this information will help us take a realistic look at our current relationships so we know what we are really giving up should the relationship come to an end. Let's look at romance, or showing love.

As we saw in chapter 2, romance is knowing what our partners want and value, and being willing to do the little things that support them in feeling loved. When it came to small romantic acts, Milo and I were not very conscious of looking after each other. In fact, I was unaware of what I really wanted from my relationship or what it even meant to express love to my partner. Yet it was something that I came to yearn for in my relationship with Milo.

In *The Five Love Languages*, Gary Chapman gives examples of how we can express love, including acts of service, or doing things for our partners; spending quality time together; giving and receiving gifts; speaking words of affirmation; and sharing physical touch. Here's how this translated into my relationship with Milo.

Acts of Service

Milo was very good at sharing domestic duties of laundry and dishes and keeping the house tidy, and I appreciated what he did. My act of service was to cook and prepare healthy meals. I don't think food was Milo's love language though, so although I enjoyed cooking, I don't think it ever felt like love to him. If I asked Milo to build something for me, he always did it quite willingly. I didn't consider these acts of love at the time, but in hindsight I realize that building things was in fact a way that he showed love. Unfortunately, I had felt I was imposing on him when I asked him to build something for me. Was this due to my own inability to receive love? When we don't feel that we are deserving, this gets in the way of our being grateful.

Quality Time

Milo and I had lots of fun during our whole relationship. Perhaps we could have used all this time together to communicate more and create a deeper connection. We spent lots of quiet time together, which was very peaceful but did not deepen our relationship the way it could have.

Gift Giving and Receiving

When it came to expressing love through gifts, Milo and I both came up a little short. We bought each other great gifts for birthdays and at Christmas, but little romantic "I love you" gifts were virtually absent. In the last six months, while Milo was uncertain what to do, he bought me more little gifts than he had during our whole relationship. I often felt disappointed after giving Milo a gift. I would stop on the way home and buy him a dessert, but he usually found something not quite up to his high standards, and so I always felt like my love wasn't really received. As gift givers we seemed often to be at cross-purposes and we missed out on expressing and receiving love.

Words of Affirmation

I told Milo I loved him every night. Sometime during the latter part of our relationship, he stopped being able to say that he loved me. He told me that he didn't know what love was and that when he had told me previously that he loved me, it was just an automatic response. It feels very sad to think that he couldn't receive the love that I had been giving to him for all those years. Other words of affirmation were almost nonexistent. I often wondered what it was that Milo really appreciated about me.

Physical Touch

Milo loved to touch, but he did not like to kiss, and he would often turn his lips to avoid any real contact with me. The only time he would really kiss me was in the heat of sexual intercourse. It was hard to be denied access to this connection with him. With Milo there were no little caresses or fondling in quiet private moments when it was just the two of us. Oh how I would have loved for him to touch me romantically.

For the most part the quality of our sex life felt satisfying. In the last eighteen months of our relationship our sex life deteriorated, and I suspect this was because Milo was in a physical or emotional relationship with Claire. A friend once told me that to keep a relationship healthy we need to stoke the fires every day. When we are in a new relationship, this is exactly what we do — we think about our partners every day. We think about how much we love them and how much we want to be with them. Once we settle down, however, we may quit stoking the relationship fires. If we neglect our campfires for too long and a rainstorm of conflict comes along, or if there is a long spell of the constant drizzle of challenges, the fire will go out. It is important that we keep putting wood on the fires of our passion by being romantic.

Romance only works if we are willing to receive the love that our partners send our way. If we keep repelling acts of love, we won't feel loved, nor will our partners. David shared the disappointment and confusion he felt about trying to be romantic with his wife, Sandra. David thought he was a romantic man, and he tried to do romantic things. One anniversary he had booked a room at an upscale hotel, made dinner reservations at a very nice restaurant, and had a limousine pick them up, with champagne. Earlier in the day he had gone to the hotel and put flowers and candles in the room. But it all kind of fell flat. Sandra didn't respond the way he had anticipated. Later she told him that she did not feel it was authentic, it was like he had read it in a book or in a movie.

So what? Does everything have to be brand-new for us to accept something as an act of love? David had put a lot of effort into arranging that evening, and he felt disappointed and rejected. He felt like his efforts just never seemed to be enough.

When we don't graciously accept what our partners give to us, we are sending a signal that they shouldn't bother to put any more logs on the campfire of passion. If we want to keep our campfires burning, it's valuable to know both what we want and what we are prepared to give to our partners. Both parties have to keep stoking the fires of relationship.

SELF-REFLECTION QUESTIONS

- Is one of you doing all the the paddling in your love life?
- Is the other partner responding?
- Would you like more sex?
- Would you like more loving touch?
- What would make you feel really loved at your core?
- What experiment might you try to see if the love can be rekindled in your relationship?

Treat Yourself as You Would be Treated

One of the things that I wanted most in my relationship was to feel precious. But what does it mean to be treated preciously? Before I could be treated preciously by someone else, I needed to define what *preciously* meant to me. I began by thinking about all the times when I didn't feel precious, and then redefined them into what I really wanted.

I began to think about what I wanted from Milo that I didn't seem to get. In general he did not want to accompany me in any of the small special things that I liked to do. I wanted to be taken out on dates, and I wanted him to enjoy himself. When I arranged for us to go to the theater, he often made negative comments about the production I had chosen. I would have loved it if he had made arrangements to go to a concert or a play. I felt very frustrated when I organized the date, and then he couldn't even be appreciative. I loved to go for walks, but when I asked Milo to come with me, it seemed like he felt I was imposing on him. When I reached to hold his hand in public, he would shake it off as if he were embarrassed to be seen with me.

My second step was to redefine all of my complaints into positive statements about what I wanted. I wanted to do a variety of the little things that made life feel special to me. I wanted to receive little gifts that showed me Milo was thinking of me. Going for a walk would represent an offer of time where we would give freely of ourselves and spend time talking. For me feeling precious is about feeling special and feeling connected. Holding hands is about connection. All of these little acts I longed for were about feeling loved. When I feel loved I feel an expansion of energy within my heart and body.

SELF-REFLECTION QUESTIONS

- What is not happening in your relationship that would help to make you feel precious?
- What does make you feel precious?
- How does that feel within your body?
- How do you love yourself?

I received some excellent advice from one of my teachers when I was focusing on wanting to be treated preciously. He said I should treat myself *preciously*. When I asked myself, "What does it mean to treat myself preciously?" I read through my journals, and lots of clues started to reveal themselves. I loved golf, so I would ensure that I got out golfing once a week. I felt special when I took a bath, so I'd take a nice hot bath in beautiful scented bubbles, dim the lights and burn a candle, or read one of my favorite magazines. Another way to treat myself preciously was to keep a log of my accomplishments and acknowledge what I had achieved. I became aware that I did a lot of fun things. Part of my journey was to become present to what already existed in my life that I was not appreciating.

In my quest to feel precious I started to keep my surroundings much tidier and cleaner. I started by throwing things out that I didn't love, clearing the clutter. The more I let stuff go, the more I was aware that keeping my environment impeccable was a way of treating myself as precious.

I noticed when staying at other people's homes that the feeling of preciousness did not come from the size of home or quality of furniture, but from the sense of peacefulness in the home. For me this was related to whether the house was tidy and clean and things were put away. Once I stayed in a friend's home in a very tidy little room that had a comfortable chair and a cute old table placed by a window where I could sit and look out at the trees and urban backyards. A sense of peace pervaded me as I sat and wrote at the table. This felt precious.

I became aware that feeling precious required me to be present to what I was doing and the feelings that I was experiencing in the moment. If we are not present to our feelings, if we don't let those feelings in, then we will totally miss that a precious moment is taking place.

I listed some of the ways I could treat myself more preciously:

- Give up habits that are not supportive.
- Exercise and work out.
- Play sports, ride my bike, swim, golf, and ski.
- Go camping.
- Go to the theater.
- Have good friends over for dinner.
- Keep my environment impeccably tidy and clean.
- Eat healthy food.
- Wear pretty dresses and sexy clothing.
- Get a great haircut.
- Buy myself a gift once in a while in honor of being me.
- Be grateful and tell myself, "I love you."

The first step in giving and receiving love is to love ourselves and to feel the love in our own hearts. In order to love myself, I needed to do loving things for myself and then pay attention and feel the love inside. It is only when we feel love that we can send that love outward to others.

▶ **TOOL: FEELING LOVE**

Notice your own heart, feel love in it, expand that love in your body, think of a person you love, and send love outward with each exhalation of your breath.

SELF-REFLECTION QUESTIONS

• What could you do to show yourself more love?
• What could you let go of that does not serve you?
• What do you love that brings joy to your heart?

How Could My Partner Show Me Love?

When it comes to showing our partners love, there are tangible and also intangible aspects of how we show up and behave in our relationships. The intangibles have a huge impact upon the quality of our relationships. We often focus on the tangible aspects of what we are doing in the relationship and forget that how we are being has an even bigger impact on long-term satisfaction. I wrote the following lists when contemplating what I wanted from a partner.

Tangible Aspects — Doing

- Fix things in the house that are broken.
- Help me clean up and finish up at the end of project, such as cooking or gardening.
- Make dinner.
- Take me on dates to listen to music, go for dinner, or do any other activity together.
- Be willing to help me when I ask.
- Buy me gifts for my hobbies or for me.
- Give me a massage or foot rub.
- Engage in conversation and be able to listen.
- Show me affection, hold my hand, give me a kiss, hug me.

Intangible Aspects — Being

- Be emotionally available — express love, gentleness, kindness, and caring.
- Offer undivided attention and be willing to communicate.
- Have a positive attitude, joy, and vigor in his life.
- Have an intimate, passionate, and creative sexual relationship.
- Be outgoing and adventurous.
- See, accept, and cherish me for who I am.
- Have a desire to grow and develop.
- Be loyal and committed to our relationship; see me as his special woman.
- See the depth of my beauty and support me to grow, flower, and blossom as a woman.

There is a double-edged sword in these lists. Yes, I want these things because I believe they will give me feelings of happiness, joy, and love. On the other hand, these may be feelings I need to learn to give to myself. Another thing about the lists is that they define how I want my partner to fulfill my needs, and if he doesn't, then I may feel hurt and unloved. I am putting conditions on how I want to receive love. If my partner would only fulfill my needs, then I would feel love. This is the thinking of a codependent or stage two relationship. It means that I will only feel loved when someone else is satisfying my needs.

It is valuable to recognize that many of the things we desire from our partners come from our emotional conditioning and unmet needs, and that it is part of our responsibility to fulfill these things for ourselves. This takes some of the pressure off our partners. It is within the realm of love that we heal ourselves. You can refer back to the description of a stage four relationship, earlier in this chapter, for more about what this looks like.

Unmet Needs

We can satisfy many of our own needs, and at the same time it is absolutely wonderful when our partners know what is important to us and show love from this perspective. When needs are unmet, we don't feel complete and happy. We are constantly looking for more. As we show ourselves love, our needs start to transform into desires. We don't need these things from our partners, but life feels so delicious and juicy when our partners can satisfy our desires. We feel deeply satisfied and appreciated. It feels heavenly. And if we could make our partners feel heavenly, why wouldn't we?

Tom wanted his wife, Clara, to clean the house and be tidier so that the house would stay clean. He believed he would feel more love for Clara if she was a better housekeeper. I asked Tom about his own habits, and he admitted that he didn't always fold his clothes and put them away, and that the top of his dresser was a mess. I suggested that if he wanted to feel more love in his life, then he should love himself and clean up his own things first. When his own personal environment was clean, he would feel better about himself and less judgmental of Clara. Next he could work with his daughter to keep her space clean. When he reached this point, then it would be an appropriate time to invite his wife to work with him to tidy the rest of the house, if she hadn't already offered. Afterward they could have a conversation about how it felt to live in a clean and tidy house, and they could decide together whether this was the way that they wanted to live. It would be a mutual decision about how to keep the house. Keeping the house clean would no longer be a condition that he imposed on his wife before showing love. In this way Tom learned to treat himself as a precious person and then to invite Clara along.

SELF-REFLECTION QUESTIONS

- How do you want your partner to show you love?
- What are the tangible things your partner could do to show you love?
- What are the intangible aspects of who your partner is being that support you to feel loved?
- How can you show yourself more love?
- Which of these items are needs that come from your conditioning and could be resolved?
- How can you show your partner love?

In the previous section we focused on what we want to get from our relationships. The other side of the coin is this: Whom do I want to be when I am in relationship? How do I want to behave and what do I want to bring? Don't forget that our partners also want to receive love. We need to be aware of what gifts we want to bring to them. It is important not to attach conditions to our gifts, not to expect something in return. When we come from a conditional place, both of us are likely to start withholding our love from each other, waiting for the other person to give first. Here's my list of what I want to give to my partner:

- Come from a place of love even when it is difficult.
- Be open to learning, growing, and developing, and keep practicing.
- Be responsible for my own emotional reactions.
- Give my partner my undivided attention when he is feeling the burdens of life.
- Be supportive of my partner's dreams, passions, hopes, and challenges, and celebrate wins.
- See and cherish my partner's brilliance; understand who he is at the core.
- Be open, flexible, caring, and curious.
- Listen and understand my partner's point of view.
- Create a warm safe, comfortable, loving home.
- Allow my partner to take care of me in the way that is natural for him, and trust that he will make the right decisions for us.
- Be fully feminine and allow my partner to take the lead.
- Be intimately and sexually available in our relationship.
- Express love to my partner in a way that is important to him.

SELF-REFLECTION QUESTIONS

- What are you willing to give to the person you are in relationship with?
- What conditions do you put on your love?
- What could you do for your partner that would make you feel good?

The Final Decision

My desire for a stage four, being-centered relationship drove me to make the final decision to leave Milo. I realized that he would never do the work necessary for us to move from a third-stage (sometimes second-stage) relationship to a fourth-stage relation-ship. I had become more and more resourceful over the years, and with the Emotional Hot Button Removal techniques, I knew that I was capable of a fourth-stage relationship. I sensed that God had brought me a gift that would enable me to truly resolve my emo-tional conditioning and move forward to a whole new place. With the four stages of relationship, Masters had given me the idea of what a magical, passionate, intimate relationship could look like. And I wanted it. I deserved a man who would be my partner, who would look after me with care and passion, and who would treat me as a lady. I was committed to doing the work that would some day bring the ideal man into my life — the man with whom I could have a magical, fun, vibrant, and exciting relationship.

On the tenth of December, driving down the twisty Sea to Sky highway from our first ski weekend of the year in Whistler, I announced to Milo that our relationship was over. It had been almost six months since Milo had announced that he wanted to leave. This time it was I who came to the realization that this re-lationship would not be able to fulfill my dreams and desires for a passionate, deep, loving connection. I wanted a man who had similar desires, who had zip in his life and something that he wanted to accomplish. Milo had none of this. He was letting life live him, rather than living life himself. I wanted so much more, and I was no longer going to settle for "good enough."

CHAPTER 10

The Jungle Looms

ONCE I SEPARATED FROM MILO, I was alone on the shore of the river, looking into the jungle. The canopy of trees stretched out above me a hundred feet in the air, completely shading the ground below. The ground was undulating; I would have to climb hills and scramble over fallen palm fronds. Vines with two-inch thorns twisted their way up through the trees searching for light. Some trees provided medicine for healing, but others had sap that would burn my skin. There was no clear path through the jungle—I would have to hack my way and hope I could maintain a heading that would take me to safety. Fear crept into my heart. Did I have the courage to face the traumas from my childhood conditioning, or would it be better to wait on the shore and hope that someone would rescue me?

Exploring our emotional jungle can seem a daunting and overwhelming task. When we start personal development work, some of us remember traumas that happened in childhood and in our early adult years; hence we already know what is in the jungle. But some of us are just like me: I had no memory of anything bad happening, so I had no idea what was in my emotional jungle. Uncovering it was an adventure in itself. Whether we know what is there or not, the emotional energy we carry around with us has a negative impact on our lives.

We have two decisions to make. First, do we want a different life? Second, are we willing to let go of the trauma that has affected us? Letting go can be difficult, because we need to be willing as an adult to face the emotional energy we could not face as children.

The tools I shared in chapter 4 and the principles I shared in chapter 7 are a great place to start the journey, but they don't serve to process old trauma. When we use these tools and principles, however, we start building our willingness to deal with the past; we gather resourcefulness. Understand that if we don't deal with the emotional energy of the past, it will limit the effectiveness of all our other learning. Many disciplines require followers to delve into and intellectually understand past experiences, and this often causes us to relive our emotional trauma.

But I have good news for you. First, our adult brains are bigger than our child brains were, and we are more mature; hence we have a greater capacity to process the traumas of the past. Second, the Emotional Hot Button Removal techniques that are covered in chapter 13 don't require us to have an intellectual understanding of past events; they just require us to be present to the energy.

I had never had to enter the jungle in the past because my first husband and then Milo had rescued me. Maybe some other man would come along and rescue me, and then I would never have to face this dark and daunting place. But I knew in my heart that no one had truly rescued me; they had just delayed my having to face my past. The sense of security they provided was just an illusion. The jungle of unresolved emotional energy still lived in my body, and if I didn't face it now, it would continue to haunt me for the rest of my life. To give myself a better chance of making it through the jungle I decided to do a little recognizance and become more aware of the dangers that I faced. I decided to look back at my life and take stock of the events that had created emotional trauma. What exactly was the emotional jungle that I needed to make my way through before I could achieve a sense of strength, self-worth, and centeredness?

Abuse

Abuse can take many different forms: verbal, physical, emotional, and sexual. Verbal abuse can take the form of yelling at children and using demeaning language. Physical abuse may involve hitting, choking, biting, punching, burning, and poisoning. Emotional abuse takes the form of belittling a person and threatening to withdraw love. Sexual abuse can take the form of incest. Children often blame themselves for the abuse, or family members blame them. All of these forms of abuse have a devastating impact, leaving permanent scars on a child's psyche that last long into adulthood. Of course abuse is not limited to children; it often continues into adulthood.

Verbal and Physical Abuse

Sometimes there is a fine line between abuse and normal behavior. My father lost his temper on a regular basis, with us kids and especially with my mother, and he'd yell and hit us kids. When I was a young child, all my father had to do was give me a stern look and I knew that if I didn't stop misbehaving I would be in trouble, meaning that he would grab me by the arm and hit me on the backside. He didn't leave bruises, but he definitely scared me and hurt my feelings. I learned early not to misbehave.

My parents argued about money and politics. My father would yell at my mother. He was brutal, and yet Mom did not back down. They had some amazing arguments with my father yelling, "For Christ's sake, woman, you don't know what you are talking about."

My father's behaviors had several negative effects on me. Growing up, I thought that noise, anger, and yelling were normal behavior. In my own partner relationships I'd yell and stomp off when I got angry, just like Dad. I did not know how to have a quiet, calm conversation with my partner. When Milo and I got together I had to stop yelling. Milo came from the opposite kind of household; he had never heard his parents argue and fight. Any conflict in our relationship caused his stomach to knot up and feel sick. I didn't really like my behavior, and I agreed to Milo's request.

My father's behavior during my childhood caused me to feel intense fear any time I was confronted with anger or conflict, especially if the anger was directed at me. I'd get a sick feeling in my stomach as though I had done something wrong. These conflict issues were a problem for me at work, as when my boss was upset, I always thought it was my fault. In personal relationships, I would quickly leap to defend myself, taking a righteous attitude to fend off the "attack." After all, my father had always been right, and since I had idolized him, I imitated his behavior as an adult. And when it really mattered, I kept silent rather than speak my truth for fear of being rejected, or losing the other person's love.

My father's spankings were not the end of my experience with physical abuse, either. During my first marriage, Gary put me down, demeaned me in front of other people, and attempted to control me, and in return I rebelled. One evening Gary and I got into an ugly fight. He was drunk and I was afraid of him, so I tried to get into my car and drive away without him. He forced his way into the backseat and berated me as I drove. I was terrified. I drove to his mother's house so that he could get out and stay there overnight to cool off. When Gary got out of the car he was so angry that I thought he was going to hit me. I turned and ran as fast as I could to the police station two blocks away. I sat on the front lawn of the police station crying my eyes out until eventually a policeman came out and walked me back to my car. I found the car door kicked in, but no Gary. Shakily I got into the car and drove off. The next morning the thing that I was most angry about was not the threat to my safety, but that he had had the audacity to kick my car door in. If he was willing to damage my car, perhaps next time I would be the one wearing the damage. It was over. I wasn't willing to stick around to find out what might happen next.

Emotional Abuse

There are many different forms of emotional abuse. It may occur on its own or may accompany other forms of abuse. Children and adults alike may suffer from emotional abuse and manipulative behavior at the hands of parents or partners. People who have low self-esteem are more susceptible to emotional abuse, as they feel they are not worthy of being treated with respect.

These are some of the forms emotional abuse can take:

- Rejecting — refusing to acknowledge a person's presence, value, or worth; communicating to a person that she or he is useless or inferior; devaluing a person's thoughts and feelings.
- Degrading — insulting, ridiculing, name calling, imitating, and infantilizing a person; behaviors that diminish a person's identity, dignity, and self-worth.
- Terrorizing — inducing terror or extreme fear in a person; coercing by intimidation; placing or threatening to place a person in an unfit or dangerous environment.
- Isolating — physically confining a person; restricting normal contact with others; limiting freedom within a person's own environment.
- Corrupting/exploiting — socializing a person into accepting ideas or behaviors that oppose legal standards; using a person for advantage or profit (for example, enticing a person into the sex trade); training a child to serve the interests of the abuser and not of the child (for example, child sexual abuse, enticing a child to use alcohol or drugs or look at pornography).
- Denying emotional responsiveness — failing to provide care in a sensitive and responsive manner; being detached and uninvolved; interacting only when necessary; ignoring a person's mental health needs.

Sexual Abuse

I have come to learn that my story of abuse is not unique; it happens to far too many children. I was fourteen years old. My parents had just sold the farm to my brother and we'd moved seven miles away, into the local town. I had been taken out of a comfortable environment where I was the queen of my domain. I felt poor, as I wasn't able to afford clothing like the other town kids. As a budding teenage girl, being in a new environment and not fitting in resulted in emotional instability.

Looking for someone to love me, I became the victim of sexual improprieties from a friend of the family, who was more than twenty years older, married, with children. When this man kissed me and touched me, the flood of new physical sensations in my body made me feel good. I was lonely, and his attentions were like a forbidden drug; even though I felt very uncomfortable, I could not seem to get enough. I was totally naïve about sex, and what I was feeling was new, wonderful, and exciting. I knew that what we were doing was wrong, but he was the older man so I just followed his lead. As with many fourteen-year-old girls, I didn't take responsibility for myself and my behavior. One day this man took me into the bedroom and took off my pants and his own. It was the first time I had ever seen a man naked, and I wasn't even really sure what he was doing with me on the bed. Afterward I was shocked to see the blood trickle from my body. Suddenly it dawned on me: I had lost my virginity to this man. Luckily the encounter didn't result in my becoming pregnant. This relationship continued for almost two years. I was mesmerized; I could not seem to break away. It was like an addiction. Someone finally seemed to love me.

It wasn't until I was sixteen and had my first boyfriend that I was able to break away from this man. The thought of him touching me suddenly made me feel sick. I told him I wanted him to stop touching me, but he ignored my requests. I finally had to threaten to tell my family what he was doing. I just wanted to forget that any of it had ever occurred. I felt guilty and embarrassed and thought I was responsible for the whole situation. I took this guilt and shame and stuffed it away, pretending that nothing ever happened. When my boyfriend and I had sex for the first time, I somehow managed to lie to him about my virginity.

I carried this shame in silence for thirty years.

Shortly after Milo told me he was going to leave, I realized that I had been only a young girl and was not responsible for what had happened to me at age fourteen. In fact, I had been sexually abused. I told Milo about my realization, and he said it had nothing to do with him.

His lack of empathy shocked me. I felt so alone. I began to shake and feel cold as the emotional trauma came to the surface. I called my friend Ethel, crying uncontrollably as the full weight of the realization surfaced in my body. Ethel told me to crawl into bed and stack the pillows around me. I lay in bed for at least three hours, until I finally had the strength to run a hot bath and sit in the tub letting warm water soothe my body. After my bath, although it was a hot July afternoon, I sat under a warm blanket and simply felt the pain that was rising in my chest. I had just been introduced to the Emotional Hot Button Removal techniques that will be introduced in chapter 13, and I used them then to deal with the trauma and pain I was experiencing.

Sexual abuse can have an impact on our future sexual relationships. Though I wanted to have sex in my intimate relationships, the memory of what had happened always flooded back into me, and I felt great shame. I liked having sexual contact, but my vagina was always very dry, and it hurt to be penetrated. In my thirties I learned about lubricants, which made intercourse easier, but I still never had an orgasm. A pleasure button had been short-circuited inside me, robbing me of the sensual ecstasy that comes from making love.

Unconsciously I could not forgive myself for the natural sexual stimulation I had felt as a young girl. I had cut myself off from the right to feel sexual stimulation, to relax and enjoy having a man make love to me. As an adult, then, I needed to convince my body that it was OK to feel sexually stimulated. It took many hours of working with the Emotional Hot Button Removal techniques and training my body to respond before the natural lubrication of my own body once again came alive. Today I know that I am a beautiful, dynamic, sexy woman who deserves to be fully aroused by a man. It is OK and natural to experience sexual pleasure.

Impact of Abuse

All varieties of abuse have devastating effects on our lives and relationships, including low self-esteem, fear of rejection, lack of trust, and challenges with social relationships to list just a few. Low self-esteem tells us we are not good enough, we are always wrong. Children who have been sexually abused try to cope with this emotional pain in ways that often cause them even more suffering: eating disorders, self-inflicted injuries, inability to have sex or obsession with sex, poor body image, generalized separation from and disregard for one's body. Other forms of abuse lead to anger, hostility, fear, and humiliation. Problematic coping behaviors related to abuse include addictions, prostitution, over-work or inability to work, becoming super high functioning or low functioning, becoming argumentative, avoiding conflict, and feeling a need to please others at all costs.

If you have been victimized by abuse, you don't have to continue to be a victim of these old traumas. It is possible to resolve your old traumas by learning to be present to and feel into the emotional energy that is stored in your body. (See chapter 13 to learn how.) This was the gift that Milo gave me by bringing our relationship to completion. Between Milo and God, I had everything I needed to resolve the emotional baggage I carried from sexual abuse.

SELF-REFLECTION QUESTIONS

- Were you abused?
- Physically? Verbally? Emotionally? Sexually? What form did this abuse take?
- What impact has it had on you?
- How has this affected your relationships?
- Are you ready to let go of this emotional energy?

Shame and Embarrassment

When my relationship with Gary ended, I felt shame and embarrassment. I had been so very lonely as a teenager, had so desperately wanted to fit in, and Gary had become my lifeline. Our relationship had allowed me to feel connected, to feel at last that I fit in somewhere. When I walked down the aisle to get married at age twenty-two, I was terrified. I knew I was making a big mistake, but I couldn't turn back with all those people watching. When Gary and I separated within ten months, I felt really stupid. I was ashamed that I was so desperate to get married. When I released my emotional baggage around this marriage, I realized that for thirty years I had worked nonstop to avoid doing anything that might cause me to feel embarrassed. This amounted to emotional bondage and a huge sadness.

Why did I look to Gary to feel safe and loved? I had always felt like an outsider, like I didn't belong. Maybe it was related to having survived childhood sexual abuse, as I had never felt safe in my body. The world was not a safe place for me, so I toughened up. I hooked up with both Gary and Milo mainly to make the world feel safer and more manageable.

The Jungle Is Thicker Than I Expected

Like most people, I wanted to believe that I had a normal child-hood. As I participated in personal development work, however, I learned that a lot more had happened to me than I originally remembered or realized. The emotional jungle I was facing was thicker than I had originally thought. Many of us are afraid to learn what happened when we were children and would prefer to remain in the dark. Yet it is only by being willing to face this darkness that we are able to heal the past fully and live into the ecstasy of the future.

You might be wondering whether it is advisable for you to enter the jungle. My recommendation is a resounding *yes*. My jungle revealed itself to me gradually over time as I practiced the techniques I share with you in this book. When the emotional energy was released, I became conscious of the events associated with it. As I slowly walked into the jungle, more energy was released, and more awareness of my past was revealed to me.

Even when we have healed the past, we still need to be vigilant to ensure that we don't attract other abusive people into our lives. We may feel very much at home with such people because their behavior is so familiar to what we experienced growing up. Subconsciously we may attract these people to complete the healing process, but we must be careful. If our partners are not willing to do their own healing, we need to make the tough decision to move on. We cannot cause other people to change, but with love we can hold space for them and be open to their willingness to change.

I was ready to be responsible for my own life and cut down the thorny emotional vines that were in the way of my experiencing the true and wonderful person that I am. Ready to find out how to deal with your own vines?

CHAPTER 11

Emotions, Dark and Light

WE ALL HAVE EMOTIONAL CONDITIONING from childhood that creates a jungle of emotional reactions we must navigate every day. My jungle seemed to be full of twisted vines with inch-long thorns! Some people seem to have fewer thorny vines (or maybe they've just tied their vines into nice, orderly bunches so they're not as noticeable).

You may be afraid of what might be hiding behind the thorny vines on your path, or you may have become so used to them that you don't feel it necessary to clear them out of the way. Maybe the vines feel like a part of you, as though if you were to cut them down you might no longer recognize yourself. It may sound strange, but our jungles can bring us a sense of security, if we have become comfortable living in the shade and darkness they provide. Perhaps we fear losing a partner or friend if our emotional trauma were cleared away and a strong light began to shine on our relationships. It is not uncommon for people to be terrified to let go of emotional trauma, merely because it has been with them for so long that they can't imagine life without it.

We are taught how to read, write, and do arithmetic in school, but we are not taught about emotions and feelings. Most people are very uncomfortable talking about emotions. We may be ashamed of how we feel, afraid that others might judge our feelings. We may not know a safe way to express our feelings. The truth is that emotions and feelings are just another source of information, like thinking. Our objective is not to eliminate our feelings, but to stay centered and respond appropriately. This takes practice.

There is a dynamic feedback loop between our emotional system and our thinking. When provoked, our emotions fuel our thinking and, in turn, our thinking adds more fuel to keep the emotional fires burning. Once I had a better understanding of my emotional conditioning, I found it easier to be self-aware and observe this dynamic process. I was able to see how my thinking contributed to my emotional reactions. Two coaching clients, Lynn and Peter, shared their story, which demonstrates many aspects of the thorny vines of old emotional conditioning and accompanying reactions.

Lynn and Peter Engage with Their Emotions

Lynn's father used to say things like "Stop it! How many times do I have to tell you, just listen — children should be seen and not heard." As a sensitive little girl, Lynn became timid. As a teenager she had to sneak around to make phone calls and see her girlfriends. By the time she was an adult Lynn's voice had become very small. She had bundled all her childhood anger away inside of her since she had no safe way of expressing it.

Lynn married her high school sweetheart, a smart, good-looking, popular boy. At the beginning of her marriage she was in heaven. However the marriage lasted only four years. The breaking point was when her husband chose to stay out partying rather than join her at the hospital for the birth of their first child. When Lynn finally set out on her own she had a three-month-old baby boy in her arms and another baby developing in her womb.

Fast-forward, through a second marriage and two more children. Thirty years later Lynn was with a loving man named Peter. Unfortunately all the old issues were coming up again and driving a wedge into their relationship. Lynn was still starving for love and had many unmet needs. She said, "When Peter comes home from work I want him to talk to me, to tell me about his day and to ask about mine. I would like him to hug me and say something sweet to me."

Peter had his own emotional conditioning, including a tendency to withdraw into himself. "He comes home and plunks himself down into that big lounge chair, turns on the TV and disappears for the rest of the night," Lynn said. "It is like I don't even exist." The more Peter disengaged from Lynn, the harder she pushed to receive his attention. Although both parties desired a supportive relationship, conflict and unhappiness started to brew as they pushed each other's emotional hot buttons.

Lynn's hot buttons were associated with feeling dismissed by her father and not deserving of love. All three of her adult relationships with men had actively pushed these buttons. Lynn was plagued by the thought that she was missing out on something, so she tried to force things to happen according to her wishes.

During our session together one night, I could sense Lynn was about to be overwhelmed by the storm of emotional energy swirling through her body. Rather than have this hurricane touch down, I worked with Lynn and Peter to turn the situation into an opportunity for learning about this recurring dynamic in their relationship.

But let's say Peter didn't want to be engaged in any growth and development. Lynn could still use the emotional provocations inherent in their relationship to resolve her own emotional conditioning. In *Transformation through Intimacy*, Robert Masters writes about using negative energy to create positive change. "We can become crazily jealous, possessive, obsessed, angry in ways we never thought possible ... If we take hold of it, we start to recognize what's right about what's wrong; we treat the shit as compost; we let the pain tear open our heart; we learn to love when we are not being loved or don't feel loved, and to give what we ache to be given." Lynn can't force Peter to show love, but she can embrace the emotional hurt and feel into it so deeply that she starts to resolve the emotional pain. By continuing to feel into one hurt after the other, she will divest herself of her past emotional conditioning. Over time Lynn can gently invite Peter to come and join her, and in time, she may receive from him what she so deeply desires.

If Peter decides that he does not want to engage in the relationship, it will likely come to an end. Lynn, however, will be in a much better place to attract a new partner more capable of expressing love, and in turn, she won't be so desperate to hear it. Lynn will then have the opportunity to experience what it's like to receive loving attention not because she desperately needs it to feel whole, but because it brings a deeper sense of closeness and intimacy between her partner and herself. It may also happen that when Lynn stops demanding love from him, Peter will have the space to offer her more of what she wants. A host of positive possibilities open up when we change our own personal dynamics!

SELF-REFLECTION QUESTIONS

- What is your childhood story that you carry around?
- What is it that you most deeply desire in your relationship?
- Have you communicated this desire clearly to your partner?
- Notice if you are in a place of need. Do you demand that your partner show up in a certain way?
- Can you gently invite your partner to show up and join you?
- Are you emotionally triggered on a regular basis?
- What emotions are you experiencing?

Sources of Emotional Conditioning

Emotional conditioning begins even before we are born and rapidly develops during the first four years of childhood when the neural connections in the brain are developing most actively.

What emotionally impacts us during this stage of our early development creates the foundation for our adult behavioral patterns, including feelings, thoughts and actions.

As newborns, we are suddenly exposed to a foreign and cold world with new sights, sounds, and sensations. Everyone knows that babies cry a lot. Crying is both a form of communication and a method of releasing the emotional energy of overwhelm. Unfortunately crying does not release all the emotional energy a child is experiencing. The remaining unprocessed energy is stored in the cells to be dealt with at a later time. As adults the cognitive processing ability of our brains is better developed, and we are able to process emotional situations more easily. Now is when we can be resourceful enough to process the emotional experiences that were overwhelming to us as children. Unfortunately most of us don't know how to do this in an easy and specific way.

When we experience emotional trauma, two things are occurring: a mental process and a physical process. An interactive dynamic occurs between the body and the brain, with memories being stored in the brain and energy being stored in the cells of the body. As adults we tend to relate to our memories as if they are the actual past. True, memories record the past, but in the way we wrote and recorded the events in our child minds. Memories may not be identical to the actual events. Children make sense of the world by being at the center of every event, and so they make each story about themselves. This is how a child ends up taking responsibility for what is going on in their world. Painful trauma is recorded and gets stuck in the mind and body at whatever age the trauma occurred; it does not grow up. As we continue through life, the energy from our traumas continues to be provoked, causing negative emotional reactions that often result in more traumatic events. This further trauma causes more pain, which we store on top of the old, forming our collections of emotional baggage. Emotional baggage is usually so painful that the energy we have repressed in our bodies will not resurface until we feel ready and resourceful enough to deal with it.

The Mind and the Emotions

There is a common perception that the mind is the dominant player and that it controls our behaviors. Our thinking causes our feelings and thus determines the actions that we take, our behaviors. Many of us are very judgmental of ourselves; our minds chatter at us, constantly telling us negative stories about ourselves. Our minds also make up negative stories about other people as a way to justify our own behavior.

Many of the tools outlined in chapter 4 help us manage and change our thinking. With consistent practice we can change our thinking and perspective on life, which will allow us to look at situations from a different point of view. When we change our thinking, then we can take a different set of actions. This is most effective, however, when we are calm and not emotionally provoked.

When it comes to how thinking affects our behaviors, our thoughts are only half of the story. Our emotions affect our thinking as well. When we have an emotional reaction, our logical thinking is suppressed. Because of this dynamic a significant amount of counseling focuses on teaching us how to control our emotions. Being more emotionally aware may help. However, when we are emotionally provoked it is very difficult to control or even manage emotions. Our ability to control our emotions depends upon the amount of unresolved emotional energy that we have relative to the situation. If we have a lot of unresolved energy, we are likely to have a large emotional reaction — anger, perhaps — and we may be unable to control it. When we get out of control we often experience regret after the fact.

I was once a semi-silent investor in a business venture with Eric, a man I was dating. I provided the working capital, and he operated the business. Yet I had a huge fear of losing money and being poor and helpless. When Eric needed more money for the business, I had doubts about what he was doing and opinions about what should be done. My mind started to churn out thoughts like a river after a rainstorm. Why was he purchasing inventory for the tourist market, when we had mostly locals as customers? I came up with all sorts of reasons why I was right and Eric was wrong, and why Eric's actions didn't make sense. My emotional reactions provided fuel for what some call a "monkey mind," a mind that constantly chatters.

When I was born my parents were very poor. They had suffered some crop failures and were having a hard time feeding, clothing, and schooling six kids. This energy dynamic of poverty and fear would have formed some of the first neural connections in my brain. Thinking affects emotions and in turn emotions affect thinking. Both emotions and thinking affect our actions. There is a direct interactive connection between body and mind; they always operate together.

SELF-REFLECTION QUESTIONS

- What do you notice about your thinking when you are emotionally provoked?
- When do you notice that you have a "monkey mind"?
- What subject does your mind often focus on?

What Are Emotions?

The energy we hold in our bodies drives our emotions, feelings, and thinking. Emotions are quite simply energy in motion— E-motion. People often think of emotions as being either positive (love, joy, happiness) or negative (anger, sadness, fear). Actually all emotions are positive, because they contain information about what is important to us. It is more accurate to speak of emotions as desirable or undesirable, meaning that we either desire to feel more of these emotions, or we would like to feel less of them. An undesirable emotion gives us the valuable information that the situation that triggered it is not working for us.

The following is a list of common emotions:

Desirable — want more intensity	Undesirable — want less intensity
Love: affection, caring, compassion, desire, liking, longing, passion	Anger: bitterness, contempt, frustration, hate, hostility, jealousy, rage, resentment, vengefulness
Joy: enthusiasm, excitement, hope, optimism, pleasure, pride, thrill, zest	Sadness: depression, disappointment, hopelessness, hurt, grief, melancholy, misery, sorrow, suffering
Cheerfulness: bliss, ecstasy, elation, enjoyment, happiness, satisfaction	Shame: guilt, regret, remorse
Surprise: amazement, astonishment	Neglect: isolation, loneliness, rejection
	Fear: fright, panic, shock, terror
	Nervousness: anxiety, distress, dread, uneasiness, worry

Undesirable emotions are our emotional hot buttons. They can be pushed by others or by ourselves. When we trigger our own egos or become judgmental, we can push our own buttons — we don't need anyone else to do it for us! However most of the time it is others who push our emotional hot buttons, intentionally or, usually, unintentionally, just by being who they are and acting out of their own emotional conditioning. The emotions we experience are inside of us — they are our own energy. Other people's emotions occur outside of us.

It is highly valuable to be aware of our emotions and the information they contain. Some people have an underdeveloped emotional vocabulary; for example, when asked how they are doing, they say, "Fine, OK, good." We can increase our emotional vocabulary and awareness by practicing the self-reflection exercise Feeling Emotions on page 223.

Feelings and Emotions

Feelings and emotions are different yet highly interrelated. *Feelings* are physical sensations that occur in the body when an emotion is triggered. *Emotions* are linked to judgment, our mental concepts about the situation, whether desirable or undesirable. According to the research of Joseph E. LeDoux, a neuroscientist at New York University, feelings are a conscious experience, while emotions originate from deep within the brain at an unconscious level.

When we are conscious of our feelings, the physical sensations that we may experience are as follows: Anxiety or worry may be felt as tightness in the belly. Hurt feelings may be experienced as a constriction in the chest. Fear of speaking may be felt as tightness in the throat or mouth. These physical sensations are due to emotional hot buttons being triggered. The self-reflection exercise Feeling Emotions, on page 223. will help you notice the physical feelings in your body that are associated with each emotion, desirable or undesirable.

When we are provoked or have unmet expectations, we might notice a subtle feeling of energy occurring outside or over the surface of the body, not localized in one spot. We are often provoked by identification, which is an attachment to or a story about something in our lives. I identified with my gardens even after we sold the house. The gardens were mine; it felt like they were a part of me. I had an unmet expectation that my partner Eric could run our business without additional injections of capital. Lynn had an unmet expectation that Peter would come home and greet her with words of affection.

Unmet expectations often result in the emotion of frustration. When frustrated, I often sense a subtle energy around my head, around my body, and sometimes over my chest, like a heavy weight. This subtle sensation can be like a fog or mist that surrounds some area of my body, or it may feel like a vibration throughout my body. It can be difficult to notice this feeling at first, but with practice you will be able to identify it quickly. Just close your eyes and sense what is occurring around or over your body.

We have several subtle senses. Imagine biting into a lemon: what do you notice? You will likely notice that your mouth is watering; this is the subtle sense of taste. Close your eyes and imagine a red apple. In your mind's eye you will see an apple; this is the subtle sense of sight. Have you ever had a conversation with yourself? You can hear yourself talking, and this is the subtle sense of hearing. Feeling your subtle senses is a matter of becoming aware of what you might not have been conscious of before.

Some people are very tuned in to their bodies and the physical sensations they are experiencing. Others are like me when I first started, unaware of our physical sensations. I had developed the idea that I was not safe in my body, and I had shut down my ability to feel, afraid of being overwhelmed. Eventually I reached a place where my body knew it was safe to be open to feelings. Post-traumatic stress often causes people to become desensitized to feeling and as a result they can't easily feel the sensations associated with negative emotions, especially the subtle feelings.

When we dissociate from the body to avoid sensing negative feelings, then we can't fully sense feelings from positive emotions either. As a result we miss out on the full impact of love and joy, and on experiencing the more elusive feelings of tenderness, ecstasy, and pleasure. To experience greater happiness, we need to do more of the activities we love and to be fully aware of our feelings. My life with Milo was a series of great activities, but I was not able to feel them fully. I was numb to my own feelings; hence I was missing out on experiencing the magic of life. After resolving a significant amount of old emotional energy, I became more conscious of my positive emotions.

When we don't experience the feelings associated with the emotion of being hurt, we might believe that we have resolved our emotional conditioning. There are two signals that indicate our conditioning has not been resolved, however. First is the presence of emotional reactions, which are fuelled by unresolved emotional energy in the body. Second is behaviors that signal that emotional energy may be stuffed down inside and has not risen to the surface. For example, we may act very independent, avoiding getting into relationships and choosing to remain single. We may be dependent on our partners, having the sense that we cannot live without them, and as a result rush into new relationships too quickly. We may sacrifice ourselves, giving too much to others while doing without ourselves. These are avoidance behaviors that people use to avoid overwhelming feelings. If we want to resolve the energy associated with these behaviors, first we must be willing to experience the emotional energy from undesirable feelings. Being willing to experience these feelings sends a message to the subconscious mind that we are resourceful enough to deal with whatever comes our way.

SELF-REFLECTION EXERCISE:

FEELING EMOTIONS

This exercise will help you become very aware of your feelings and what the sensations in your body are signaling to you.

- Three times a day, stop what you are doing, close your eyes, and focus on the sensations in your body. You may want to set a reminder on your phone or your electronic calendar, or do it before each time you eat.
- Describe each sensation, and then find a word on the list of emotions (see page 220.) that is appropriate for the sensation you are feeling.
- Also note what you are doing when you experience this feeling.
- What information is this feeling communicating to you?
- Maintain a list of your emotions and associated feelings. Over time, notice the patterns that emerge.

Organize Your Vines

The world of emotions and their corresponding feelings can be a complicated tangle of plant life to push through. Luckily, Tom Stone came up with a very simple model to help us categorize the vines that are growing in our emotional jungles, and he wrote about it in *The Power of How*. This model assisted me to quickly identify the root causes of my emotional reactions. It has given me insight into the emotional reactions of others, too, which has allowed me to respond better to their situations.

Tom calls this model the Core Dynamics of Common Problems. There are three major categories of common problems: "Resisting Feeling Things Fully," "Looking for Yourself Where You Are Not," and "Trying to Force an Outcome." I call these Core Problems. They are interconnected and interrelated, and they can all come into play at the same time in a given situation. You'll find that most of your emotional reactions will come from one of the Core Problems, and sometimes they'll come from an interaction of several Core Problems. Each one has something to say about the emotional reactions that can be provoked by divorce.

Resisting Feeling Things Fully

When we resist feeling the emotions provoked by traumatic events, we end up with the energy from emotional events that overwhelmed us as children plus what was added as we encountered additional emotional challenges over time. This emotional energy is stored in our emotional baggage until we find a way to release it.

I have often heard people say, "Time will heal your pain." Chuck Spezzano, in *If It Hurts, It Isn't Love*, says that what most of us do with the pain of a breakup is push it back inside us so we can go on. Unfortunately, the pain lies dormant, just waiting to break into our consciousness when provoked at a later time. Past pain is disguised as current pain. We carry these unresolved emotional experiences around in our subconscious minds and in our bodies until an external event triggers the suppressed energy. The pain can manifest as oversensitivity or as blindness to life, and it attracts further unpleasant events that add to the pain we already have stored away. Very few of us actively and consciously seek to feel more pain in our lives, but we end up adding to our pain anyway. Consciously experiencing past pain can be as frightening as entering into a jungle at nightfall, with all the haunting and unfamiliar noises. Yet this is exactly what we need to do to resolve incomplete emotional experiences from the past that are masquerading as current emotional pain.

In classic therapy, *transference* means that we project our pain onto people in the present who represent the significant players in our past emotional traumas. Our present partners are often targets for this past pain, as we witnessed in Lynn's story. Lynn projected onto Peter all the hurt she felt from her father, which had been compounded by two failed marriages.

I denied and hid the pain that I had stuffed into my body in childhood. This caused me to appear as a very tough and independent woman, and yet on the inside I was vulnerable and easily hurt. The more I denied my pain, the more prolific the thorny vines in my jungle of emotional conditioning.

Power struggles and conflict represent internal conflict within ourselves, and we often attract people who will help us bring the internal conflict out into the open. With awareness, we can take a close look at ourselves. When we are in the heat of the moment and experiencing overwhelm, the greatest challenge is to respond appropriately in the moment. Often when our emotions are triggered and the undesirable energy from past pain has been put into motion, we behave like the hurt child that has been stored away inside of us, rather than like a mature adult. It is great to know that our partners can bring out the kid in us!

The good news is we can learn to witness when unmet needs are ripe for resolving. I have learned to welcome feeling things fully in my life as a way to resolve my past pain and hence not be overwhelmed by the same emotions in the future.

Looking for Yourself Where You Are Not

The second dynamic area where our emotional conditioning from the past is evident is when we are looking for love outside of ourselves. Tom Stone indicates that this Core Problem begins when we are born. When we were in our mothers' wombs, everything was looked after for us. Once we were born there were lots of times when our immediate needs were not being looked after, and we had no language to communicate our needs. At the level of feeling, we conclude that the part of ourselves that meets our needs is missing.

Many of us look for other people to meet our needs and show us love. In particular, we look to our partners. If we only had love expressed to us the way we want love to be expressed, we think, then everything would feel right in our world. We would feel whole and complete. As mentioned in chapter 9, we may look for this love in the form of terms of endearment, touch, gifts, acts of service, or quality time together. These can be wonderful moments. But when we have a sense of need rather than desire, that the act must happen for us to feel joy or happiness, then we are looking for love outside of ourselves. The problem is that we are not feeling enough love for ourselves from within ourselves. When we look for love outside of ourselves we create all sorts of turmoil, often about quite simple things.

For example, Milo thought I was much better at laundry. For me, if Milo did the laundry, it was a sign that he loved me. It was amazing the amount of emotional turmoil that something as simple as laundry brought into our relationship. When quite frankly, doing laundry had nothing to do with love, it was just a domestic necessity.

SELF-REFLECTION QUESTIONS

- When do you not feel loved?
- What do you need someone to do or say to help you feel loved?
- What are your expectations around being loved?
- What does your partner want from you to feel loved?

The Ego

Before moving on, allow me to give you a very simplified introduction to the ego. Whole books have been written on the ego, but for our purposes a simplified view is sufficient to show how the ego creates problems in our relationships.

Our egos have taken on their own self-importance and at the same time have created a separation between us and others around us. Our egos create a trap in our thinking:

- I am what I have.
- I am what I do.
- I am what people think of me.
- I am separate from others.
- I am separate from everything that is missing in my life.

It is this feeling of separateness from others that creates the great fear in us of being judged as not good enough. We feel alone and begin to look for love and approval outside ourselves, demanding that our partners love us the way we want to be loved ... or else.

Our egos remember all the hurtful situations from the past and keep bringing them forward in current conversations and arguments, as Lynn did with Peter. The ego is the dynamic link between the mind and emotional system. The ego remembers the hurt and pushes the button on the emotional energy stored in our body. Of course our partners have egos too, and start to pull away as a defense. For example, both Lynn and Peter felt like they were losing the other's love, which in turn provoked their stored emotional energy. Before long they found themselves spending most of their time stewing in isolation and feeling unloved. Until we release the fear of not "getting" love, and forgive our partners for not filling that imaginary missing piece, this dynamic plays out again and again.

Craving Control

We often think that controlling what goes on in our lives would make us feel secure. If I do things "my way," then I know they will work out OK, right? Then I won't have to worry about being lonely, embarrassed, and so forth. I believed this: If I am an expert in my chosen field and I know everything there is to know, then I will never look stupid. These thoughts were a major cause of the way I behaved and hence the way people experienced me. Now that you know what was occurring on the inside, you might label me as having been very insecure. Exactly right, but I covered up for my insecurity on the outside by being an expert and a know-it-all. I appeared as tough as nails. I tried to be in control so that I would not have to deal with uncertainty or the unknown.

Doing things "my way" caused friction between Milo and me. When we worked on a project together, such as building raised garden vegetable beds. I would always be asking why he was doing something a certain way and then suggesting another way for it to be done. I made suggestions about how the pieces of wood should be fitted together, and he did it a different way. Building was something that Milo was really good at, but I had this compulsion to control things. This meant that I was not present to feel the love that Milo was investing in building the vegetable boxes, and it likely took away Milo's pleasure of doing this service for me. The bottom line was that my ego got in the way of both me and Milo experiencing more love in our relationship.

The bad news is that each of us has an ego that creates the illusion that we are separate from each other and gets in the way of us making heartfelt connections. The good news is that the ego provides each of us with our uniqueness. It's what allows us to grow into individual human beings. Our egos provide us with our strength and determination to survive; this is what keeps us from quitting and giving up.

Our egos are active forces in our minds and our lives, so it is well worth learning to manage them. When I recognized how much willpower my ego had, and how it attempted to dominate so many aspects of my life, I realized that if I didn't learn to manage my ego, it would continue to manage *me*.

TOOL: MANAGING THE EGO

(CONTROL-ALT-DELETE BUTTON)

Ask yourself the following questions:

- Is there an outcome I am trying to force right now?
- What am I insisting upon?
- What am I afraid of?
- Could I let these things go?

When we are in a heartbreaking situation such as a divorce, it is the drive of the ego, our willpower, that helps us to keep getting out of bed every day. Our willpower is what propels us forward to achieve goals and objectives. It activates us to learn, to be creative, to develop new ideas and share them with others. Our egos are by no means bad, but it is problematic when we allow our egos to make our decisions from the ego's fear-based point of view.

SELF-REFLECTION QUESTIONS

- When do you notice that you try to control situations?
- What are you afraid of?
- When is your willpower hindering your relationship?
- When is your willpower useful and serving you?

Trying to Force an Outcome

How does the ego cause so many problems? Well, begin by asking yourself how forceful your willpower is. I learned to notice a forceful energy that occurred in my body whenever I was trying to make something happen, to push something forward. This is the third Core Problem: trying to force an outcome. When my willpower was becoming too forceful, I noticed, I tended to encounter resistance from others. When others don't share our desires or perspectives, their egos will establish a protective force.

I used to greet my former neighbor, Carlos, on the street almost every day and we would chat briefly. I could tell Carlos was attracted to me and wanted to ask me out. One day I had an invitation to come to his house for lunch, at noon. I was a few minutes late, and at 12:05 he showed up at my door wondering where I was. I could feel his forceful energy and need to control the situation, which was unattractive to me. From that day on, I kept my distance from him. My ego was protecting me from that unwanted outcome.

Just because a relationship no longer suits us doesn't mean there's a need for anyone to be at fault. It's most helpful to me when I use these situations to observe what I am not comfortable about in myself. I look at what the situation is mirroring. I look at where I need to forgive myself. When Milo wanted to move on from our relationship, I didn't need to make him wrong for wanting to try out a new relationship. It felt terrible to me, to be sure, but when I stepped back from the situation I realized I had done the same thing Milo was now doing, many years ago. When my relationship with Gary did not work, I had sought company elsewhere. Such situations give us practice at forgiving both ourselves and the other person. They help us learn to let life move forward on its own terms, and to welcome new situations rather than struggle to fight off the changes that inevitably come along. Why should our partners stay in relationship with us? Because we want them to! When we create a self-serving story about who's right and who's wrong, we are using willpower to try to force an outcome. Then we tend to ignore other people's perspectives about the situation. When things don't go our way, we may overreact out of frustration or anger, especially if we are expecting to extract love from the situation. We may feel a great sense of struggle at these times, as if everything is too much.

Intertwining of the Vines

The ego is the one aspect of our conditioning that we can really manage. We can determine the degree to which our egos manifest in our lives. Looking for ourselves where we are not and avoiding feeling things fully are both patterns rooted in our past emotional conditioning. The underlying energy of these two Core Problems must be released and resolved if we are to achieve freedom from their emotional grip. The ego, however, is a different matter: it provokes the unresolved energy of these other two dynamics, causing most of our emotional reactions.

As we venture into the jungle of our emotional conditioning we must learn to recognize the different types of vines we will encounter, and how to cut through them. Each of these vines has a unique growth habit, some of them starting high and away where we hardly see them until they grow downward and end up firmly rooted, obstructing the path forward. Other vines grow upward from deep within, wrapping themselves around us as though we were a host tree. Some have giant thorns that can gouge us if we grab onto them too tightly. In the next few chapters we will encounter each of these vines and learn how to cut them down permanently. How exciting to enter this jungle knowing we have the ability to clear away every obstacle!

CHAPTER 12

Entering the Jungle
of Emotional Conditioning

WE CAN ENTER THE JUNGLE WITH the intent to use the emotional turmoil of a divorce or breakup to permanently resolve our emotional conditioning from childhood. It's a great opportunity, and we're not going to waste it! All our lives we've used up so much energy struggling to manage all sorts of emotional situations: fear of setting out on our own and being alone, anger at being rejected by our partners, or guilt for leaving our partners. We may be feeling intense pain about all the things that we have had to leave behind, as I did with the beautiful gardens I had nurtured for years. We may be stuck in a place of depression and suffering, the way Henry was when he could not understand why his wife left him after having been married for only two months. These feelings can seem overwhelming. Many of my clients have stated that they just want the pain to go away. We long for the days when we felt some sense of happiness; even numbness would feel better than this, we may think.

All this pain is due to the thick growth of thorny emotional vines. There's the Lawyer Vine (being judgmental), the Wait-a-While Vine (resisting change), and the Mile-a-Minute Vine (manufacturing interpretations). This chapter uses the Core Dynamics model that Tom Stone laid out in *The Power of How* as a frame of reference to shed more light on the emotions that we experience when going through a divorce or other relationship ordeal. Emotions, or our labels for them, are really just intellectual concepts. What we are dealing with now, in the thick of the jungle, are the physical sensations that let us know we're *feeling* those emotions.

This isn't counseling. We are not dealing with our conditioning at the intellectual level anymore. We are resolving it at the
physical level, where we feel it, where it touches us most deeply.
To resolve these problems permanently we need to cut down the
troublemaking vines and remove them from the jungle, leaving
a clear path for us to move forward in life. First we'll classify the
vines we may find growing in our jungles, and learn a few strategies for managing them in the short term. Then, in chapter 13, I
will show you how to cut these vines down for good.

Core Problems — The Vines in the Jungle

Resisting Feeling Things Fully	Trumpet Vine: Avoiding the Present
	Strangler Vine: Ignoring Your Intuition
	Lawyer Vine: Being Judgmental
Looking for Yourself Where You Are Not	Headache Vine: Mistaking Need for Love
	Tape Vine: Limiting Self-Expression
	Wait-a-While Vine: Resisting Change
Trying to Force an Outcome	Cockspur Thorn: Excluding Other Perspectives
	Mile-A-Minute Vine: Manufacturing Interpretation
	Barbed Wire Vine: Overreacting to Circumstances

Resisting Feeling Things Fully

In the first category of Core Problems, Tom Stone has provided us with three subclasses of problems associated with resisting feeling things fully. From not being willing to feel our past emotional experiences fully, we are "Avoiding the Present" — the Trumpet Vine. The second problem is "Being Judgmental," also known as the Lawyer Vine. The final problem is "Ignoring Your Intuition," or the Strangler Vine. According to Tom Stone, this overall category is based on our being emotionally overwhelmed in childhood and making a feeling-level decision to avoid feeling intense emotions fully. As a result, we don't feel any of our emotions fully, not even the pleasurable ones. The real trouble here is that if we avoid our feelings, we can't feel life. Gradually, over time, the vines of resisting our feelings grow a tangled barrier that prevents us from living the way we would ideally like to live. Let's take a closer look.

Trumpet Vine — Avoiding the Present

Have you noticed that sometimes your mind gets stuck on something that happened in the past and you just can't let it go? Maybe someone has wronged you in some way and the Trumpet Vine continues to play past tunes in the present moment. This was exactly what happened to Henry. He felt deeply rejected when his wife decided to leave the marriage after only two months. Henry felt so terrible about the short duration of his marriage that he spent the next five years asking himself, "Why?" He was stuck in the past, unable to experience the present moment.

Or maybe you have caught yourself living in the future, focusing on an event that may happen. You fantasize that when this event occurs you will be happier. When we are not living in the present, we create stories focused on either negative events from the past or wishful thinking about the future. We focus on these events as a way of avoiding our feelings in this moment. For some of us, our minds are addicted to living in the past or the future. We live anywhere but the present.

Eckhert Tolle says the pain that we experience in the Now is a form of unconscious resistance, that we are making a judgment about what is occurring and then attempting to avoid feeling whatever is happening. When we resist feeling our current emotional experiences fully, we do not bring them to completion. It is this lack of emotional completion that causes the buildup of energy I refer to as emotional baggage. When someone pushes our emotional hot buttons, we activate the past pain stored in our emotional baggage and bring it forward to the present. Because we don't know how to resolve this pain, we keep experiencing it over and over again when our buttons get pushed. As we reexperience this past pain, we tend to retell the stories associated with it. Our friends often get tired of hearing these stories and may distance themselves from us. This is especially true if we complain about a former partner and all the nasty things he or she did. All our unhappiness and anger gets replayed out into our current lives in the present moment. If we don't deal with this pain, we relive it over and over again.

The other thing that we do when we avoid the present is that we worry about some possible negative event in the future. Our mind makes up stories about what we fear and projects these stories into an imaginary future. When this happens, we experience the emotions associated with our negative projections just as though the events were actually happening right now.

In this way we bombard our poor bodies with negative feelings about past events — and even future events that have never occurred! Obsessed with what is behind or possibly ahead of us, we are unable to experience what pleasure there may be in the moment we're living now.

Due to my conditioning and fear of overwhelm, I lived in anything but the present moment. When my mother was alive, I cried myself to sleep many nights afraid of how alone I would feel when she passed away. After she passed away, this fear of being alone stayed with me. The pain resurfaced again and again, as though it had punctured a deep hole in my chest. It felt dark. I wished the pain and fear would go away, and yet at that time I did not know how to get free of it. Maybe you have felt this way, too. If I can learn how to let go of this kind of pain, you can do the same thing.

SELF-REFLECTION QUESTIONS

- What stories do you retell from the past?
- Are they happy stories, or are they stories of upset?
- What is the purpose of telling these stories?
- Do you spend time daydreaming about the future?
- What are you hoping will occur that is not occurring now?
- Do you spend time worrying about the future?
- How does focusing on the past or the future affect what is happening in your life now?

Strangler Vine—Ignoring Your Intuition

Due to my fear of being overwhelmed, I unintentionally suppressed my ability to be aware of what I was sensing in my body. My mind resisted feeling the pain that was stored in my body, and like the Strangler Vine, it formed a thick web that barred me from being present to my intuition. Intuition, or our "gut feeling," recognizes subtle sensations associated with knowing what to do. When we are not present to our intuition, we miss the messages that it sends to us. As you will see later in this book, being present and having full access to our intuition is vital if we are to live into our ideal and magical lives.

The second barrier to ignoring our intuition is the feeling of doubt. Feelings of doubt override the intuitive messages that the body's sensing system sends to our brains. I might have a sense of knowing that I should do something or take a particular action, but my mind enters in with a thought and feeling of doubt that cancels my intuitive knowing.

One day I parked my car at a metered parking spot on the street and went to have lunch with a friend. I had only enough change for one hour of parking. It occurred to me that our lunch would last for more than an hour and that I should get some more change to put into the meter. My mind leaped in to help. It said, "Oh no, it will be all right." An hour and fifteen minutes later as I left the restaurant, I saw that I had been given a thirty-dollar parking ticket. I told myself thirty dollars was a cheap lesson for not paying attention to my intuition. The next time I doubted my intuition, the cost, or the lost opportunity, might set me back far more than thirty dollars.

For me, the knowing of intuition is like an energy in my body that has a message attached to it, or just a feeling that a certain course of action is to be followed. Or it might be a knowing that for the moment I need to sit still and wait until the appropriate course of action becomes clear. Doubt shows up in the form of an energy pattern that overrides and cancels out the original energy of the intuition. My mind then enters the process and, rather than supporting the intuitive knowing, provides all sorts of reasons as to why my feeling of doubt is correct. It is often said that opportunities are presented only once, and when we don't act upon them, they are gone. I actually find that when I am really paying attention, when I am present, there are a few signals that indicate to me the appropriate course of action to follow, and when I am clear on what the signals are pointing to, then I take action.

When we resolve the emotional energy that we have stored in our emotional baggage, we will cut the roots of the Strangler Vine that chokes our awareness of our intuition. Reducing the energy from my emotional conditioning reduced the fear and the associated doubt that I was taking the wrong course of action. I became significantly better at listening to my intuition and allowing it to guide me rather than using my mind to logically figure everything out. When I live this way, I find that I place myself in more and more situations that bring me joy.

SELF-REFLECTION QUESTIONS

- When do you ignore your intuition?
- What is the cost of ignoring your intuition?

Lawyer Vine — Being Judgmental

When we resist feeling things, we separate ourselves from others. We experience things as being outside of us rather than coming from inside of us, because we really don't want to admit that at some point in time we behaved that way too. When I was judgmental of others, it was because I was judging myself. I was noticing something in others that I was critical about within myself. It is the mirror effect that I talked about in our relationships with our partners. What I am uncomfortable with might be current or might be in the past. For instance, I was angry that Milo cheated on me. Who I was really angry with was the young woman who cheated on her first husband, Gary.

Getting over being judgmental was a major challenge for me in my relationship with Milo and in all other areas of my life. Here's one example: On the weekend, Milo and I always did the laundry for the coming week. Milo would often take the laundry out of the dryer and leave it in the laundry basket, which just ensured permanent wrinkles. I hate ironing clothes. I was angry that Milo did not take more responsibility for ensuring that the laundry got completed, with the clothes folded and in our dresser drawers.

Let's look at the emotion of being critical and judgmental. First, as with any emotion, the emotional energy that I felt resided inside of me and not Milo. It was the energy inside of me that was being provoked by my expectation that Milo should ensure that the laundry was done and wrinkle free.

I had a judgment of myself that I should take to completion any activities I began. Guess what—this was one of my biggest challenges. I was constantly starting projects and getting 80 to 90 percent complete and then leaving them unfinished. I sewed all the curtains for the house except the ones for our bedroom window. The sewing machine sat out for weeks while I intended to sew the last set of curtains, which never got done.

The wrinkled laundry was just a proxy for the negative judgment that I had about myself for not completing projects. It was a mirror of my own behavior, which in my own estimation needed to change. Until I changed my thinking and resolved the emotional energy in me that made me feel uncomfortable about my own behavior, I would continue to be critical of anyone who did not take things to completion.

▶ ### TOOL: CRITICAL AND JUDGMENTAL

Being critical and judgmental has a mirror effect: what we see in others is really just a reflection of what we see in ourselves.

- What is it that you are critical or judgmental of in another person?
- When have you done something similar?
- How is what you are observing related to yourself?

▶ **TOOL: FORGIVENESS**

We often need to forgive ourselves before we can forgive others and let go of our criticisms.

• What do you need to forgive yourself for?
• What do you need to let go of?

SELF-REFLECTION QUESTIONS

• What are you critical or judgmental about in your partner?
• How does this situation apply to you?
• What emotion are you experiencing?
• What feeling is associated with the emotion?

Looking for Yourself Where You Are Not

When we feel like there's something missing in our lives, we tend to look for that piece outside ourselves—by finding the right romantic partner, a powerful car, a gorgeous house, or children that live up to our expectations. When we have all of this, we think, then we will feel satisfied and complete. But this is all an illusion because we are already whole and complete. Nothing is really missing. However, as long as we don't feel our wholeness, we look for love outside ourselves.

The Headache Vine has us mistaking getting our needs met

for love. We look to our partners to meet our needs, and when they do, we feel loved, at least for a short time. When we have a sense of security, when things stay the same, we feel more comfortable and secure in ourselves. The Wait-a-While Vine doesn't like to rush into significant life changes if they can be avoided, even when our lives or our relationships are not working. When we feel insecure it is better to keep quiet than to rock the boat. And if we were to say what we really thought, we might put our relationships in jeopardy, so the Tape Vine helps us to limit our self-expression and keep the peace. Generally when we are looking for ourselves where we are not, we are looking for love and acceptance outside of ourselves. When we don't get it, we may experience frustration or a sense of isolation.

There are three sub classifications of vines that have us looking for love outside of ourselves. The Headache Vine has us constantly trying to get our unmet needs met, and when we do, we call this love. The Wait-a-While Vine doesn't like to rush into significant life changes if they can be avoided, even when our lives or our relationships are not working. It is better to wait and avoid changes. Tape Vine helps us to limit our self-expression and keep the peace.

SELF-REFLECTION QUESTIONS

- What emotions arise if you imagine not having your partner around anymore?
- What are the physical sensations you feel?

Headache Vine — Mistaking Need for Love

Gary Chapman's five love languages, which we talked about earlier, focus on developing good management strategies to meet our partners' unmet needs. When we know what our partners' needs are, then we can satisfy those needs and our partners will feel more loved, at least for a while. The challenge is that we are constantly serving our partners' needs, and when we make mistakes, they don't feel loved. Our relationships would be significantly more fulfilling if each of us was able to permanently resolve our own underlying unmet needs. We want to absent the energy inside of us that feels like "If I don't have this then there is something wrong with our relationship." This is the dynamic that Lynn and Peter were playing out in their relationship. When Peter did not come home from work and engage Lynn in a conversation, Lynn did not feel loved. She needed Peter's attention; she needed Peter to speak words of affirmation for her to feel loved.

Unmet needs are something that we desire to have to feel our absolute best. However when the desire is transformed into something that we must have from others, or we feel like there is something missing from our lives, we become "needy." When people around us don't provide what we need, we are left feeling empty inside. When I wasn't feeling appreciated by Milo, in my own heart I knew that for me to feel appreciation required that I change my behaviors and spend as much time on myself as I was on working around the house. I would also have to resolve some of my deeper emotional energy that left me feeling unloved and unable to feel the love that was being expressed to me.

If and when Lynn resolves her underlying energy of "need," then what will be left is a simple desire to hear words of affirmation from Peter, but she will not need to hear them to feel loved. When Peter does speak words of affirmation, they will touch Lynn's heart in a new way. Lynn will experience a deeper sense of joy.

Another place we look for love is in recognition from others. This is what Lynn really wanted from her father, and it was why she married her first husband, to gain the recognition of her peers. When we have unresolved emotional conditioning around the area of recognition, we may be receiving recognition from others but not accepting it and fully taking it in. As much as I had desired to be recognized, I often felt uncomfortable and embarrassed when I was being recognized. I was deflecting it. My golf coach would tell me how great my golf swing was. Friends would give me nice gifts for my birthday. I received these gifts and compliments graciously, yet I wasn't taking in the love that they conveyed. Milo also gave me very nice gifts for my birthday and at Christmas, and yet I still did not feel appreciated and recognized. I looked for love and recognition from outside of me and often felt disappointed because I could not feel that love.

Real appreciation meant that I had to treat myself better. For example, take more time on the weekends for myself and quit pushing myself to do more and more. I needed to learn to acknowledge myself for what I was doing and feel a sense of satisfaction about it. Setting up some rewards for myself, such as time to read or go hiking in the forest or go to a café and sit and have a coffee and just people-watch. Over time, as I started to treat myself better, I let go of the suffering that I was feeling due to others, Milo in particular, not fulfilling my needs. I started to take time to read novels, take long baths, and go for a massage once in a while, all in honor of recognizing myself. Doing these things for myself greatly eased the old sense of there being something missing in my heart, but it did not resolve the underlying emotional hurt that I had stored away.

When I resolved much of my hurt and gave myself the appreciation I deserved, I started to experience the world in a different way. Now when someone fulfills one of my desires it feels juicy and sweet, like the icing on the cake — rather than it being the whole cake, or the only piece of cake I'll ever have. Recognition feels good, but I don't "need it" to feel happy.

SELF-REFLECTION QUESTIONS

- Who are looking for recognition from?
- Who do you want to be accepted by?

- How do you feel when you are not recognized or accepted?
- What could you do to recognize yourself more?
- How do you feel when you recognize yourself?

In addition to resolving the energy of our unmet needs, we also can do a lot more to treat ourselves with love and build a stronger sense of love. For instance, we can go back to chapter 4 and practice the mirror exercise to gain a stronger sense of self-love. When we resolve the emotional energy that keeps telling us we are not good enough, we will drop off a whole pile of unmet needs that have us behaving in ways that don't serve us.

The good news is that the Headache Vine has some medicinal properties and can be used to clear up the headaches that we cause ourselves when we look for love outside of ourselves, or when we look for ourselves where we are not. By being conscious of our behavior, we can start to become aware of when a desire becomes a need that we feel like we can't live without. We can notice when we are depending upon our partners to get a need met or when we are blaming our partners for this need not being met. When we have this level of awareness, then we can start making different choices about our behavior.

SELF-REFLECTION QUESTIONS

A need feels like something that you must have, something that is missing in your life, that you will not be complete without. When you think of a need that you have, be it acceptance, accomplishment, acknowledgment, caring, freedom, power, recognition, or safety, to name a few, you can ask yourself the following questions:

- Why is this need so important?
- Who am I when I have this need met? How do I act? What do I think about?
- Who am I when I don't get this need met? How do I behave? How do I feel about myself? How do I feel about others? About life?
- What three changes would I have to make in my life to fully meet and satisfy this need?

Tape Vine — Limiting Self-Expression

When we are looking for love outside of ourselves, it can be very frightening to speak up and say what we are thinking. This leads to tolerating toxic behavior, among other issues. The fear of losing our partners' love or our parents' love is a primary reason many people don't speak up about what is bothering them. Like the Tape Vine, which grows very close to the ground, we tend to keep a low profile and keep our thoughts to ourselves.

Lynn had grown up with a very small voice; she was afraid of losing her father's love and, later, her husband's love, if she spoke about how she felt. I have encountered many people in my coaching who are afraid to talk to their partners about concerns they have about their relationship. They are afraid that if they bring up their concerns it will make the relationship worse, and that their partners will not want to work on the relationship. So rather than face losing the relationship, they keep quiet and tolerate what is not working, with the hope that someday their partners might change. One client said his partner no longer wanted to have sex. This had been going on for years, but he had never told his wife how unhappy this made him, because he was afraid to lose her love. After many years he found a solution he thought would be acceptable to keep his relationship intact, but his solution backfired, forcing both of them to confront the problems in their relationship. At that point they could no longer live in denial.

With Milo I was always afraid to speak up about the really important things that bothered me. It was the personal and intimate things between us that I had difficulty talking about. I would have a conversation in my head with him, but when it actually came to speaking about it, I ended up suppressing what I had to say. And I couldn't speak to him about how unhappy I was with our lack of communication; I was afraid he would reject me and ignore me if I tried to raise the subject.

My conditioning around not speaking up came from my father; I had listened to him for thirty years tell my mother to shut up, that she did not know what she was talking about. It became ingrained in me that speaking up meant conflict and being degraded. When I was thinking about something that I really wanted to open up a conversation about, I often had all sorts of doubt about how my message would be received. I would feel afraid and would constantly put off the conversation for "the right time." Because I was afraid of losing Milo's love, the right time never came.

Because the Tape Vine grows low to the ground, it can be pulled out and cleared out of the jungle with consistent effort. Not speaking up becomes a habit, and with conscious effort we can change old habits that don't serve us. When I notice I am holding back speaking what is on my mind, I ask myself the following questions: What is it that I want to say? How can I say what I need to say without hurting the other person? What am I afraid will happen when I say it? Speaking up became a lot easier when I let go of the anger around the way my father treated my mother. I now recognize that when I tolerate things and don't speak up, I am showing a lack of love and respect for myself, and I want to treat myself with love.

SELF-REFLECTION QUESTIONS

- What is that you are not saying in your relationship that needs to be said?
- What is holding you back?
- How could you say what needs to be said without hurting your partner?
- What are you afraid will happen?

Wait-a-While Vine—Resisting Change

When we are uncertain of an outcome, we can become paralyzed with fear of the unknown. The unknown feels like jumping off the edge of a cliff into swirling water. This was how all change used to look to me. I was afraid to allow situations to unfold. Instead, I tried to manipulate things so that they would produce the results I wanted.

Jed McKenna, in *Spiritual Warfare*, makes the point that we often buy into our own judgments that certain things are "bad" and other things are "good." What this does is keep us locked into the fear that the "bad" might happen to us. If we are patient and allow the unknown to unfold without forcing any outcomes, we can observe the situation as it happens. Then we can decide if the situation works for us or not. When we live in fear that bad things are going to happen, we usually send out negative energy that in turn causes us to behave in ways that attract and help cause "bad" things to happen.

Once I got over the worst of the immediate emotional turmoil from my divorce, what I found was that there was no bad or good about it. Things were just different. When I accepted the situation I was in and started focusing on how I really wanted to feel, I started to take the actions and do the things that helped me to feel the way I wanted to feel.

Sometimes the river of life presents big waterfalls, sometimes it gives us long stretches of quiet water, and sometimes there are series of nonstop rapids. As we learn and grow our experience of life changes. Where my life flows to in the future will present a different kind of challenge. Will one path be better or worse than another? Only I can apply that judgment. And if I am truly living in the present moment, fully embracing life, then whatever path I am on will be an adventure. It is only when I choose a particular path out of ego, some sense that this is the way life *must* be, that I am likely to encounter suffering.

We suffer when we keep holding on to things, ideas, or people after it is time to let them go. We don't always know in that moment why we need to let them go. Did I know at the time why it was important to let go of Milo? No. Do I know now? Yes. I have an idea that I needed to set myself free because there was more growth available to me out in the big "bad" world, where I could face my fears. I consciously chose to let go of control, to remove the Wait-a-While Vine from my jungle, and to let life show me what direction to take. As I have embraced the unknown, it has become clear to me that there is some greater purpose for me than the life I was living before. I am now allowing intuition to guide me as I move through the world.

SELF-REFLECTION QUESTIONS

- What do you want to stay exactly as it is in your life?
- What is it that you need to control?
- What would happen if you made a change and it didn't work out?
- How would you feel?

Trying to Force an Outcome

The third category of Core Problems, trying to force an outcome, has our egos standing front and center in our emotional conditioning. It should be no surprise that when our egos are involved, we are forcing something to happen—because our egos' role is to keep us safe. When the ego interacts directly with energy that we have stored away from resisting feeling things fully, we often feel a huge sense of struggle in our lives. Things just don't seem to go the way we want them to go. We have an expectation of something happening, and then things don't work out. A classic example was the store that Eric and I opened; most things that we tried to do just did not work out. I can't tell you why they didn't work, but they very consistently did not work, and we forced an outcome by keeping the store open much longer than we should have. We were optimistic and got tangled up in the Barbed Wire Vine by overreacting and doing things too quickly.

When we are looking for ourselves where we are not, we can often feel frustrated, hurt, and angry when we don't receive the love we seek from others. In these circumstances the Mile-a-Minute Vine writes stories about how it would like things ideally to be, and at the same time the Cockspur Thorn excludes other people's perspectives, resulting in unmet expectations and disappointment.

Given the amount of emotional baggage that I carried around, I was no stranger to forcing outcomes. When I got an idea into my head I tended to push forward and take action, while ignoring other information about the circumstances. A simple example was when Milo and I went golfing late one Saturday morning, which meant that we did not get home until about four in the afternoon. I had it in my head that I wanted to make a nice dinner; Milo just wanted me to make hamburgers. When we got home we were both tired, and I had to negotiate with myself to let go of making a more formal dinner in favor of making a simple, practical dinner. For Milo food was fuel; for me making a nice dinner was a celebration and a way that I showed love for myself and him. But making a more elaborate dinner when we were both tired didn't make sense. Even though I knew that it didn't make logical sense, there was some energy from within that drove me to force the issue around what we were going to eat.

The issue around food was just one small example. Forcing things to happen played itself out over and over in all my relationships in all areas of my life. If you are wondering whether you force outcomes, notice if you have had people in your life label you thick-headed, stubborn, or pushy. Now ask yourself, did they have a point? Be honest. These labels certainly applied to me. I am not proud of it, but that is the way I was. I was a queen at forcing outcomes. Forcing outcomes has a lot to do with wanting to be right, wanting things our way, and being afraid of losing someone's love.

SELF-REFLECTION QUESTION

- In what situations do you notice yourself insisting something needs to be a certain way?
- What would happen if you just allowed the situation to unfold?

Cockspur Thorn — Excluding Other Perspectives

The ego tends to ignore other peoples' perspectives and needs to have things its own way. For most of my life I only accepted other people's perspectives if they had a well-articulated argument. Otherwise I considered my perspective to be right. This meant I was a very poor listener. I often became impatient listening to someone's perspective, especially if they did not explain things clearly. It was more important to me to go ahead with my idea than to consider using someone else's idea. After all, I had thought my idea through and was pretty sure of the outcome. By excluding other people's perspectives and wanting to be right, I was much like the Cockspur Thorn to deal with: very prickly. People tended to deal with me with a certain degree of caution. The irony was that I just wanted to be accepted, and I thought that if my solution worked, then I would not look stupid — I would gain people's approval, maintain their love, and everything would be fine.

One of my most traumatic events around ignoring people's perspectives occurred at a workshop about six years ago. One evening the leaders conducted an exercise where they asked each one of us a question privately, and that question determined whether we were to participate in a group exercise the next day or not. I and a few other people were eliminated from participating with no explanation. I felt isolated and left out, which hurt and embarrassed me. I fumed about the situation overnight. By morning I was absolutely livid and convinced in my own mind that what they had done was wrong and hurtful. To this day I do not understand the purpose of that exercise! What I do know is that it really hurt my ego and sense of self and that it was about the angriest that I can ever remember being. It pushed on a whole pile of my emotional hot buttons all at the same time

My ego said, "They were wrong to do this and not provide some explanation or learning." Even though this event occurred six years ago, my ego still holds the perspective that what they did was wrong. How open do you think I would be to hearing why they did the exercise after feeling so much hurt? You're right — not very open. It is extremely hard to be open to listening and having good communication when our egos are protecting us. It is even harder to have good communication when we are in the grips of an emotional reaction. Perhaps they had a purpose for the exercise, and I was so angry that I did not hear them provide that explanation. I was too proud to ask what the point of the whole exercise was, for fear that my ego would be served up a mortal blow. So I stifled my self-expression and withdrew emotionally from this event that my ego had deemed unsafe.

SELF-REFLECTION QUESTIONS

- What do you make others wrong for?
- When do you notice making yourself right?
- What are you ignoring about your partner's perspective?
- What perspective would a wise, neutral onlooker have of the situation?

Mile-a-Minute Vine — Manufacturing Interpretations

Worry and anxiety come from underlying fear about emotional and physical safety. The mind makes up stories, negative projections on the future, and these stories create a sense of unease in our bodies. This is what I call the Mile-a-Minute Vine. Its speed of growth depends upon how much emotional energy we have stored in our baggage. The more energy stored, the more vigorous the vine grows, choking out the tender growth as it scrambles upward. The more emotional conditioning we have, the faster our minds make up negative stories that bad things will happen to us if we don't have sufficient money, or love, or food. We may have real concerns that need some well-thought-out action. However, our worries can be blown out of proportion if they are based only on the fearful stories that our minds make up.

I had always worried about money. Even when I earned a six-figure income and had virtually no personal debt, my mind made up stories that terrified me. I would be broke, we would not be able to afford our house, and I would not be able to survive. The fact that I was in a relationship with Milo, who had a good job and could support us if necessary, did not alleviate this fear in me. The fear was much deeper. I believe this fear started when

I was a baby in my mother's womb, due to the severe poverty that the family was experiencing when I was conceived and born. As discussed in chapter 11, our early family conditioning is very powerful in the first three years of our lives and can set the scene for these underlying fears to plague us throughout our lives.

The Mile-a-Minute Vine can grow out of control. When I went to bed at night I used to feel the terror of poverty coursing through my body. I would repeat a mantra—"Happiness comes from inside"—over and over again until I fell asleep. If I woke up in the middle of the night with the fear gripping my belly, I would repeat the mantra until I was able to fall asleep again. After about six months the fear began to subside. I started to feel more happiness in my body and the worry receded. I also started to consciously choose to interrupt my mind and stop it from telling me negative stories. Letting go of my need for control and changing the stories my mind was telling resulted in me taking some significant steps to achieve greater happiness.

▶ TOOL: MANTRAS AND AFFORMATION

Mantras are short statements we repeat many times, like a talking meditation. Mantras have roots in spiritual chants that go back thousands of years in yogic traditions. The type of mantra discussed here rewires the brain by making a set of positive statements which eventually change our underlying internal language and some of our beliefs.

The negative story that is going on inside of your head or the feeling you want to create in yourself will determine the exact mantra that you will want to state. Here are some examples that I and others have used:

• Happiness comes from inside.
• I am a beautiful, dynamic, sexy woman.
• I am a competent and capable person.

If your brain does not believe the positive statement, you may notice a sensation of "No, this is not true." Then start with an afformation rather than a mantra. Afformations are questions we ask ourselves to engage our brains to provide an answer. For example:

• Why am I pleasantly pleasing to myself?
• Why am I highly attractive to other people?
• Why am I excellent at my work?

Let your brain fill in all the reasons why the statement is true. Then repeat the question and answer it again. Do this as many times as you like.

When we are writing our negative stories, we are pushing our egos' fear button. When this button is pushed, we are often provoking old emotional conditioning that is linked to a lack of safety. To eradicate the Mile-a-Minute Vine we need to resolve the underlying energy in our bodies that weaves the story that we are not good enough and that we are not safe. When this underlying energy is absent from our bodies, our minds will stop making up the negative stories. We will be able to live in the present moment and be aware of the truth of what is occurring now. Unfortunately, when we focus on our negative stories we tend to attract more negative energy into our lives, which make things worse.

SELF-REFLECTION QUESTIONS

- What stories are you writing about the situations in your life?
- How often do you find yourself writing negative stories about the future?
- How do they make you feel?
- What other stories might you write?

Barbed Wire Vine — Overreacting to Circumstances

When we use a lot of willpower in our lives, we have a tendency to overreact to situations. It can feel like we have fallen into a dense thicket of Barbed Wire Vines full of prickles. Other people also often get snagged on our prickles. Overreacting has three distinct characteristics: the frequency of overreacting, the size of the emotional reaction, and the speed with which we react. I have been aware ever since I was a child that I felt frustrated with a lot of situations. I was someone who had a high frequency of emotional reactions. When I worked for the bank it seemed like I was constantly upset about something, most of it having to do with abiding by a set of regimented rules or with our quality of customer service. I made up my own stories about what the rules should be and how we should serve customers; I was constantly forcing an outcome. Working in this way felt really hard.

When I first became conscious that I had the ability to exercise some level of control over my emotional reactions I realized that most of my emotional reactions occurred at a relatively low level. For example, something would be bothering me and my mind would go over and over the situation, trying to figure out what to do or how to respond. From this low level I then often exploded;

I didn't seem to have any middle ground. My emotional reactions were like a dimmer switch that had only two levels, low and full-on bright. When I was fully provoked I had almost no ability to manage my reaction. I often yelled at people and damaged relationships. The emotional energy seemed to explode inside of me and I could not contain it.

My emotional reactions came and went swiftly, most of the time. I wasn't someone who became angrier the more I stewed on something. Given my emotional volatility, it was not surprising that Milo preferred to limit his self-expression. He might have considered this the safest way to be in our relationship. At least it kept him from falling victim to the Barbed Wire Vine himself!

Our objective is to respond appropriately to the given situation. If we are in grave danger, we want to have an immediate response and take immediate corrective action to remove ourselves from danger. The challenge is that our egos often overreact to dangers that don't really exist. Our egos are often protecting our pride or supporting our position of being right; then when we are challenged, we overreact to defend our positions. This is where our sense of struggle comes from in life, where it feels like things are not working out for us. The emotional energy we have stored from resisting feeling things fully fuels the emotional reactions of our egos, which want to have things our way and be right. The problem with this behavior is it damages our relationships with our partners and others around us.

Initially, anger management strategies helped with managing my emotional reactions. The best technique that I encountered for shifting negative emotional energy was to laugh. Big, deep belly laughs have often helped me shift the energy of frustration when it became stuck in my body. The other thing that I did was choose to contain my anger, even when I wanted to explode, until I could remove myself from the situation. Once alone, I could fully express my anger and make it really loud, saying everything that I wanted to say. This helped burn off a lot of the energy that used to course through my body when I got angry. These tools were often useful in dealing with an emotional reaction in the moment. They didn't reduce the frequency or magnitude of my emotional reactions, however. That only changed when I started to resolve the emotional energy that was locked away, deep in my emotional baggage.

TOOL: BELLY LAUGH

In private, when you are feeling upset, start to belly laugh. Laugh for up to a minute and then check in with how you feel.

TOOL: MAKE IT BIG

In private, whatever you are upset about, make it really big: say everything you would like to say and animate your expression. Turn around in the other direction and have a good belly laugh! Notice how you feel.

SELF-REFLECTION QUESTIONS

- How often do you get upset?
- What do you notice about the intensity of your emotional reactions?
- How fast do you get upset? Are you someone who gets worked up gradually, or do you explode quickly?
- What causes you to become upset?
- If you were to see that the cause of your upset was actually coming from inside of you and not outside of you, what might you be reacting to?

JACQUE SMALL

It's a Dynamic System

All the Core Problems of our emotional conditioning work together at the same time. It is just a question of which is the dominant player at any moment.

It was Sunday morning and Milo was still angry with me from Saturday for not fertilizing the evergreens that ringed the backyard as he had requested. I had simply refused to do it. From my perspective he was perfectly capable of doing it himself, and I had my own work agenda for the day. The rose bushes and the grass garden and all the other flower beds needed weeding. I didn't need another job added to my plate. I was feeling unappreciated and hard done by. But from Milo's perspective, this was just one more example of how I was not supportive of his needs. But how much more work did I need to do around the house to show my support?

What we don't resolve in our current relationships gets carried forward to future relationships. I had a sense of being hard done by in my relationship with Milo. A year after Milo and I separated, I was at my new boyfriend's house helping him scrub the deck of his condo. I could have stopped at a reasonable time to have lunch, but I was forcing an outcome. I wanted to finish scrubbing that deck, and I was down on my hands and knees, scrubbing away, when I heard my boyfriend say he wanted some poached eggs. My mind immediately interpreted that statement to mean that he wanted me to make him poached eggs. How dare he! Couldn't he see me here on my hands and knees, working so hard? Haughtily I blurted out, "You'll have to make your own poached eggs!" The fireworks started as he took my comments as a rejection of him. I hadn't stopped to think that maybe he meant to cook his own eggs all along. And he didn't stop to consider my perspective, either.

The moral is that it is not just the big emotional traumas we carry into our next relationships that can cause conflict and trouble; it can be a whole host of little frustrations accumulated over the years. And all that it takes is an idle thought about poached eggs for a new relationship to become tangled up in some very thorny vines. The choice we are faced with is either to carefully pick our way through all the thorny vines that are present in our relationships, or to take out the machete and cut the vines down to clear an easier path for our relationships and our lives. What to do?

Tools like afformations and belly laughs help us manage our thinking and change our behavior but they don't empty out our emotional baggage. These tools merely assist us to tidy up the jungle floor and make it less dangerous. In order to permanently resolve our underlying emotional conditioning, we're going to have to cut down some deeply rooted vines. This is what we'll cover in the next two chapters.

CHAPTER 13

Cutting Through the Jungle of Feeling

FINALLY IT IS TIME TO CHOP DOWN the vines in the jungle. We have talked about emotions in many different sections of this book. We have looked at the whole spectrum of emotions that we encounter when our relationships are in turmoil, and especially when we end up separating from a partner and getting a divorce. We have accumulated a backpack full of tools to manage our thinking and emotions as we navigate our way through the white water of our relationships. In the last chapter I shared a framework developed by Tom Stone within which we can identify the emotions that we are experiencing and the dynamic interaction of these emotions.

Remember that emotions have feelings — physical sensations — associated with them. In this chapter we focus on these physical sensations, which allow us to cut down the vines of our emotional conditioning. I share with you my experiences of using the Emotional Hot Button Removal techniques, which are very simple and elegant. These techniques can change our lives permanently if we are willing to practice — and I mean practice. (See chapter 4 for more on the importance of practice with our new tools.)

When an outside event pushes our emotional hot buttons, we have an emotional reaction which is fuelled by the emotional energy held in our bodies. The emotional reaction has a physical sensation to it, a feeling, often located inside our bodies and sometimes around our bodies. As discussed before, we don't like to be overwhelmed, so we often make a feeling-level decision not to feel the pain. However, we can bring emotional pain to completion if we instead welcome the feelings into our body and feel into the energy. Chuck Spezzano, in *If It Hurts, It Isn't Love*, describes this practice. He suggests allowing yourself to simply feel dramatic, painful, or unpleasant situations and concentrate on the strongest sensation in your body, noticing how it changes as you focus on it. Physical and emotional pain can then be released as you welcome each new situation and heal yourself as you go, using this simple approach.

Tom Stone, in *The Power of How*, takes this concept to the next level. He describes two techniques for bringing emotional energy to completion. The first technique is the CORE Technique, which resolves intense emotional experiences from the past: our emotional baggage. The second technique is the SEE Technique, which dissolves emotional identifications and attachments. Identifications come from our egos and the stories they weave in the form of expectations, which, when not met, lead many of us to feel disappointment, sadness, or frustration.

It might seem sometimes like emotional pain is a permanent part of us; however, based on my experience Tom Stone is right when he says that even though we can feel the pain in or around our body, that pain is not part of us. Instead it is a temporary condition that brings us some kind of experiential wisdom. Now let's focus on resolving the energy inside of our bodies that comes from incomplete emotional experiences from the past.

Resolving Energy Inside—The CORE Technique

Tom Stone's CORE Technique allows us to experience and feel into the deepest emotional pain that we hold in our bodies—without becoming so overwhelmed by the emotional experience that we dissolve into crying. As a technique for resolving emotional energy, crying is like using an old DOS computer, when we now have Intel CORE processors. Anyone want to go back thirty years and use your old computer? No, I didn't think so.

The CORE in CORE Technique stands for Center of Remaining Energy, which is the intense emotional energy we've stored in our bodies. Because we are feeling into the most intense part of the energy in our bodies, we release the energy faster than by feeling the energy in a more general way. The CORE Technique involves, first, feeling into the most intense part of the energy, and second, doing this technique repeatedly whenever we are provoked. When we use the CORE Technique repeatedly, we free our bodies permanently of our emotional baggage. It is the secret of how to feel into the energy that most practitioners have overlooked, and soon you will know the secret that can change your life!

Most people feel anxiety like they have a knot or ball in the stomach. When we have hurt feelings, it might feel like a pain or constriction in the middle of the chest. Sometimes there is a constriction at the base of the throat, and we feel like we can't speak. The trunk of the body and the throat are the most common places where we feel the physical sensations of energy in our bodies. Some people have stored energy in their extremities, hands, feet, and legs, and some in their back, but these are less common.

Going back to the belly, imagine that the sensation of anxiety is the size of a basketball. The basketball has a black rubber plug in it, and in the center of that plug is a hole where we insert the needle to fill the ball with air. When we put our attention on the feeling in our bodies, it is the black rubber plug that we want to focus on. The black rubber plug corresponds to the place where the energy is most intense in our bodies. Once we have our attention focused there, then the next step is to observe the little hole where the needle goes in and allow ourselves to feel down through that.

We don't want to do anything with the energy; we are not trying to make it go away. We are simply putting our attention on the spot that feels most intense and holding it there. Then it is just a matter of being present to the energy until it starts to dissolve. Sometimes it will become more intense before it starts to dissolve, and other times it will soften and start to disappear. The key is to keep your attention on the most intense part of the sensation until there is nothing left. And I mean nothing, or it will grow back like a virus. "Good enough" or "It's better" are not good times to stop putting your attention on the energy. Keep going until there is nothing left to feel.

> ### TIP #1: CORE TECHNIQUE
>
> Stick with the energy to the end, until there is nothing left to feel. Most people want to quit too fast and are in a hurry for it to be over. Sometimes we will complete the exercise in two minutes, sometimes in twenty minutes, and on rare occasions, in two hours. You can break up the two-hour sessions. If the energy is this big, it will be there later!

There are times when the energy inside the body does not change at all. When this happens, it means we have encountered some kind of resistance to feeling into our energy. Sometimes we have had this emotional energy for such a long time that it feels like the energy is a part of us and subconsciously we don't want to let it go. This is often true with depression or emotional hurt that occurred when we were very young: we identify with the energy. Or we may be afraid that if we start feeling into the physical sensations in our bodies, something awful is going to happen. And sometimes we have no idea what the resistance is about, but the feeling just won't budge. Then it is time for the second technique: the SEE Technique.

Resolving Energy Outside—The SEE Technique

The SEE Technique, also originally developed by Tom Stone, feels into quite a different sensation than the CORE energy. SEE stands for Side Entrance Expansion. I like to think of it as seeing energy everywhere. The physical sensation is very subtle; it might feel like a vibration or tingling all over our bodies. It might feel like a heaviness that sits on the chest or shoulders. It might feel like a fog around our heads or bodies. As in all these examples, the energy is usually big and widely dispersed.

The trick is to use our subtle senses to feel this energy. What are the subtle senses? Imagine biting into a lemon, does your mouth water? This is the subtle sense of taste. Have you ever had a conversation with yourself and heard yourself talk? That is the subtle sense of hearing. Now we are going to use the subtle sense of feeling to feel into the general sensation of energy that is over or around our bodies.

Let's start with a metaphor again. Put your attention on the energy that is all over your body. Notice that the energy has an outside edge. As you put your attention on the energy, imagine that it expands outward like filling a balloon with air. As the energy expands, continue to keep your attention on the outside edge. After a couple of minutes, when the energy has fully expanded, then open up a little gap in the edge of the balloon and slide outside. Take your attention outside and beyond.

You will notice that the energy that you slide out into has a different quality; it feels very calm and quiet. If you have ever meditated, you might be familiar with this energy. I like to think of this space as being the universal energy where we are all connected. Some call it pure awareness. It is a place of infinite possibility that we can tap into for insight and a sense of knowing, when our minds are very quiet.

Allow yourself to be immersed in pure awareness for a few minutes and really enjoy being here. Then turn your attention back to the other energy, and notice what you see. Usually you will notice that it has become smaller and is starting to fade away. If it has not started to fade yet, or if it has not completely faded away, then turn your attention back to the quiet, silent background and immerse yourself in that more deeply for a few minutes. Notice the peace and quiet of pure awareness and really enjoy the sensation of immersing yourself in this energy. Now turn your attention back to the original energy that you were inside of. Has it shrunk away? If so, then scan your body to determine if any CORE energy has revealed itself to you. Then use the CORE Technique to resolve that energy. If there is no CORE energy, then you are complete for the moment, until more energy is provoked in your body again.

TIP #1: SEE TECHNIQUE

I find that the SEE energy takes two forms. The first is a general sensation that occurs over the body and sometimes just around the head. Notice that you are inside of this energy. Notice whether this energy is close to the body or extends far outside of the body. Be present to the energy and see if it expands, and as it expands, follow the outside edge of the energy until it stops expanding — then go to pure awareness.

TIP #2: SEE TECHNIQUE

If the energy feels like it is a heavy weight on your body, such as on your chest or shoulders, then put your attention on the weight and visualize the energy vaporizing and filling a balloon. As the weight finishes vaporizing, then find the outside edge of the balloon. Then transfer your attention to pure awareness.

TIP #3: SEE TECHNIQUE

If you can't seem to get out of the balloon of energy, then look up into the right-hand corner of your eye, fold an edge of the balloon back, and allow your attention to slide out through the gap.

That's it. That's all there is to feeling into the emotional energy stored in our emotional baggage. Simply brilliant, yet no one has ever taught us how to do this! Imagine what would be possible if we were to teach children how to do this. They wouldn't have to haul major baggage around for most or all of their lives.

Once you have learned the techniques, however, there is one big challenge: you need to practice and use them at every opportunity. If you don't use them to cut down the vines in your emotional jungle, then those vines will be growing as vigorously next year as they are this year. Yet those of my clients who have practiced regularly have had huge success making major changes.

Since I have been doing this work I have had many conversations with people about emotions and feeling. Someone will say to me quite indignantly, "Yes of course I 'feel' the physical sensations in my body." I then explain that what is really happening is that they are aware of physical sensations in their body. They are not, however, feeling these sensations in a way that will *cause the emotional energy to come to completion quickly*. Eckhart Tolle, like Spezzano, knows that we need to feel into the energy field of the pain in our bodies in order to break our identification with it. Tom Stone, however, forged a better machete, uncovering the key to resolving emotional energy quickly with his techniques for feeling into the most intense part of the energy.

Cutting the Cord

When we are in close relationship with someone, especially an intimate partner, but also perhaps a family member or business partner, we may become energetically attached to that person in a way that does not serve us. This usually occurs due to looking for love outside of ourselves: we become attached to someone in an attempt to get our needs met or to feel love. The energetic thread between us may seem to become thick, like a cord that fuses us to the other person. When we are fused, we no longer bring our gifts to this person from a place of freedom, instead we act from a place of our own neediness. To set ourselves free, we can use another process to cut this energetic cord.

Cutting the cord does not necessarily mean ending the relationship; it means we are cutting the energy cord that has us fused to the person. When the cord is cut, then we are able to come from an unattached place and offer our true gifts without needing to get anything in return.

I'm often aware how easily I become attached to a partner in a way that does not serve either of us. Should you feel very attached to someone and want to free up that energy to be in a more resourceful place, there are many "cord cutting" rituals. One day when I was in a coaching session, my coach asked me to visualize the energy connection between my boyfriend, Conrad, and me. I immediately sensed a thick energetic cord, about three inches in diameter, thick as a piece of beef tenderloin, extending from the core of my body and stretched out in space toward Conrad. My coach asked if I would be willing to cut the cord with him. I wouldn't be ending the relationship; I would just be freeing myself of the energetic attachment. As I thought about this, I could feel my fear of letting go. It felt like I would lose him. I needed to sit in that place for a few moments to realize that I would be releasing my fusion to him; I would not be releasing my relationship, unless that was what I wanted. Which I didn't. I still wanted to be in relationship with Conrad. I visualized picking up a pair of golden scissors, and slowly I cut the cord. I immediately felt free of the energy that had been gripping me. My energy felt much more expansive, and I was much more resourceful and able to deal with the decisions I needed to make. I appreciated having my coach's support as I let this energy go.

Feeling Physical Sensations

Some people have difficulty being aware of any physical sensations in their bodies. When one of my students was first learning the CORE Technique, she thought that feeling into the most intense part of the energy in her body meant intensifying the emotional energy, in other words, making the sadness (or any other energy) bigger. This just intensified the degree of overwhelm that she felt. She did not understand that feeling into the most intense part of the energy in her body meant feeling into the physical pain in her body, not the emotional pain—and this was because she was not actually aware of the physical sensations in her body.

Some of us have faced overwhelming feelings that led us to subconsciously decide to not be sensitive to our physical sensations. We have numbed out. The problem with numbing out is that we rob ourselves of the ability to feel desirable emotions as well as unpleasant ones, except on those rare occasions when we are suddenly flooded with good feelings. To become more aware of the sensations in your body, you may want to revisit the Self-Reflection Exercise: Feeling Emotions in chapter 11. This exercise will help you become aware of your emotions and the physical feelings associated with them.

Resolving Your Emotional Energy

Let's go to work, shall we? When you first start resolving energy, you will likely be presented with small amounts of energy to resolve at a time. As your ego becomes more comfortable with the idea that it is safe to feel energy in the body, larger chunks of energy may be presented to you. The more emotional energy I resolved, the bigger the physical sensations that arose in my body. I had the sense that my subconscious gained a sense of security that it was OK to start feeling the big areas of emotional energy that I had been stuffing away. When this energy arose in my body, it filled my whole chest and took many hours to resolve. After that, the feelings that were once again provoked went back to being small sensations within my body.

When a feeling is small, it might take five minutes to forty minutes to resolve. When a feeling is big it might take a couple of hours. When it is huge, it might take a few days or even a couple of weeks. The speed with which we resolve our emotional energy depends upon whether we are doing it on our own or with a coach. There is a concept of the power of two: energy is resolved faster when we have a witness. So when you have something that feels really big to resolve, I recommend doing it with a coach. To use the techniques in this book, you will need to find a coach who has been trained by Great Life Technologies; these coaches may use the title Human Software Engineer. Private coaching and practice sessions are also offered through Divine Divorce. When you become adept at using the techniques, you will be able to resolve a lot of energy on your own.

The other thing to remember is that we all have different amounts of emotional conditioning and hence different amounts of energy stored in our bodies. I have coached many people who have never experienced the size of emotional energy that arose in my body when I faced the sexual abuse that I experienced. When it first arose in my body, it seemed to form a solid block and did not seem to have a spot that was most intense. I thought of it as an iceberg, and I put my attention on it and thawed it one little bit at a time. Eventually the physical sensations in my body dissolved away, and I have had no further triggers associated with sexual abuse or my sexuality. That area appears to be complete.

One of the things that you need to understand in applying these techniques is that my stories describe experiences that I have had. From using these techniques myself and coaching clients to use these techniques, it is apparent to me that we all have different physical experiences. When we place our attention on physical sensation, some of us see vividly colorful images and some of us see nothing. Sometimes we receive a clear message as we cut down our emotional vines, and at other times there is no message at all. I can only remember one clear image, though I have had several vague insights as to where the original emotional energy came from. Most of the time I had no knowledge about which underlying event caused the energy to be deposited in my body. Unlike psychology work that attempts to unravel and understand past events, we don't need to understand where the feelings came from to resolve them. We are not trying to unearth the original story. We are simply bringing incomplete emotional experiences to completion by feeling them in a very specific way. When physical sensations are present in our bodies, all we need to do is focus on the most intense part of the feeling and release it from our bodies.

The reason that we do not need to understand the story is that the story is in the past. The place we are at is the Now, and where we are going is the future. When we resolve the emotional energy stored in our bodies, the stories that go along with this emotional energy will also be dissolved and will disappear.

The next thing that will happen as our emotional baggage starts to disappear is that we will have more access to our intuition. Plus, by practicing the tools in chapter 4 and the concepts in chapter 15, we will be able to consciously choose who we would like to be and how we would like our lives to be. We will no longer have to live our lives based on our emotional conditioning. By resolving our emotional baggage, we change the perceived hardwiring that has been driving us for most of our lives.

Now that we have the intellectual freedom and the emotional freedom to choose who we want to be, understanding the old stories is a waste of our time and creative energy. We have more fun things to do and more important things to contribute to the world than understanding some event twenty or thirty years ago that we can't do anything about anyhow.

You may be asking how long all of this will take. I'll be honest with you: it will take a while. It all depends upon how much energy you have stored in your body and on how willing you are to practice. Some people release energy in their first coaching session with me, and it causes a significant shift in them. For other people it takes a couple of sessions for them to start noticing a shift in their reactivity. The one thing I do know is that every person who has used and practiced these techniques on a consistent basis has noticed a major shift in the way they show up in life. When past emotional energy is absent from our bodies, we no longer have over-the-top emotional reactions associated with that button. The benefits of eliminating our hot buttons are that we have no more major emotional reactions and that energy is no longer present in our bodies to promote dis-ease that may turn into the medical form of disease and illness. A third benefit is that without this negative energy in our bodies, it is significantly easier for us to experience the pleasant energies of joy, happiness, and love. One of my students, Albert, who is almost sixty years old, has done most of this work on his own. He called me early one morning to say he had just resolved some big energy of dread in his abdomen that he had woken up with every morning for almost as long as he can remember. With absolute glee in his voice, Albert said, "I can tell, I am finally getting my life back."

Isn't that what we really want, to live our lives fully and have more good feelings?

CHAPTER 14

Clearing My Path Vine by Vine

I N THIS CHAPTER I WILL DESCRIBE the physical sensations
that occurred in my body as I cut down each of the thorny vines
in my own emotional jungle. I will share tips on using the tools in
the backpack as I tell the story of how I forged through my jungle
to reach a safe place on the other side of the pain.

Resolving Grief and Loss

Sometimes one vine is almost indistinguishable from another; it's
just one big mess. This was certainly how it felt as I faced the emotional trauma at the thought of Milo leaving. Much as I didn't want
to accept that Milo was no longer invested in our relationship, subconsciously this was the conclusion I was coming to in November
as we drove up to our cabin for a ski weekend for just the two of
us. On the drive up I could feel a huge pain in my chest; this was
the Headache Vine—the fear of our relationship dissolving. I knew
the pain was connected to our relationship coming to a close, but
as I felt into the pain in my chest, some new piece of information
was coming to me. Some of the pain I was feeling belonged to older
vines from childhood, and the emotion was deeply connected to my
mother. I could sense these two vines were intertwined; each had its
own piece of sadness and grief, but I didn't know where one left off
and the other began. It all felt like one big tangled mass of sadness.

As I was feeling into the pain in my body, I was grateful that I
didn't have to release the emotional pain the old-fashioned way, by

crying. Or worse yet, have to suffer through the pain and slowly push it back into my body. The CORE Technique was proving to be magical in this case.

As Milo drove the car up the mountain on the dark, twisting sea-to-sky highway, I sat with my eyes closed and focused my attention like a laser on the spot in my chest where it felt like there was a deep hole. I sat there swaying back and forth as Milo took one curve after the other, breathing into my belly and feeling the deep hurt in my chest. I knew I needed to keep my attention on it and keep feeling it until there was nothing left to feel.

As I felt into the most intense part of the pain, it started to dissipate. The hole in the middle of my chest and extending out along my sternum was starting to dissolve. But as the sensation in my sternum lightened, I became aware of tightness in my right breast. I started to feel into that pain, and it dissolved, while a slight remnant returned to the center of my chest. I felt into these remnants of emotional energy until my body was free of the pain and there was nothing left to feel.

▶ **TIP: FOLLOW THE INTERTWINED VINES**

When it feels like the pain is moving around in your body, what is actually happening is that you are cutting down several different vines associated with the same issue. An issue might have only a couple of vines or up to twenty or thirty vines, and a few very big issues will have a dense snarl of vines that need to be removed. The current issue is bringing up the related energy stream back in time, and who knows what is back there.

In the car, I then thought about my mom passing away and not being here anymore. I felt the sadness well up in my body, and a constriction occurred again in my chest. There was a sharp pain on the outside edge of my left breast, and as I breathed and felt into it, it softened and the sensation slowly moved into the center of the breast. I continued to breathe and feel into the most intense part of the sensation, just observing it. I focused my attention like a laser and sensed where the constriction felt the most intense as I continued to breathe deeply. A minor amount of tightness was left in my sternum. There was a last little bit of emotional energy to bring to completion, and then there seemed to be nothing. No more pain. It was all gone.

I felt tired and a little shaky from having moved so much energy. First having felt into losing Milo, and then finally feeling into the loss of my mom three years earlier. When she died, I was numb; her death had overwhelmed me and I had pushed the hurt and grief that I felt away. Over time the pain went away. But I hadn't resolved the pain; I had just pushed it down into my body. This is typically what happens to the emotional pain when we "allow time to heal all." It doesn't actually get resolved; it just gets buried away in our bodies. Then the thought of losing the person I loved most in my life pushed the emotional hot button on the energy that I had stored away from losing my mother. The topic area of the energy I had tapped into was loss and grief.

The current loss provoked the unresolved energy from my previous losses. Because so much energy had been stored in my body, the pain of loss was truly overwhelming for me. This is the problem with not being able to feel into the energy from an emotional event at the time it takes place; it accumulates in our bodies and is reactivated when a similar situation occurs. If we are unable to deal with it, then it gets shoved back into the body once more. Luckily this time I knew how to feel into the energy to free myself from this sense of loss.

Resolving Anger and Rage

You never know what will push your buttons on old energy or what subject area will come up. I had been renting a room from Denise for about four months when one day in February, I came home with my friend Lynne after spending a day skiing in Whistler. It was my first day of skiing that winter. We were both tired and hungry, and I quickly heated up some food while Lynne waited for her husband to pick her up.

Denise was drunk when we got home and in a foul mood. To avoid conflict, I took some food out of the freezer and heated it up for Denise. During the dinner conversation, Denise was very aggressive, which often happens when we use alcohol to numb out our pain. At one point in the conversation, Denise told me, "No, you don't feel unsure about your relationship with him, you feel contempt for him."

I exploded inside. The rage was so strong in my body, I was vibrating. It felt like my hair was standing on end. It was all I could do to say, "Thank you for your opinion," and excuse myself from the table.

Luckily Lynne's husband arrived shortly thereafter; I cleaned up from our dinner and went straight up to my bedroom. I was livid. I could feel the energy swirling in my body all night; I was hardly able to sleep. In the morning when I awoke, my whole chest was completely filled with pain. It felt like someone had set a hundred-pound weight on it. I sat in bed and started to feel into it. As I felt into it, I began to recognize that the emotional energy came from repressed feelings about my father. I had heard him tell my mom over and over again, "Shut up, you don't know what you are talking about." Then I heard Denise tell me to shut up and that I didn't know what my own feelings were. I was incensed that someone would presume that they knew more about how I felt than I did myself. The truth is that we can never know how someone else feels. We may be able to relate to their emotions, but we can't actually feel how they feel. Their feelings are within their bodies, not ours.

It took about ten hours of work over several days for me to feel into the core of the energy in my chest. I finally dissolved the rage in me about the way my father treated my mother. While I dissolved this energy, I made a point of not interacting with Denise. I sensed that as long as this rage was up front and center in my body, talking with Denise would only lead to an ugly conflict. After dissolving this energy, I was grateful to Denise for pushing my buttons! It was "free coaching" that gave me the opportunity to resolve big energy in my body that fuelled the emotions of anger. This partially explained why I was always angry, even as a child I was angry, and now I was getting to release this anger.

► TIP: TAKE ADVANTAGE OF FREE COACHING

Rather than blaming another person for pushing your buttons and making you angry, silently thank them for showing you what needs to be resolved in you. They are providing you with free coaching. Take advantage of it: remember to sit down and feel into the energy that arises in your body and bring it to completion.

However grateful we are to someone for helping us to release our emotional baggage, we still may decide not to remain in their company. Subjecting ourselves to other people's toxic behaviors is not good for our long-term health.

In this case, Denise was not my partner, and I had no other emotional attachments to her that needed to be resolved. Within a couple of days of resolving the emotional energy in my body, I received a clear message from my intuition that it was time for me to leave.

When I moved into my new home with Cindy, just six blocks away, I could feel the energetic walls of protection that I had built up around my body melt away. Over the next several months as I wrote this book, all sorts of major energy from old emotional baggage began to arise in my body. I spent an hour a day feeling into the flow of old emotional energy that was being released. My intuition had known that in order to heal myself and do this new work, I needed to be in a different environment.

Releasing Attachments

One day after I had moved out, my intuition sent me to see my gardens at the house I had lived in with Milo. I wanted to see all the spring flowers coming up. I was shocked and devastated when I saw my gardens paved over with grass. It was all I could do to keep from breaking down into tears in my car. Letting go of my relationship with Milo, my house, and my gardens, felt like I was losing a piece of myself. It took me a couple of hours using the CORE Technique to feel into the emotional energy that flooded into my chest: I had lost everything that I had worked for for the past twenty years. It was all gone.

I had attached meaning to my work, my relationship, my house, and especially my gardens. There was a great deal of emotion around these attachments, and by releasing them I created a greater sense of freedom for myself to take on something totally new. Maybe I would decide to have gardens again somewhere else, and maybe not.

The more things we let go of physically and emotionally, the freer we become. Freedom comes from cleaning our closets of emotional baggage, as well as of physical things we no longer need.

We are attached to the objects, people, and activities in our lives because that is what we have given meaning to. These things become how we identify ourselves. Very often we are focused on acquiring more objects in our lives: a nicer car, new furniture, a bigger and better home. These are all things that we use as a measuring stick of our status or level of success in life. Resolving the attachments to our partners is the most difficult, because we often define our lives based on family. This is my partner, these are my children, I am a mother, and together this is my family. This feels like a known entity, providing safety and security. When a marriage ends many of the "my" attachments end, especially for men as these days children usually end up with their mother.

It may sound crazy, but attachment also occurs for those of us who have had traumatic events occur to us as children. We have been carrying around the emotional pain ever since we were little, and that pain has become a part of us. To let go of the pain would be letting go of a part of ourselves. Intellectually we may know this pain is causing suffering in our lives, yet we are terrified of not having these feelings with us anymore.

When we release these emotional attachments, be they to things, people, or our own pain, we create a lightness and freedom within our bodies. We no longer carry with us the fear of losing the people or the things that we have become attached to. We no longer need to hoard things. The good memories are with us — they are in our bodies, love is in the body — and we will never lose these memories. When we let go, our minds become less constricted in thinking about what is possible in our lives. New opportunities start to arise as the energy in our bodies starts to change. As we focus on this new, softer, more joyous energy, we start to attract into our lives what we really want.

Resolving Depression

Depression can be one of those energies that have been with us for a long time that we are afraid to let go of. Jason was caught in the place of having long-term depression and also having to let go of his partner. In this letter Jason shares how hard it is:

> I hear people say, and I hate hearing it that this too shall pass, or give it time and you will be OK. I don't want to be just OK, I don't want to give it time, and no, this too

shall not pass. I have turned to God for answers to my problems and it doesn't seem he is listening. Each day is worse than the last. For the life of me, why can't I let go?

Jason was very attached to his wife, and his attachment created suffering in his life in the form of depression and a significant amount of sadness. Jason cried to try and release some of the overwhelming energy. But it was not enough.

When we focus on our loss and have no way of releasing the energy of the attachment in our bodies, we start to numb out. I believe a portion of the cause of depression is due to our inability to feel all the intense pain that is occurring in our bodies. The emotional energy that we feel overwhelms us, and to cope with it our bodies create a heavy energy, like a heavy thick blanket, so that our feelings will not be so intense.

I have coached people with depression to use the SEE Technique to lift the heavy energy of depression. The energy of depression causes us to have low energy and it keeps us stuck in a place of dissatisfaction. It seems like we have no ability to break free of the energy and move forward. Underneath the blanket of heavy energy, we have often found lots of incomplete emotional experiences to use the CORE Technique on. However we could not get to the energy inside the body without first lifting off the heavy blanket of energy. The depressive energy acts like a gatekeeper to the energy stored inside our bodies. We need to resolve the depressive energy that we have identified with first, before we can release the emotional energy from past experiences.

▶ **TIP: FEEL THE SUBTLE ENERGY**

If you are having trouble feeling into the energy inside of your body, then look for a subtle layer of energy all over your body on the outside. The energy on the outside of your body acts like a gatekeeper and will need to be resolved before you resolve the energy on the inside of your body.

Resolving Financial Fears and Anxiety

Going through divorce or other major life transitions can cause us to become caught in the grip of fear about our financial well-being. Our minds start to make up doom and gloom stories, painting worst-case scenarios that cause anxiety within our bodies. This anxiety creates an overall body energy that might show up as a tingling sensation all over the body, tightness and churning in the stomach, or a heaviness that sits on top of the chest. It may also show up as depression.

This was Heather's experience as she faced a financial crisis and career transition after having gotten back on her feet from being divorced five years previously. When she went to bed, her mind was very active and kept running all the negative scenarios over and over again in her head. Heather was terrified that she would lose the house she and her new partner, Martin, had built. When she kept telling herself the negative stories, she began to have severe panic attacks. These were getting in the way of her being able to function properly and find a new job. The stress was taking a huge toll on her and Martin's life. Heather and Martin both felt like maybe there was something really mentally wrong with her, and she became terrified of becoming mentally ill.

I worked with Heather to feel into the emotional energy in her body. Her most dominant sensation was a buzzing all over her body, and below this buzzing energy there was a tightness in her stomach. She used the CORE Technique to feel into the most intense part of the physical sensation in her stomach. After a few minutes, she found that it did not change.

Then she turned her attention to the overall buzzing feeling in her body. Putting her attention on this feeling, she imagined that it expanded, as if she were filling a hot air balloon. She was using the SEE Technique to expand the energy, keeping her attention on the outside edge of the energy. When it was fully expanded, she turned her attention to the silent background of pure awareness and allowed herself to fully enjoy the sensations of calm and peace. It took several minutes for the energy that filled the balloon to shrink and disappear.

She then turned her attention back to her body and scanned it for any physical sensation. She noticed the tight feeling in her stomach again and used the CORE Technique to feel into the spot that was most intense. As she kept her attention on this spot, she noticed that it became more intense. She was now able to feel energy that she had not been willing to feel. After several minutes the energy began to soften, and then it eventually disappeared. I provoked her again by talking about the negative things that might happen due to her financial challenges, and the sensation came back. Once again she used the CORE Technique to resolve this energy. We repeated this process until my provoking her did not bring up any more physical sensations.

▶ TIP: PROVOKE YOUR EMOTIONAL ENERGY

The key to resolving old emotional energy is to provoke as much energy as possible, and then put your attention on it until there is nothing left to feel. You may have to repeat the cycle of provoking and feeling many times depending upon the magnitude of the issue.

Dealing with financial challenges is a two-step process. First we have to sit down and feel into the emotional sensations that are being generated by our bodies. These sensations are either created in the moment due to our minds forming a negative projection of the future, or come from emotional energy that has been stored away in our bodies from the past. Either way, this emotional energy is debilitating and slows us down from taking consistent focused action.

The second step is to get clear on what our objectives are. In Heather's case it was to find a new job to generate cash flow to make the mortgage payments. She needed to be able to hold the vision of finding an ideal job and have a daily objective and action plan for conducting her job search. By having this focus and consistently taking the action steps to achieve her objective, results would start to occur and momentum would build. There is a universal law that where attention goes energy flows and results occur.

I had Heather use one of the tools from the backpack: When she went to bed at night, she was to focus on how happy she was to be living in her house and working at a fantastic new job she had landed. By taking these positive steps to release her emotional baggage and focus on what she wanted, she started to send more positive energy out into the universe. Heather established strategic targets for new work and then took consistent action to secure a position with one of these companies. When we send out positive energy and take consistent action, the universe starts to reward us with positive results. Our positive energy causes the people in our lives to respond to us differently. Lying in bed worrying and feeling sorry for ourselves will not turn around the situation. The situation will only turn around if we keep putting one foot in front of the other and start feeling the way we want to feel. Dropping off our emotional baggage clears away the barriers to our feeling the way we want to.

Through our coaching a new awareness opened up for Heather:

> Something you said resonated in the service at
> church today. Today was the Epiphany, when the three
> wise men visited the infant Jesus. "By choosing to be

vulnerable and risk a leap of faith, they discovered an unexpected gift much greater than the ones they were ready to offer. Each day we are called to leave the safety and security of what we know, the conventions that rule our lives, the control we think we have. We are called to step into the unknown, to let go, to be vulnerable in order to discover our answers."

I think that this experience has happened because without it I could not really let go. I had let go, partially, by leaving my executive position to look for a more meaningful job. But I had not really given up on the idea of following the rules to a successful life. I didn't even realize the risk we had taken on by building this house. But now that it has happened, I will get through it. I will hopefully have more faith in myself to venture outside of the "rules."

This story has a happy ending: Heather found a job; she and Martin remortgaged the house; they won an award for building design; and Martin became swamped with new work. What they wanted actually happened! Then they had a whole new set of challenges. Heather continued to work on releasing her emotional baggage so that she could deal with all of her new challenges from a centered and stable footing.

When we are walking through life, we need good hiking boots: they keep us stable while we use our machetes to cut through the emotional vines that we will continue to encounter. The CORE Technique and the SEE Technique are excellent machetes that we would do well to keep sharp and close by our sides. Knowing how to feel into our emotional feelings is key to having a smoother, more magical life.

Working with the Power of Two

Being in connection with other people is vitally important when we are dealing with emotional trauma. One of the worst things that we can do is to isolate ourselves, which can be a tendency when we feel depressed and are suffering. However, we also need to be careful that we are not a burden on our friends. We need to have a sense of balance.

I made a connection with a man that I met on holidays, Arturo. Some months later I reconnected with him on Facebook and started a kind of pen pal correspondence, which turned out to be a journal of my adventure through my emotional jungle as I cleared huge thickets of emotional vines while writing this book.

Here I will share a few of my letters to Arturo with you. As we work our way through these letters I will highlight for you the Core Problems (CP) from my emotional conditioning that these letters reflect.

Journaling provokes energy release, as you will see. These letters were a way for me to journal what was occurring with me, and they were even more powerful than a journal as they were being received by another who just held space for me without needing to respond to every point, or make it all right for me. I am not sure that Arturo even read all my writing, and it really wasn't important. What was important was to feel that someone received what I wrote.

▶ ### TOOL: JOURNALING AS A

SELF-PROVOKING EXERCISE

One of the ways to push your own hot buttons is to do some journaling. What is bothering you? What is not happening the way you want it to in your life? Go back to earlier chapters of this book and start answering the self-reflection questions, or reread what you wrote previously.

When you write down what you are thinking, it will likely provoke the emotional energy attached to your thoughts. As you are writing, notice what is occurring in or around your body. Have any sensations started to arise from your exploration? If so, then stop writing and feel into whatever energy has arisen and bring this energy to completion. When the physical sensation is complete, reread what you wrote. If more physical sensations occur, then resolve them first. If no physical sensations are present but more thoughts come up, then write them down and notice if more physical sensations come up.

Keep doing this until you resolve whatever energy is arising. This could take twenty minutes, an hour, or several hours. You can do it all at once or over a series of days. I have noticed once my energy is up and I am willing to feel it, it will stay up or return easily until I deal with it.

Resolving the Fear of Not Being Loved

As we face a current relationship coming to an end, many of us fear that we will not find anyone who will love us. This is the intersection of two Core Problems: looking for ourselves where we are not, and resisting feeling things. It causes us to feel isolated and alone.

Dear Arturo,

A huge pain arose in my chest today; it stabs me right in the middle of my breasts. I was working on my book this morning.

As I started to feel into it, I started bawling my eyes out. If I love you, I am so afraid that you won't love me back. In fact it feels terrifying. Why didn't Milo love me? I loved him so much. It really hurts that I loved him so deeply, and to not have that returned. Wow, I really stuffed this one away! When I reread this it feels like there is a big hole drilled through the center of my chest and running through to my back. It is excruciatingly painful.

What a nut bar I am! I am being judgmental of myself, worrying about what you must be thinking. Really I am quite normal and sane. OK, I am not normal. Most people stuff away their feelings or act them out in anger or depression, or carry them into their next relationship. I am facing my feelings head on, being open and vulnerable with you. I trust that you understand this. Apparently I am a little afraid that you will think of me as a nut bar. The energy of this feels like I am in a big heavy bubble that is squeezing me so tight, squeezing me and keeping me all glued together. It is as if I am afraid that somehow I will fall apart if I don't keep myself tightly contained. The story is that I need to keep myself all tightly contained so that I will be safe. That if I put up this tough, got-it-all-together image, I will be OK. When the truth is that I would just like to be a wreck for a moment and have you hold me and love me.

▶ CP: Resisting Feeling Things Fully, Being Judgmental
TECHNIQUE: SEE Technique to dissolve the bubble around me

I am really tired of being tough and looking like I have all my shit together. I can feel the weight of this on my shoulders; it feels very heavy to be carrying around. And the interesting thing is that I do have my shit together in a lot of ways. Just at moments like these it doesn't feel like it.

▶ TECHNIQUE: SEE Technique to lift the weight off my shoulders

It is interesting how opening up my heart to you, being open, loving, and vulnerable, creates this portal to allow emotions that are buried deep in the past to rise up and be dealt with. I am really clear that the emotion is not about you, but that you are a conduit to access the emotion. What is true about you is that my heart is open and loving. Anything else that is arising about you in my mind is a story that is being fuelled by these old emotions, that I then project on to you.

A fantasy story that occurs in my mind is that if I were to be in long-term relationship with you, eventually you would leave me for someone younger, because I will get old. The story never has the fairy-tale ending that we would be together forever. It always has this sad ending where I get ditched and then I am out on my own again, only now I am an old woman. I can feel the pain in the center of my chest.

▶ CP: Trying to Force an Outcome, Manufacturing
Interpretations
TECHNIQUE: CORE Technique

By the way, telling you this is very scary for me. This feels very real. It feels like if I communicate my truth, if I speak my truth, you will turn your back and walk away. I will lose you. Fear. I think this is why when we are married – we don't communicate the truth of what is going on for us. We fear that we will lose our partners, and we are more afraid of being alone than we are of living in a hollow relationship where we don't speak what is most important to us. Some place I was not speaking my truth to Milo. Actually I was not asking for what I wanted in our relationship. I wanted him to step up and be more committed in our relationship, for us to develop a joint vision of what we wanted in our life together. He never wanted to have this conversation, I think because he never really saw a joint life with me. OK, this hurts, there is a very sharp stabbing pain in the middle of my chest.

▶ CP: Looking for Yourself Where You Are Not, Limiting
Self-Expression
TECHNIQUE: CORE Technique

*As I sit here and feel into my pain, I realize that my future will not
be a continuation of my past because I am unravelling the emotional
turmoil that would have me relive my past. If I were to continue to hold
on to these old hurts, the feeling of not fitting in, the feeling of loving
someone deeply and then being rejected, I would likely carry this fear
into my next relationship.*

▶ CP: Looking for Yourself Where You Are Not
TECHNIQUE: CORE Technique

If I don't resolve the fear, then being rejected by my partner
will likely be a self-fulfilling prophecy, and I will attract to me
what I least want. If I fear that my partner will leave me for another woman, as Milo did, then I will likely be insecure in future
relationships. This insecurity will lead to jealousy, which is made
up of many negative emotions such as loss, unworthiness, and
heartbreak. I would always be questioning, Can I trust my partner to love me deeply? Can I trust that at some point in time he
will not reject me? This lack of trust in itself is very wearing on
both people. One person is eaten up on the inside with insecurity,
and the other person gets weary of trying to prove their love. The
only thing to do is to heal the old wounds that lead to this insecurity in the first place.

▶ CP: Looking for Yourself Where You Are Not, Mistaking
Need for Love
CP: Forcing an Outcome, Manufacturing Interpretations
TECHNIQUE: CORE Technique to feel into successive
waves of physical sensations in my chest

By resolving all this stuff, I get to choose a whole new future, which will be on some totally different path than if I followed the course of life that I was on. I have let go of most of my possessions. I am a gypsy at the moment, living in other people's houses for six months at a time. I have no ties. I am even letting go of the old emotions that would tie me down to the past. The future is totally unknown for me. Somehow I know the new life journey will really start when I am in Belize. I don't have any idea what it looks like, but I get a sense that something new is going to start unfolding.

▶ CP: Absent: I trust and act on my intuition.

Maybe with luck this will come to completion today. Thank you for receiving this.

Lots of love,
Jacque

Resolving the Fear of Being Alone

The profound feeling of loneliness and being alone are very common at the end of a relationship, as I mentioned in chapter 6.
When this feeling of being alone finally hit me, a year after my
divorce, it left me feeling very ungrounded. I felt like there was
nothing to hold me to this earth, there was no reason to be here. If
I were a balloon filled with hot air, I would just float away. One of
my letters to Arturo demonstrates how I used the Emotional Hot
Button Removal techniques to let go of the emotions connected to
loneliness. I then used an exercise to ground myself.

Dear Arturo,

I think this is the most alone I have felt since Milo left.

*I have no house. I rent a room from an acquaintance in an apart-
ment building. I have no gardens, no flowers to go and tend, no weeds
to pick. I have no furniture to speak of. No history hanging around me. I
don't even have children to identify with that they are mine. I am on my
own. I don't even have a lot of clients at the moment. I don't even have
them to hold me down and ground me. It feels like I am free-floating with
nothing to anchor me. I am truly on my own. All alone.*

▶ CP: Resisting Feeling Things Fully, Avoiding the Present
CP: Looking for Yourself Where You Are Not, Resisting
Change

*It feels like someone has stabbed me in the middle of my chest. There
is a big hole there. I can feel the pain extend out over my rib cage and
into my right breast. Interesting, why do I feel so much more pain on
the right side of my body than my left. The tears flow from my eyes and*

I mop them up with tissues, and then it is back to putting my attention on those spots in my body where the sensation feels most intense.

▶ TECHNIQUE: CORE Technique

I am also feeling disappointed that I am feeling this sense of aloneness one year after I moved out rather than last year. There must have been so much emotional energy that I had to deal with last year that I stored some of it away to be dealt with later. But I have had some really happy times in the fall, over Christmas, and in January. I thought I was finished with the emotional energy of the divorce. Guess I was wrong.

▶ CP: Trying to Force an Outcome, Manufacturing
Interpretations
CP: Resisting Feeling Things Fully, Being Judgmental

I have a good sense of what direction I am traveling, but I really have no idea what I will encounter on the journey. I know that there is bright sunshine and happiness on the other side of this doom and gloom that I feel in my body. It just feels frustrating that I am not out of the jungle yet; my ego has decided that I should be complete.

▶ CP: Trying to Force an Outcome, Manufacturing
Interpretations

The great void I feel in my chest is about having nothing to feel attached to. You are the one tiny stake in the ground that I have attached a very thin string to that keeps me anchored. Other than writing this book and my plan to work abroad in the fall, I have nothing concrete to attach myself to. Both of these things I can visualize and see in my mind. The rest of my life feels like a void. The pain and sadness has not left my body.

 CP: Looking for Yourself Where You Are Not, Resisting Change
TECHNIQUE: CORE Technique

It is not that I haven't been on my own before. I packed a small amount of clothing and headed off to Europe in 1985 to go backpacking for three months, by myself. I didn't have any fear of being alone then. Here I am twenty-six years later caught in the emotional grip of being alone. Yet I know that I have lots of friends, and it doesn't make any difference relative to the emotional feeling in my body. Bringing a man into my life will not resolve the emotional feelings that I am having; he may mask it or be a distraction such that it returns to its hiding spot in my body, no longer provoked. This would be the act of finding a partner to assist me to feel whole, rather than resolving the old emotional energy and having me feel whole from the inside.

CP – Looking for Yourself Where You Are Not, Mistaking Need for Love

As I have been going through this for the last couple of hours, I have been in contact with friends and I have been able to express myself. This has assisted with getting the energy to move in my body. It is

hugely valuable to have some close friends to be able to express what is going on and being received by them. They don't need to fix anything. We need friends to provide contact and energetic support; we are fully capable and resourceful to resolve this within ourselves. And it has been wonderful for me to have moral support to keep me grounded in the moment.

Thank you for being there to receive all my messages and hold space for me. I really appreciate that you have been there to listen as I feel through the pain in my body and bring it to completion.

▶ TECHNIQUE: CORE Technique

Lots of love,
Jacque

▶ **TOOL: GROUNDING EXERCISE**

The objective is to be grounded in your being and in integrity without being attached to anything. We all are energetic beings, and we can coalesce our energy in and around our bodies. We are here and grounded on the planet to experience life in physical form.

Imagine a point in the center of your head. Imagine it is a spark of light. Focus your attention and energy on this spark of light. If you don't see a spark of light, just focus your attention within your head. Notice when you do this that your head is very quiet and peaceful.

This spark of light is the essence of you and your consciousness. Be present to it. Next, anchor yourself to the earth by imagining that you are attached from the core of your body down and through to the core of the earth. You will now feel grounded to the earth rather than feeling like you might float away or disappear.

Finally Letting Go

When we are overwhelmed by emotion, we are no longer able to manage effectively. We become a victim of the emotion, and most of the management tools presented in chapter 4 are useless. It is like we are treading water in the rushing cold river of life and trying to open the backpack to pull out just the right tool — but none of the tools work effectively because we are drowning. What we needed was a life vest, and we didn't take it with us because we'd decided that we wouldn't get wet.

Resolving our emotional baggage makes us lighter so that we can float and be much more resourceful as life presents us with challenges.

Dear Arturo,

I woke up this morning to the realization that my relationship with Milo is really at an end. I know — what didn't I get about this before? It has been a full year since we sold the house. It seems to take the emotions time to catch up to reality.

 CP: Resisting Feeling Things Fully, Avoiding the Present

I have been working on a project for the last four months putting all the pictures and video footage together from my holiday in Belize. Dur-

ing this time Milo and I have spent a lot of time together as he taught me how to use the video editing software to make a movie.

The project is now finished, and so is our time together. There is really no reason for me to spend any more time with Milo. We really have nothing to talk about anymore. I bring him up to date on a few friends, he does the same for me, and then we are at the end of things to talk about. When I asked what didn't work for him about our past relationship, he simply said, "There wasn't enough sex and I was emotionally and mentally unfulfilled." The sex part I understood. It was too bad that he didn't initiate more of it if more was what he wanted! When I asked what **emotionally and mentally unfulfilled** meant, he believed those words explained it all. I shook my head and walked away no more informed than before the conversation. With that as an example of our communication, it wasn't surprising that we did not make it.

So I sit here today with the insight that Milo and I are really finished. We have no reason to spend any time together. I can feel the sadness in my chest. Letting go of what I have not fully let go of before. I think my body has known that I am reaching this point, it is just that my mind had been in denial that the time has arrived to fully let go. I have had lots of pain in my body all this week and have not been aware of what the specific trigger was. Plus I have been very tired. I have not run or worked out for a couple of days to give my muscles time to recuperate, and I am still tired.

► CP: Resisting Feeling Things Fully
TECHNIQUE: CORE Technique

It feels like I am resisting letting go, and it takes a huge amount of energy to hold on to the past. I know that if I were to make myself busy, I could distract myself from what I am feeling and not have to feel it. It would have the effect of stuffing the energy back into my body. The great thing about where I live and my living circumstances is that I can take *the time to feel what is occurring and fully experience it, so that I can bring it to conclusion.*

I must be breaking out of the emotional heavy lifting that I was doing. I have noticed that I am feeling excited and vibrant once again. Only a little bit of energy left in my chest. When I ask myself what this energy is about, it is about letting Milo go completely and permanently. Being in relationship with him has been so much a part of my life, and now it is completely coming to an end. I can feel the sadness in my chest and my throat as the tears roll down my cheeks.

▶ TECHNIQUE: CORE Technique

As I was sitting here and feeling into this energy, I realized that I am determined to keep doing this work, because I am focused on transitioning from being a Human Child who is full of emotional reactions and tantrums, be they small or large. I am determined to become a Human Adult, who is well-grounded, present, and aware of what God or the universe has to present in terms of opportunities for my life. To be able to listen to my intuition and recognize when I have a "knowing" of what the right next step for me is. I want to be able to live my life with a quiet peaceful confidence in a world of uncertainty, knowing that I can perceive and feel my way through it. I am focused on living life to its fullest, living ecstasy.

Take care, my friend. I love you very much and appreciate your receiving this letter.

Jacque

As you may have noticed, when we journal, our minds free-flow from one area of thought to another. As emotional energy arose in my body, I stopped writing and felt into the energy using either the SEE Technique or the CORE Technique. I mostly used the CORE Technique, as what I was resolving was past emotional experiences that had not come to completion. We tend to use the SEE Technique to let go of our identifications and negative projections of the future. When you journal, I suggest using a pen and paper and just letting your mind take you to wherever it takes you. It tends to know the areas where you are resisting and holding emotional energy. When you notice a physical sensation occurring in your body, stop and feel into it. To see if you are complete, read back over what you wrote previously and see if any more sensations arise in your body.

You will also notice that my emotions and physical feelings were often a result of more than one Core Problem occurring at a time. Often a particular emotional reaction involves two and sometimes all three Core Problems. It's not necessary to know the Core Problem to resolve the emotional conditioning. However, when we are emotionally provoked and want to understand the nature of the provocation, we can often associate it with one of the Core Problems. The Core Problems provide us with a simple way to identify the dynamics of our emotional reactions.

Suzette and Brandon Chop Down Their Vines

Things were not going well for Suzette and Brandon. They had been married for seven years, and for the last four years, things just weren't like they used to be. Suzette told me that Brandon did not seem to be engaged in the relationship anymore. He would agree to do things and then not do them. He didn't seem to be willing to engage in conversations, and couldn't look her in the eye when they did have a conversation. I assured her that the Emotional Hot Button Removal techniques required a minimum of talking for a major transition to occur.

Brandon came along to the introductory session and spent most of the time looking at the ground, hardly able to speak. Four weeks later, he felt so much lighter. Things were going great in their relationship. Brandon could hardly wipe the smile off his face to get down and do some more work. Suzette and Brandon were having conversations together, giggling and having fun for the first time in several years. It was their emotional baggage that had been clashing and creating problems.

With the downturn in the economy, Suzette and Brandon like many people had had employment challenges and hence some financial challenges that put pressure on their relationship. This had seemed to cause Brandon's withdrawal in the first place. Brandon's withdrawal pushed on Suzette's hot button of "having to be responsible for everything." It turned out that Brandon was terrified of conflict, and his Core Problem was looking for yourself where you are not.

In fact, Brandon seemed to have a huge thicket of Headache Vines — mistaking need for love — causing him a headache! Due to resisting feeling things fully, Brandon had been avoiding the present moment in his relationship and had virtually closed down his self-expression; the Tape Vine literally stopped him from speaking. Suzette, on the other hand, had had no idea what the problem was, she just knew that something needed to change or she was going to try to force an outcome, which would likely look something like divorce. Suzette kept pricking herself on the Barbed Wire Vine, overreacting to circumstances — at least in Brandon's view of the situation. The more Suzette got upset, the more Brandon withdrew, because he was terrified of conflict.

In our sessions, Brandon told us that he felt angry, hurt, and left out. All of these feelings can be attributed to looking for yourself where you are not. I simply provoked Brandon, and he went to work cutting down the huge thickets of Headache Vines and Tape Vines that were growing in his emotional jungle.

While Brandon went to work on his jungle, I started to work with Suzette. Her emotional conditioning was buried much deeper than Brandon's and needed to be provoked to come to the surface. I think for years Suzette had been resisting feeling things fully and had been carrying the weight of her family on her shoulders, starting with the breakdown of her first marriage and raising children on her own, and then feeling unsupported by Brandon over the past few years. Suzette suppressed much of her emotional energy and was ready to implode if something didn't change. She had no idea that it was her frustration that was helping to cause Brandon to shut down.

With Suzette releasing her frustration and Brandon letting go of the emotional energy that was causing his sense of hurt and anger, all of a sudden the dynamic in the relationship changed. First, they gained some significant insight as to how they could use their relationship to resolve the emotional conditioning that was causing many of their relationship problems. They could reach the beginnings of the fourth-stage relationship Robert Masters described in *Transformation through Intimacy* (see chapter 9). They now know what provokes the other person, so they can choose to not provoke their partner, or just to have more empathy when their partner is provoked. Each of them is responsible for resolving their own emotional upset.

Second, when they are provoked they can just sit down and resolve the emotional energy; they no longer have to push it away and resist it or project their upset onto their partner. Third, they can actively choose to sit down for an hour a week and be each other's coach, provoking whatever emotional energy they can to keep chopping down their vines. Ultimately this will create more space for love in their relationship. Divorcing your partner becomes optional; divorcing your emotional baggage is highly recommended.

Blue Sky Ahead

There came a time when I could see a break in the canopy up ahead: rays of sunshine were reaching all the way down to the ground below. Excitement filled my belly. Maybe I was finally out of the jungle. It had felt like it would never end.

I have often felt disappointed when another big piece of energy arose in my body to be brought to completion. Would I ever be finished? Would I ever stop hurting? But when I saw the sunshine, I knew it was all worth it. I felt a sense of freedom in my body that I had never felt before. I sensed that somehow I had become profoundly different than who I had been. I was calmer, I talked slower, my voice had changed, and I walked differently. It was like a new Jacque was emerging from the jungle.

To get through the jungle of my emotions, I had to be willing to feel the physical sensations in my body. For you to get through the jungle of your emotions, you will have to be willing to feel these physical sensations. You will need to be willing to take the time to focus your attention on the physical sensations in your body. If you ignore them like you have in the past, then the energy will stay in your body and continue to plague you in the future. But if you do the work, magic is possible.

Eckhart Tolle has said that if we put our attention on the pain-body and shed light on it, we will break our identification with it. He was absolutely correct. I had broken my identifications. I had left piles of thorny vines in my wake as I made my way through the jungle.

The CORE and SEE Techniques are relatively simple once you learn them; there are a few intricacies to using them, like when you have an identification and your body does not want to let go of the energy. But with a little coaching support you can overcome these barriers. If you and your partner both know the techniques, then you can help each other out and hold space for each other to chop through the clusters of vines.

The choice is now yours. Would you really like to drop off your emotional baggage? Are you ready to cut down the vines in your emotional jungle and experience the radiance of sunshine in your life? If you are, you will have new ground to work and the opportunity to plant a new crop in fertile soil.

CHAPTER 15

Tilling the Soil

THERE IT WAS: A CLEARING. No more thick jungle canopy overhead. I could feel the beautiful tropical sunshine on my face. Joy and happiness filled my heart and my body vibrated in excitement. I had done it! Yahoo! I had done the heavy lifting.

I had accumulated many key principles for living a happy life over the six years of personal development work I had done, traveling from village to village listening to the wise elders speak. I had practiced putting many of these principles into place in my life, in my business, and in my relationship with Milo. They all worked to a certain degree, but they weren't enough for me to fully experience the magic of the true me. Imagine filling a hot air balloon with hot air, pumping more and more air into it, until slowly, when it has enough air in it, it rises from the ground. The problem is that even with my backpack of tools in hand, I had still had all the weights, my emotional baggage, tied to the sides of the basket. So although things had gotten better in my life and I was feeling happier, I just wasn't flying very high at first, and I was still running into lots of obstacles. I needed to drop off my emotional baggage to soar. Now that I have done that—cut down most of the vines in my emotional jungle—I want to take you on a journey through the key principles of living a magical life so that we can all soar in our lives.

100 Percent Responsibility

"You are 100 percent responsible for everything that happens in your life." I first heard these words at a Jack Canfield personal development seminar in 2004. What, I am 100 percent responsible for what happens in my life? How could I be responsible for my boss having a mental breakdown at work? How am I responsible for Milo saying no whenever I came up with an idea? How am I responsible for the unhappiness that I feel, when I have tried to do everything I thought one needed to do to live a good life? I went to school, just like my parents wanted. I have a master's degree in economics. When my master's degree didn't seem to be good enough to get the kind of job I wanted, I spent three years studying every weekend to get my Chartered Financial Analyst designation. How was I responsible for being turned down for a vice president title? My ego screamed. All sorts of stuff just happens to me that I have no control over.

Yes, for the most part we have no control over what happens to us, and yet, maybe we do. I am going to make a very important distinction here: *Taking 100 percent responsibility for everything that is happening in our lives is different from controlling everything around us.*

Where we need to take responsibility is within ourselves. We have the ability to choose what we think about any situation. We can choose to be present to our emotions and feelings in any situation. And most importantly, we have the ability to choose how we will respond to any situation. It is this ability to choose that allows us to take 100 percent responsibility. The question is, are we resourceful enough to make this choice or will we constantly play out the Drama Triangle?

The Drama Triangle described by Stephen Karpman, a psychiatrist who won the Eric Berne Memorial Scientific Award in 1972 for this work, has three players: Victim, Persecutor, and Rescuer. The Victim role is played out when we give up our power to another person or to a situation. The Victim role might sound like this: "There is nothing I can do about this person; I have to work with them and I can't change their behavior." In a relation-ship it might sound like this: "My husband never comes home on time for dinner, and then the kids and I have to wait for him." When playing the Victim, we blame others for our circumstances, rather than taking responsibility for our own situations. In taking responsibility, we have a choice over how we want to respond to whatever situations come up. At work we can choose to cover for the other person or not. At home we can choose to eat din-ner at a certain time whether Dad is home or not. Our coworkers and partners can only play Persecutor to our Victim if we allow ourselves to have emotional reactions based on their behavior. I am not suggesting for a moment that we need to like what they are doing, but we can choose to respond to the situation from a centered and grounded place.

The Rescuer is the white knight who comes in and saves the day. Rescuers save the Victims from themselves, which isn't very helpful. Those playing Victim usually have a "poor me" story that they are unable to do something themselves due to some unfor-tunate circumstance. Rescuers see an opportunity to help, and we rush in to provide our assistance. As Rescuers, we are often trying to please others and get our own self-worth from being of value to others. The problem with playing the Rescuer role on a regu-lar basis is that we are not valuing ourselves. We are looking for ourselves where we are not, and in the process of looking for this love, we often give away too much of ourselves.

When Rescuers do not receive the love that they expect to get, they may switch roles and become a Victim or a Persecutor. We may feel like we have been taken advantage of: "I have to do so much extra work because my coworker does not do things to the high standard that I have, and things are often done wrong." The Rescuers who work so hard can feel unappreciated and hard done by when they become the Victim.

When Rescuers or Victims become Persecutors, we are going to get even. We may become angry and lash out at the other per-son to show them how wrong they are. We make it their fault that things aren't working the way they are supposed to. The Persecutor's ego rises to the defensive position, stands in the place of being right, and excludes the other person's perspective. In the case of our coworkers, we Persecutors might say something like "If you weren't so pushy and demanding, rushing me, then I would be able to do my job better." The Persecutor takes on the aggressor's role. In the case of the husband who was always late, when he does get home the Persecutor goes on the attack and tells him, "You're a lousy father. You can't even come home and have dinner with your children. What kind of a man are you?"

Milo and I played out the roles in a more global way. I was the Rescuer; Milo was the Victim. I brought all the friends into our relationship. I was the one working hard to create a home for us. I looked after our finances. In the relationship I carried more than my fair share of the load; quite frankly, I worked way too hard. As the Rescuer, it took me a long time to figure out how to put some boundaries in place and stop doing so much. When I stopped doing some things, like planting the vegetable garden, it wasn't long before Milo took these jobs over. Those gardens became his, and he did a great job!

I also played the role of Victim, due to the fear of being alone, and Milo was the Rescuer by being my constant companion. We were codependent in this way. By this I mean that we both played both roles, Victim and Rescuer, keeping each other safe from being alone. Milo was also a Victim of life: he held everything inside of him and wouldn't communicate anything about how he felt. This made me angry and I became the Persecutor about him not communicating with me.

A couple might be playing several different roles at any one time. We can play roles in a conversation, we can play roles in a specific situation, or we can be playing general roles in a relationship. In conversations we generally play opposing roles. In relationships, we might be playing the same role. I think Milo and I both felt like victims in our lives, and by being together we were both rescuing each other.

When Milo and I were splitting up, it would have been so easy for me to play the Victim of Milo's infidelity. He could have persecuted me for not being there for him in the relationship sexually, mentally, and emotionally—which apparently was his perspective about what was missing from our relationship. But we both chose not to persecute and blame the other person for the relationship coming to an end. I purposefully chose to set an intention to bring our relationship to closure with grace and ease.

You get the idea: around and around the triangle we go, switching roles on a moment's notice. This is where the drama occurs in our conversations with our partners and other people that we are in relationship with, including our children. Not only do we have trouble sitting quietly and listening to our partners when they are talking so that we can truly hear them, we can also be caught playing one of the roles of the Drama Triangle. When we are caught in the grips of an emotional reaction, we can switch between the roles very quickly. Guess what happens to communication? It breaks down. Where do we go? Often into conflict.

However, now that we have cut down the vines in our emotional jungles and have emerged out into the sunshine, we can experience situations with a greater sense of calm. We have greater ability to take responsibility for ourselves and the way we respond to situations. We now are more resourceful and can choose in the moment an appropriate response given the situation and the conversation. When we are observing our global behavior, we can stand in a place of being centered. As the Rescuer, we can choose to set a boundary by determining when enough is enough. When we are playing Victim, we can ask ourselves, What could I do to change this situation? When we are the Persecutor, we can look inside of ourselves to see what we are angry with ourselves about. Then we can sit down and cut down another thorny vine.

When we take 100 percent responsibility for ourselves, we can stop playing in the Drama Triangle. Taking responsibility for ourselves requires that we start focusing on truly loving and honoring ourselves and being centered in the core of who we are. As we clear up our emotional baggage, we are able to take actions based on who we want to be.

SELF-REFLECTION QUESTIONS

• In your relationship, what role on the Drama Triangle do you tend to play?
• What are the main topics that you tend to create a dramatic role around?
• How could you take more responsibility in your life for each of the dramas you are participating in?
• What would taking more responsibility look like?

Intention

In all the personal development work that I did prior to learning how to feel, we always created a vision and goals. Intentions, I have come to believe, are a very powerful first step before setting a vision. Intentions inspire a focus that taps into our desirable emotions. Intentions are energy in motion.

An intention is a statement of the experience that we want to have, the feeling we would like to feel, and the emotions we would like to have. Review the list of emotions in chapter 11 and choose which emotion feels ideal for you as a way of being. In every private coaching session, my clients state their ideal intention for whatever they would like to focus on in the session, and then together we remove the barriers—the emotional baggage that blocks the realization of their intention statement. My intention statement for going through the divorce was to do it with grace and ease. My current intention statement as I write this book is to have a fun, vibrant, and thrilling life. I want to have fun, feel vibrant within my body, and have both my personal life and my business be thrilling. Thrilling is both exciting and stimulating; I want to be inspiring and inspired.

An intention statement is written in the present tense as if it were happening right now. If it is not happening right now, then what we do is start living into our intentions, working on cultivating these experiences and feelings. A lot of people ask me, What is an experience? Fun is an experience I have when I am doing things that I enjoy. Thrilling is the experience I have when I am taking on new challenges or figuring out how to do something for the first time. Thrilling is also the experience that I have when I am speaking to an audience about what I am passionate about. Adventure is an experience that I have when I go to new places and explore new things—river kayaking and camping are adventures for me. Being vulnerable is an experience that I have when I allow my life to move into unknown territory and I don't have any idea what is going to happen. When I am being vulnerable, I trust the universe will show me what I need to know to make my way through the unknown territory.

The true joy of life is not about what possessions we own, it is about the experience we have and the feeling that those experiences generate in our bodies. And it is our ability to be present to these experiences that brings us the sense of joy. The magic of life occurs when we are very present to our feelings. Therefore if we know what the experiences are that we want, and how we want to feel, we will have a better sense of what we want to attract into our lives. My intention statement is, "I have a fun, vibrant, and thrilling life."

SELF-REFLECTION QUESTIONS

- When you feel the best, what are you experiencing?
- If you were having your ideal experience, what would that be?
- If the ideal you were walking down the street, what would you see?

• Hold this new person in your mind's eye. How do you feel?
• Intention statement: What experience would you like to have and how would you like to feel?

I hold a picture of a happy, smiling woman in a yellow sweater walking down the street with a bounce in her step. People see me and feel me coming. They feel wonderful when they have been touched by my presence. I brighten up their day and my day at the same time.

What Do We Really Want?

This is the million-dollar question for a lot of people. Most of us don't really know what we want in life. We might have an idea of what we are supposed to want — the big house, beautiful furniture and paintings, an expensive car, nice clothes. Holidays that involve travel to foreign destinations: hiking in the Himalayas, white-water rafting in Costa Rica, beautiful beaches in the Caribbean. These are some of the things that we might want. Notice that my first list contained physical things, and my second list encompassed things to do. Which of these lists is more appealing to you? Is it the list of things you own, or the list of things you might do? Notice the feelings these lists elicit in you.

When I started doing visioning work, I used many different tools to uncover what it was that I might want in life. The rest of this chapter presents these tools in the order that I learned them. You might try some of them or all of them. I still don't know exactly what I want from a physical asset perspective, but after having worked on this for the last ten years, I do know how I want to feel and what experiences that I want to have. From the place where I am now, so long as I can feel the way I want and have the experience that I want, I am relatively flexible about what I do and what I own.

▶ **TOOL: VISIONING EXERCISES**

These are several good visioning exercises. I suggest doing them in the order presented here.

▶ **TOOL: CREATE A VISION BOARD**

Choose a question that you would like to explore. It might be, What is next in my life? It might be, What is important to me? It might be, What do I want from my next career? Focus on whatever it is that you want to be attracting into your life next.

Obtain a bunch of magazines, and as you flip through the magazines cut out the pictures that you are attracted to. Don't think. Just trust your intuition. Do not cut out any words. This is an exercise in listening to the subconscious mind.

Glue your pictures on a piece of bristol board. When your board is finished, look at it. What story is it telling you? You might even want to video the story that you tell and watch it later.

If you really let your subconscious choose the pictures, the board will show you what is really important to you. Notice how you feel.

Note: This exercise can also be done from the conscious mind. In this case, choose pictures of things that you have decided that you want.

▶ **TOOL: WRITE A VISION**

Based on your vision board, write about what you want your life to look like. Where do you live? What does your house look like? What do you do for fun, recreation, work? Tell a story about your family. Tell a story about your wealth. What would you like to own, and how do you contribute to others?

When you read your vision, how do you feel?
Which pieces do you really want?
Are there any pieces that you think you "should" have?
You can delete these if you want or just notice how you feel about them.

Feeling the Magic

It is great to set a vision and know what we want, and at the same time we need to feel gratitude for what we already have. Are we able to feel the magic of what is happening in our lives at the moment? To feel the magic we need to be present to what is currently occurring in our life that gives us pleasure and joy. To experience love we need to be open to really feeling the kind gestures that our partner makes when they are expressing romance. We have to stop taking things for granted and take the time to be grateful and fully experience in our body what is already present in our lives. I was so busy doing things in my relationship with Milo that I wasn't present to all the great things that we did together except when we were camping. That is when I slowed down enough to be really present to how great my life was.

Once I had let go of a significant amount of emotional conditioning, I was able to be much more aware of and present to my emotional feelings. By letting go of the emotional barriers I was able to let in more of the pleasurable feelings and hence I experienced more of the magic of life.

Attitude Is Altitude

What we focus on grows.

I learned early on in my personal development work that my attitude was everything and that how I approached life was vital to my happiness. If I wanted to be happy, I needed to change the way I saw the world and related to people. I actively used the tools presented in chapter 4 to start changing my perspective of events that were taking place around me and my relationship to those events. I started to get the idea that not everything was about me—that people were being who they were being and their behavior had nothing to do with me! At last I was able to stop taking everything so personally.

Whether we are looking at separation or divorce or life in general, developing a positive attitude and approaching events from a learning perspective makes for far happier travels. We were designed to be happy. Some of us accumulated a lot of emotional baggage early on in life that has made it more difficult for us. It is this emotional baggage that tends to fuel our negative attitudes: "It doesn't matter" or "I can't change" or "Everyone else is wrong and treats me badly." We can look at things from a positive perspective and find the learning in everything, even when an event seems negative. From every situation we can ask ourselves, What is there for me to learn from this event?

As I progressed in my development, I adopted the attitude and intention that I was going to fully enjoy life. I was going to look for and start doing those things in life that I really enjoyed and stop doing the things that I did not enjoy or things that didn't contribute to my positive energy. From my many years of coaching I had heard people talk about what they "needed" to do. By the tone of their voice, I could tell that these activities felt like a burden to them. I asked them why they volunteered to be on the parent committee at school, the local community improvement committee, and the board of their professional association, all at the same time? It was usually because someone asked them to and they couldn't say no, or they had come to expect that this was what they were supposed to do. They often felt overwhelmed and like they didn't have any time to do what they really loved. Volunteering for so many different situations was a burden to them. Then there was the client that who volunteered for at least six organizations, felt like it was easy, and was grateful that he could contribute so much. It all depends on what speaks to our hearts and what our attitude is. If what we are involved in doesn't speak to our hearts, then it will be difficult to have a positive attitude.

Having a positive attitude affects more than our relationships. Our long-term mental health is affected by how we interpret and respond to our environment. The book *Liars, Lovers, and Heroes: What the New Brain Science Reveals about How We Become Who We Are* states that the way we view ourselves impacts our understanding of the events in our lives, which then affects our response to those events. As we go through a relationship breakup, we might start to tell ourselves stories, like "I am not a good person. No one will ever love me." These stories create a negative self-image, and then our behaviors will likely reflect the story we are telling. It is important to pay attention to the stories that we tell about ourselves. This is a difficult enough time without being judgmental of ourselves. Instead we need to write positive stories about who we would like to become.

SELF-REFLECTION QUESTIONS

- What does your attitude tend to be like?
- What would you need to do to shift your attitude to be more positive?
- What might this make possible for you?

Creating Our Reality

Once I realized how important my attitude was in determining my behavior, the next idea that I became aware of was that I actually create my own reality. My thinking and behavior have a huge impact on the experience I have in the world. I became aware that many of us seemed to be going through life on automatic pilot. I started to play a game to bring some light and happiness into other people's lives and into mine.

When I went to a store and the clerk asked me, "How are you?" I always provided an upbeat reply, like "I am excellent" or, if I was having a really great day, "I am fantastic." I remember being at a gas station one day, and the attendant asked me how I was, and I said "I am fantastic." A big smile erupted on his face. He told me I was the first person he had met that day that was fantastic and he wanted to know why. I told him, "I am alive, healthy, and happy, and life is good." Stating that I was fantastic made me feel fantastic inside. It also caused a positive response in the gas station attendant—so why not be fantastic rather than— the standard answer—"Not bad." After all not bad is just one step above bad, and is that where we really want to be?

It is really hard to feel positive and upbeat when we are in a negative space. Try this exercise out for yourself: First, slump over and say, "Life is wonderful, life is great." Notice how you feel. Second, stand up straight, with your shoulders back, and say, "Life sucks." Notice how you feel. I bet that when you were slumped over, you did not feel great, nor did life feel that bad when you were standing up tall with your shoulders back. Now try standing up straight and saying, "Life is wonderful." How do you feel? Better? We need to educate and condition our bodies to be in a position that allows us to feel great, and we need to condition our minds to generate positive thoughts and notice the emotions that go with them.

The secret to developing a more positive way of being is to focus on what we love and start doing more of it. When we focus on what we love, the things that we don't love start to fall away.

314

We don't have time and space for those things or the thoughts that they bring. Becoming happy starts to become a self-fulfilling prophecy, especially once we have dropped off our emotional baggage. The more I focused my attention on the positive aspects of life, the happier I became and the more positive experiences started to occur in my life. People started to tell me that I was the happiest person they knew.

Here is the fundamental truth — we create our own reality.

- We become what we think about.
- We become what we speak about.
- We become how we feel.
- We attract people who have the same attitude that we have.

To change our reality we need to change what we think about, what we speak about, and how we feel. Our thinking needs to focus on what we want, rather than what we don't want. We need to be impeccable with our speech, talking only about what we want and how we want to feel. In every moment we have the freedom to choose what we want. If we choose to have a positive attitude and to continue to move into positive space, then our environment will respond accordingly. This doesn't mean that we won't be presented with challenges. What it means is that even when we are presented with challenges, we can positively affect the outcome of these challenges and the impact they have on our lives.

As we assess where we are in our relationships, we will now get to actively choose who we are going to be and how we will treat our partners, regardless of how our partners treat us. When a relationship is going well, it is relatively easy to behave in an appropriate way, but when things get difficult our behavior may deteriorate. In difficult times we really have the opportunity to take a stand for who we want to be in this world. Do we want to be someone that we can be really proud of in the future? How we behave toward our partners in this difficult time of divorce will be with us for a long time. A natural default pattern and maybe the easiest route for the ego is to play Victim and blame our partners for what is happening and the way our relationships fell apart. However my observation is that we can take a stand in the early stages of the separation that will have a huge impact on how the divorce or separation unfolds.

I have noticed that when one partner is angry, it often provokes the other partner to become angry. Now two egos are standing in the place of being right, and neither partner can hear the other. Conflict erupts; each person starts establishing their position, and then negotiations have to occur from a place where both people are trying to force an outcome. Do you think this will produce a positive outcome? No, me neither.

When my buttons are pushed, I use the management strategy of choosing to keep quiet and listen. When my emotional reaction is complete and I have resolved the energy, then I will come back and have a conversation. When my buttons are pushed, I can't be who I want to be, so I choose not to engage. Engaging would not create the reality I want. So the next time you are provoked and want to engage, ask yourself, "Am I being who I want to be? What reality do I want to create?"

SELF-REFLECTION QUESTIONS

- What reality would you like to create?
- What would you like to have happening in your life that is not happening?
- How do you have to be different to invite more of that reality in your life?

Intuition

We each have a natural internal guidance system to assist us on this journey of attracting into our lives exactly what we want. It is called intuition, or gut feelings. Our intuition usually speaks to us in a much quieter voice than the one that speaks to us from our minds. I find that my intuition only sends me a message once. If I am not listening, I will miss the message. In the past I might hear the message, but my mind would override my intuition, saying, "No, that won't happen" or "I need to do something else."

Sometimes I have had general feelings of just knowing something that I am supposed to do. When I made the decision to write this book, I just knew that it was what I was supposed to be doing. Not to do it would mean turning my back on something important in my life. I chose to not think about how much this project would cost financially or the amount of time that it would take. I trusted that the universe would help me figure out exactly how I was going to finance the project and get it to completion. It must have worked, because you are now reading the book!

When we have intuitive hits or inspired thoughts, we need to take action on those thoughts to activate them in the physical world. This is the signal we send back to the universe that we have heard our intuition and we are willing to follow it. The universe will usually send more help to assist us to put our inspired thoughts into action. The key aspect is that we have to be open to help. Help will show up in all sorts of ways to assist us along the path, and it won't necessarily show up in the way that we think it should. I used to have the habit of doing everything on my own. If someone offered me help, I would often say, "No, I can do that myself." Well it doesn't matter if I could do it myself or not, I learned to start saying "Yes!" and accepting the help. It occurred to me that I was saying no to the universe's offer of assistance, and if I wanted help, I needed to be open to all help.

Be Present to What Is Showing Up

Sometimes we need to be exposed to an idea several times before it really lands. Jed McKenna, in *Spiritual Warfare*, and the
contributors to the book *Presence* agree on living life from a place
of noticing the patterns that present themselves and then allowing yourself to flow with the pattern that is being presented. My
normal way of operating had been to use my mind to decide
what direction to take and then to push forward to execute those
ideas. This is what happened with the Swing into Leadership program. I imagined what would happen if someone else launched
this program instead of me. Fear struck my heart and I forged
ahead—not because I knew this was what I should do, but because I was afraid that someone else would do it. Sometimes we
don't know when a message comes from our true intuition and
when the idea comes from ego. As I have been practicing using
my intuition more, what I have noticed is that when things come
from true intuition, or when a pattern is presenting itself, it feels
more like a knowing. It is like, "Oh, this is what I am supposed
to do." Sometimes I don't know why I am supposed to do this,
but the direction I am to take is clear. I also notice that I am rather
calm inside; I am not overexcited, nor is my mind going over and
over my decision from a place of uncertainty.

    I noticed patterns showing up in my life when I made the de-
cision to go back to Belize for a working sabbatical. Three things
moved out of my way as obstacles very quickly. The first was
that I negotiated my way out of a contract with a company to do
more personal development work. Being who I wanted to be, it
was time to graduate, so I made their woman's retreat in Tulum,
Mexico, my last event. This took me to within two hundred miles
of Belize. Second, it was January, and my landlord had told me
she was going to sell the house in May, so I would need to find a
new place to live. When it looked like I would go back to Belize
in October, she offered to delay selling the house until late summer, and then we could both move when it was time for me to
go to Belize. Third, Milo offered to store the rest of my posses-

sions if I wanted to go. All barriers removed, I would now have to make an excuse not to go to Belize. Belize was somehow part of my destiny.

Maybe you're saying to yourself, "That's great for you, but I can't just leave my life and go to Belize to find myself!" Or, "If I could go to Belize, then life would be great for me, too." But this is the voice of the ego discouraging you from taking action on behalf of your own happiness. Our egos are very good at making up all sorts of excuses not to take action. That way we can continue to feel comfortable in what is familiar. It means we don't have to deal with the Core Problem of Resisting Change. For me, it just happened that at that point in my journey, I got the message that it was time to step outside of the routine that I had created for myself. It was time to step into an adventure and take on a new challenge. I encourage you to notice what it is in your life that is speaking to you, calling you to an adventure. Magical things are happening all the time. The universe is sending you information, if you are open to hearing it, seeing it, and feeling it.

SELF-REFLECTION QUESTIONS

- What might the universe be trying to show you or teach you?
- What message is contained in these patterns?
- When you have an idea to do something, what story do you notice spinning in your mind?
- How are you feeling? Calm or superexcited?

Wait Until You Know

Often we don't know what direction life is going to send us. Sometimes we need to wait until we are shown what direction to follow. The key is being open to waiting for these messages. The book *Presence* talks about reaching clarity and inner knowing. You wait until you receive a message from your intuition or from patterns that are being presented to you. When you receive the message, you will have an inner knowing that it's the truth. Until you receive new messages, continue to take action at whatever you are doing now to the best of your ability. Be open to allowing the universe to work at its own speed.

In December I knew I was working in Belize for a reason. Life had brought me there, but I hadn't known why. I worked diligently for two months writing this book, and then I met Conrad around Christmas. Clearly Conrad had come to play a role in my life. I wasn't sure how big a role he would play — I would need to "wait" to find out. I need to allow the universe and my intuition to show me the path forward. Life is a journey that takes time to unfold. Our role in the unfolding is to fully enjoy whatever we are doing and to pay attention to what comes next.

SELF-REFLECTION QUESTIONS

- When is it difficult for you to wait for things to unfold?
- What story is your mind making up?
- What is the cost of waiting?
- What is the cost of acting now?
- What determines the cost?

Practicing Awareness

If there is something that we really want in life, then we need to keep practicing to increase our awareness. To be aware of what is occurring around us, we need to be conscious. This is a continuous and constant practice. If we stop practicing, we may take a couple of steps backward — which is fine, but then we need to wake up and start practicing again to keep moving forward purposefully. The secret is to realize that we have the absolute freedom to choose what is happening in our lives. When we take 100 percent responsibility for what is happening, we are no longer victims of others' actions, nor do we need to rescue or persecute others. Plus when we take 100 percent responsibility, we are no longer victims of our own self-judgments, which can be worse than other people's judgments of us. If we happen to fall back into our old ways, let's be honest with ourselves and ask, What is happening? What can I learn from this? What do I need to resolve? How could I have managed better in the moment? As we continue this practice our resourcefulness will increase, and over time we will become "ultimately resourceful," recognizing that we are the "cause" of the life we have.

We may find that we are stuck due to an inner conflict about letting go of what we have in our current lives and being committed to what we want in the future. I was identified with my relationship with Milo and everything that entailed; the universe had a different and better path for me to follow. This new path is ultimately giving me the life I want, because I keep moving forward based on my "knowing." All I need to do is allow this to unfold over time. We can all do this by being curious and entering into a place of wonder, rather than living from a place of fear, needing to know exactly what will happen. We let go of needing things to be a certain way; we let go of control. In my relationship with Conrad, as I write I don't know where we're headed yet, exactly. But I'm committed to staying present to how the relationship unfolds and how that fits with my intention statement. This is my intention statement for relationship: "We stand and walk beside each other in intimate relationship, treating each other preciously, feeling deep love."

Wanting Something More

I wanted something more in life, and I was willing to commit myself to doing whatever it took to be different. My objective became to live every day as if it were my last day. It might be a day of learning, or a day of being highly focused on work, or a blissful day with my family, or a day of supporting my partner to be more successful in his business or a client to step into some new realm of their life. Was I fully living my life? No matter what I was doing, I wanted to be doing it well, and I wanted to enjoy myself while doing it. This was my measure of fully living life with the greatest sense of enjoyment and happiness.

My objective was to live life with a sense of ecstasy. Was I living a fun, vibrant, and thrilling life that was full of adventure? I was the one that invited the fun into my life; I was the one who chose to be vibrant each day. I attracted into my life those things that were thrilling to me.

This is not to say that I didn't have challenging situations arise that I needed to feel and think my way through. Lots of those came up. What was important was how I responded to them. Handling each of these situations and learning from them built my resourcefulness. As I handled these situations, I opened myself up for more thrilling opportunities. Whether something was thrilling or not depended upon my attitude and how I showed up and responded to the situation.

It is time for a review of what you want. Take a moment to review the self-reflection questions that follow. What is it you really want? This is a good time to make adjustments to your vision to reflect your newest understanding of who you are and where you are going.

SELF-REFLECTION QUESTIONS

• Go back to what you said you wanted and who you wanted to be. Do you really want this? How will you feel if you get it?
• Go back to what you said you wanted in a partner. Do you really want this? How will you feel?
• Go back to what you said you would like to be doing in your life. Do you really want this? How will you feel?
• Go back to what you said you would like to have. Do you really want this? How will you feel?
• Go back to what you said about how you would like to feel. Do you really want this?

When we are willing to step into what we really want, we just might be able to be unreasonably happy. Wouldn't that be nice? If we can create this out of a divorce, I would consider it to be a pretty good outcome. If we can create this within our current marriages, I would consider that an even better outcome. But I am not attached to what journey we take. I am open to wondering what the universe will bring.

Yes, I was willing to settle for less in my relationship with Milo. It was "good enough." I was afraid to ask myself all these soul-searching questions, because I did not know what I would find out. I was afraid to lose my relationship with Milo. I looked at what I had from a material perspective and I didn't want to give that up either. Due to these fears and attachments I was not willing to ask myself the deeper questions in life. To be fair to myself, I didn't know what some of the questions were that I needed to ask myself. That is why coaching is so brilliant—coaches ask questions that we can't think of asking ourselves.

Hitting a crisis in my relationship made it possible for me to go where I was resistant to go. It hadn't even occurred to me that I needed to really look at what I wanted in my primary relationship. To some extent I was cheating both of us. By keeping the status quo I was certainly cheating myself out of a more magical life — and maybe Milo too.

Taking Action

By now you know what you really want, right? If not go back to the top, because the next step is about taking action — consistent, focused action. Oh, you thought that if you told the universe what you wanted, it would just show up on your doorstep in a nice neat package with a bow on it? Sorry, that is not the way it works. That is called a dream. Dreams are not likely to be manifested into reality unless you take some action, and I mean real action.

Reading this book is a good first start — it satisfies your mind. But real action requires you to take a pen and your journal and answer the questions in this book. Or doing some of the visioning exercises and then forming the habit of visualizing them. Or going out and having some new experiences to gather new information. As I started to have new experiences and connect with other people, learning about them, it helped me to develop more insight about myself. I did not learn in isolation. The mind is only one form of learning, and it can be pretty good at ignoring what it does not want to face. Having new experiences brings your whole body knowledge and wisdom.

Doing the work to drop your emotional baggage is a whole set of actions unto themselves. This work requires you to have a consistent, automatic habit of feeling into the sensations in your body when you notice that you are in the middle of an emotional reaction. Once you have done this work, it will make it even easier for you to take consistent focused action to manifest and live the life you most desire.

OK, so you know what you want, and you have cut down the vines in your jungle, and now you seriously want to manifest something more in your life. Consistent, focused action is what is required. This means doing whatever it is that you do and doing it well until the universe starts to show you what is next. When the universe shows you what is next, you need to take action in that area to the best of your ability. As you keep taking action, you will get feedback on the direction that you are moving. If it is the right direction, more resources will come to help you keep moving forward. By resources, I mean someone will come into your life to offer you help for free, someone will swap services with you, or, most of the time, you will swap money for the services and products that will help you. Don't wait for help to be free — and when it is free, be extra grateful that someone has given you this gift!

If no help shows up, then maybe you read the signs wrong, or maybe you just have to wait until something else comes your way. We don't know what the timing of things will be, and we don't want to force the outcome. Maybe someday my Swing into Leadership program will be just right for whatever is happening in my life at that moment, and maybe it was just a good learning exercise. The key is to keep taking action wherever you can take action and to do a very good job wherever you decide to put your attention.

Having Fun

Most importantly, go out and have fun. Life is a journey, and you were put on this earth to enjoy yourself. Whatever activity you choose to do, make sure it is fun. If it is not fun, then it had better be very valuable to your learning. Your ego doesn't really like to work hard, but you may be using a tremendous amount of willpower to obtain what you think you need to be successful in life. When you let go of fear and someone else's notion of success and put your attention on what you are passionate about, work and life become much more enjoyable. When you finally hit your stride and find work that is purposeful for you, work becomes easier, captures you and draws you forward. When you are in a relationship, connected with your partner and supporting each other to grow and fully step into your lives, life can be magical.

There is another side to life and that is doing things that are purely for the fun and pleasure of life. For me that was sports. If you are not sure what constitutes fun for you, think back about what you used to do when you were a kid. What did you do for fun? Did you read? Did you go dancing or play music? Were you in the photography class? What things have you always wanted to try out? Now might be a good time. Having a great attitude is a lot easier when we are connected with other people and having fun.

CHAPTER 16

Planting Seeds for a Magical Life

WE HAVE BEEN BUSY CUTTING DOWN our emotional jungles and have started to till the land, getting ready to plant a new crop. We are starting over in who we want to be in our lives, how we choose to interact with others, and most importantly, how we choose to relate to ourselves. We may have divorced a partner, or we may have decided to really work on ourselves and our relationships. Either way, we are in the process of divorcing our emotional baggage. No matter what the situation, we have an opportunity to plant new varieties of seeds and see what comes up. We can taste new fruits and vegetables that perhaps we haven't tried before, because we have never experienced life as the new person we are being today. Oh it is so exciting to see what will come up in our gardens. I can hardly wait.

Starting Over

In its own good time the universe provided me with opportunities to date and to become good friends with new men who came into my life. Was everything perfect in these relationships? No, but each of them occurred for a purpose and I learned many valuable lessons on my journey to becoming the kind of woman that I wanted to become. In my current relationship I am continuously learning new things about my partner and myself. I continue to be open to seeing what happens between us from different perspectives, and I practice living from a place of love in order to create the kind of home and life that I want.

Was It Worth It?

You might be wondering if doing all the work to cut down your emotional vines is worth it. After all, it seems like an awful lot of hot, sweaty work, and it takes a relatively long time before a clearing is opened up in the jungle. And now you're probably thinking, "I need to work the land and plant a garden, and the next thing you are going to tell me is that I need to weed the garden too!" Yep, you're right. We do need to weed our gardens — more emotional energy will arise throughout our lives. The good news is that picking weeds is easy compared to chopping down vines; it is like doing a meditation while we grow our garden of life.

The question is, is it worth it? Yes, every painful moment is worth it. I have become a happy, well-grounded, centered woman who is willing to be vulnerable and take on the challenge of living into a magical life. I am no longer afraid to be me, and I am OK with knowing that who I am won't suit everyone. I will suit the people who want to get at it, roll up their sleeves, and do the work. I thank a good friend for providing me with this insight, because she is exactly right: a magical life for me is being with people who can talk about their emotions and who are ready to get to work and live their own magical lives. I want to be with people who are willing to take action in alignment with what they talk about. Imagine seeing vast meadows of people growing what they want. Imagine your children being able to have a life that they love. How much better would the world be if we were all living our magical lives?

Do Painful Emotional Reactions Ever End?

By this point you may be wondering, do we ever stop having painful emotional reactions? The answer is, I don't know, and I am not sure that it matters. As long as I am having emotional reactions I know there is energy that needs to be brought to completion in my body. There have been periods of time when nothing has provoked me, and then something will happen and a new series of provocations will occur. I just accept whatever comes up without judgment and sit down and do the techniques to bring the energy to completion. It has become almost a meditation or spiritual practice just accepting what is.

I have a clear intent to remove as much emotional baggage as possible so that life will be as easeful as possible. I have an intention to be able to live into my life's purpose and fully feel joy in my life, plus to be as healthy as possible. Chuck Spezzano says that awareness of our feelings is imperative for us to feel alive, to feel joy and even to know when we are in pain and need to make a change. Famed cyclist Lance Armstrong has a goal to go fast. To do this he makes himself and his bike as aerodynamic as possible. When we drop off our emotional baggage, we make ourselves as aerodynamic as possible in life, so we can live the life that we truly want. I have an intent to be unreasonably happy, to make a difference in many people's lives, and to live a magical life. I don't want anything slowing me down or preventing me from having this experience in life. I know that I will attract all the resources that I need to live my intent, and I don't want emotional baggage to be a barrier to attracting these resources into my life.

Just to be clear: letting go of emotional reactions doesn't mean we stop feeling emotion. As I mentioned in chapter 11, all emotions have a purpose. There are no good or bad emotions. Emotions contain information about what we enjoy, about what we love, and about what does not work for us. Our objective is to have the appropriate emotional response given the situation, instead of going overboard or suppressing what we feel. Emotional reactions are responses that are over the top or non-existent for a given situation. When someone we love dies, of course we feel a huge grief. The sadness is an expression of the depth of our love. But if we are still grieving several years later, there's something besides love going on. There may also be a significant amount of emotional attachment that still needs to be resolved.

SELF-REFLECTION QUESTIONS

• Do your emotional responses seem appropriate given the situation?
• What judgments do you have about yourself and about continuing to have emotional reactions?
• What would happen if you let go of these judgments and just accepted what is?

Seeing the Possibilities Together

For couples who drop off their emotional baggage, a whole new possibility opens up. When we are emotionally provoked, our ability to communicate often breaks down. However when both of us know and use the Emotional Hot Button Removal techniques, we are not processing each other as a talk therapist would. We are simply holding space for each other to feel into whatever emotional reaction is occurring in the moment. Or if we have children, one person is looking after the kids while the other one is dropping off his or her emotional baggage. We are supporting each other to heal the past and to be able to step into our lives and our relationships from a new energetic place. We are more resourceful in our relationships. As a couple we are now divorcing our emotional baggage, which allows us to live into a fourth-stage relationship — or at least a third-stage relationship — as described by Robert Masters and discussed in chapter 9. The important point is to get our relationships out of the eddy of denial or to calm the turbulent waters of a river that is nothing but one series of rapids of conflict after another.

When we absent the old emotional energy from our bodies, we will start to feel calmer. Couples like Suzette and Brandon who have worked together to let go of their emotional baggage start to recognize the patterns that push each other's buttons. Instead of getting caught in the Drama Triangle and being a Victim or persecuting each other, they are now able to more fully take responsibility for their own emotional reactions. When we take more responsibility for what is occurring with us, we can now have different conversations with our partners. As we let energy go, we need to understand that our partners are changing and we can no longer treat them the same way as we did in the past, because they have the ability to be different. Energetically they are different, just as we are different when we release our energy. We now have to recognize that our relationships are in the middle of a dynamic system, and we need to hold a place of curiosity for both ourselves and our partners. When we avoid feeling things there is a tendency to keep living in the past and to keep treating our partners according to who they were in the past. We need to be curious about who we are becoming and who our partners are becoming as our old emotional conditioning disappears.

The Emotional Hot Button Removal techniques are simple ways to use what occurs every day in our relationships to empty our emotional baggage. I call it free coaching. Your partner is your coach simply by pushing your emotional hot buttons. When your partner pushes your buttons, say, "Thank you, my darling. I am going to go do some work now. I will be back when I am finished." I charge money to push your buttons. Your partner may push your buttons for no additional charge. I encourage you to use your relationship to let go of whatever you can.

Sometimes we will encounter big emotional energy that feels stuck or is just too big to deal with on our own. Or as a couple we may be experiencing conflict in a particular area and can't get out of the trap of living in the past. It is at these times that having an experienced guide to help us navigate through the emotional jungle is most helpful. We can think of our journeys through the emotional jungle as an adventure, because we don't really know what we are going to encounter or what is going to be on the other side. An adventure guide is hugely valuable in teaching us about the various vines that are growing in the jungle and about the most efficient way to remove these vines. When we are doing this work all on our own it can feel lonely; having people to work with is often comforting. Joining a practice class is a great way to meet other people and to hone our skill at removing thorny vines. Connecting with others who are also resolving their emotional energy increases the depth and speed at which we can resolve our own emotional conditioning. The joint energy of the group allows us to resolve energy faster, which makes working as a couple highly effective because we can support each other to resolve our energy.

SELF-REFLECTION QUESTIONS

- How open are you to your partner being different?
- What would cause you to keep treating your partner the same as you have in the past?
- How could you be more curious about who your partner is in the present moment?
- What support could you use to become really proficient at removing your emotional baggage?

Working with a Reluctant Partner

Through my own experience and through talking to hundreds of others, I've learned that there are lots of people who won't do this work, or any other kind of personal development work. And we can't make them. People will only do what they are comfortable doing and what they believe they need to do. We will only do what we perceive to be uncomfortable or scary if there is something that we want so badly it is worth pushing through the fear and discomfort. So what do we do if our partners do not want to join us?

After having read this book, you will have seen that to do nothing and accept the status quo, hoping for the best, is not a good option. My perception is that many couples are not willing to rock the boat and head out into the fast-flowing waters of the river. They accept what is. If this is the case for you, then I encourage you to develop a positive attitude. Focus on what is working in your relationship and let go of everything that is not working. After all, it is your choice to stay on this part of the river, so do your utmost to make the best of it. However, you can do much better using the tools presented in this book.

You now know how to use everything that comes up in your relationship to resolve your own emotional conditioning. Remember, we reflect our partners. As you release your emotional baggage, it will have an impact on your relationship. It is possible that your partner will notice the changes that you are making. You will be a role model for your partner and also for your children. You will be showing your children that it is OK to invest in ourselves personally. When you and others have noticed that you have made significant changes in your behaviors, then you can invite your partner to come join you. That is when you can start asking your partner what kind of a relationship he or she would like to have.

As you are doing your work to drop off your baggage and practice being who you want to be, set an intention for the kind of relationship you would like to have. What is the experience you want to have? How do you want to feel? Start focusing on attracting that into your life. Start focusing on creating those feelings and that experience now. Then notice if your partner joins you. If you are willing to listen to your intuition, it will tell you whether your partner is going to join you or not. The important thing is that you use your relationship to resolve as much as possible within yourself. If you do end up separating from your partner, you will likely have to walk through your own emotional jungle again and cut down a bunch more thorny vines. The good news is that you will be hauling less baggage around in your life and you will have an opportunity to plant new relationship seeds. Because of the work you have done, you will likely attract a different kind of person. And you will be very resourceful to handle any kind of emotional drama that might occur in the new relationship.

Either way, you win. If your partner joins you, you can work to co-create your ideal relationship. If your partner doesn't join you, you will have an opportunity to become significantly more emotionally resourceful. This way if your relationship boat does tip, you will have a life vest to keep you from drowning while you swim to shore. You will also have an excellent tool for dealing with any emotional trauma that arises.

SELF-REFLECTION QUESTIONS

- What would stop you from cutting down the vines in your jungle?
- What do you give up by not cutting down these vines?

Communication at Difficult Times

Miracles happen. Our partners decide to join us. In fact they are excited about being able to do something simple and concrete to have a better relationship. The next biggest key to success in any relationship is excellent communication. But our habitual emotional reactions can get in the way.

Our emotional reactions keep us from speaking our truth when we are afraid of losing our partners' love. When it comes to speaking what we truly think, we need to do this in a way that is not going to hurt the other person intentionally. When we have something important to say, we need to make sure that we are speaking about ourselves rather than them. This usually involves the use of the "I" word. We might say, "When you come home at eight in the evening five nights a week, I feel like our relationship is not important to you." The first part of the statement is based on observable fact, what is actually taking place. Something that both partners would likely agree is occurring. We may have to come to some agreement on what is even occurring. The second part of the statement is how we feel, and when we present it in "I" language we are talking about ourselves and not blaming our partners for our feelings. Our partners may want to dismiss this or deny it, but the bottom line is that this truth is about us, and we know how we feel.

There are times when our partner's truth may hurt or make us angry. In these situations we can call a time-out and excuse ourselves from the conversation while we deal with our emotional reaction, then come back and resume the conversation, even if it is the next day. There is no sense having an important conversation in the middle of an emotional reaction—the likelihood of it going well is next to nil. I suggest that you make an agreement with your partner that whenever you are emotionally provoked, you will call a time-out and go feel into your own emotional energy. If this is prearranged, your partner will not feel abandoned or like you are walking out on the conversation: he or she will know the conversation is to be resumed later. Just make sure you do come back and resume the conversation.

If they take our emotional reaction personally, our partner may, in turn, be provoked into an emotional reaction of their own. At this point a conversation usually breaks down into an argument, with neither partner listening and both being angry and not heard. The Drama Triangle discussed in chapter 15 is in full action at this point: Victim and Persecutor are both likely in action. We can choose to be hooked by the drama, or we can choose to be self-responsible, take a time-out, and feel into the energy of our respective emotional reactions. By practicing this process we can improve the quality of our communication and avoid falling into the trap of being critical and having contempt for our partner. After all, it is just old energy that is being provoked, and it is getting in the way of us having a high-quality conversation about the current situation.

There are a couple of communication habits and agreements that are valuable to develop. The first is to have the intention to enter into any communication from a place of love. When our hearts are open and we are approaching our partners from a place of love, then not only are we looking to be heard, but we are open and available to hear our partners.

The second is to communicate as if we are passing a talking stick back and forth. Talking sticks have been used by American Indian tribes to promote just and impartial hearing and to indicate who has the right to speak at a given time. This is a great tool for couples to use when we have something contentious that we want to talk about. Milo and I used a beanbag heart; you could use something as common as a wooden spoon. The person who is talking holds the talking stick and speaks until finished, and then passes the stick over to his or her partner. Only the person who is holding the stick is allowed to talk; the other person must remain silent. This at least determines who is going to be speaking, which is half of the solution when it comes to communication.

The quality of communication is actually based on the quality of hearing. What do I mean by this? True communication is two-way communication, which means that one person sends a message and the other person receives the message. It is like tossing a ball to your partner and having your partner catch it. Only in communication, what we are doing is tossing an idea to our partners that we want them to catch. Whether they catch our ideas or not will depend upon the quality of their hearing and the quality of our messages. We have already discussed how to send an authentic and compassionate message: using "I" language. The quality of hearing depends upon our hearts being open from a place of love to receive the message, and on our willingness to be present and put our full attention on our partners. When we are fully present to hearing both the meaning of the words our partners speak and the underlying message, then we are hearing.

This is the habit that we need to develop and to practice. Unfortunately what often happens when we are talking about a contentious issue is that our minds start crafting a response to the words we are hearing without us truly understanding the message that our partners want to convey. With a talking stick, we can take the time to think about our responses. We don't need to be in a hurry; we don't need to be afraid that we won't be heard.

If we were to practice these basic concepts, I believe communication in our relationships would improve substantially. We need to be willing to first express our truth within the relationship, and then resolve the emotional reactions that come up when we do express our truth. Having a set of ground rules for speaking and using a talking stick will greatly improve the quality of listening and hence the overall communication within a marriage or partnership. And finally, speaking and listening with love in our hearts makes everything go much more smoothly.

SELF-REFLECTION QUESTIONS

- How would you rate the quality of your communication with your partner?
- What would you be committed to doing to improve the quality of your communication with your partner?
- What is the first step that you need to take?

Living a Magical Life

To live into a magical life, we need to be willing to live into uncertainty, to not need to know how things are going to work, to give up controlling most aspects of our lives, and to be vulnerable. The ability to be vulnerable and take risks has been the greatest gift of my adventure through divorce. It has allowed me to live life from a new place and in a totally new way. I am being someone totally different today than I was three years ago when Milo told me he wanted to leave. I have been able to step into a place where I am fully enjoying and wondering what life will bring me. And I am not even scared! I have this absolute sense of confidence that my life is going to take off and I am going to soar.

It is when I live from this place of faith and love that I enter into the flow of life and allow the magic to happen. It is then that I begin to manifest what I truly want.

There is a saying that there is nothing like experience. From my experience there is more to living than just changing our thinking and managing our emotions. Even after we have resolved our old emotional conditioning, we must continue practicing courage on a daily basis. Fortunately, once we've made our way past our tangled vines, practicing courage, compassion, and connection comes easily, and all we really have to do is live life from a place of love for ourselves. Self-love makes it possible to truly love others, whether or not they are behaving in a way that seems lovable.

When we've come this far in our journey, we will have traveled in relationship with our partners (whether through an ending or a new beginning) in a way that cultivates the seeds of a magical life. Whether we divorce a partner, or divorce only our emotional baggage, the outcome will be the same: we will be empowered to live the life we desire.

I don't know about you, but my memory isn't all it could be. So I'm glad that to live my best life, I only have to remember two things:

- Live life from a place of love.
- Feel.

Pretty simple, eh?

Endnotes

1   Questions adapted from the Quick Inventory of Depressive
    Symptomatology (Self-Report); see Rush et al., "The 16-Item
    Quick Inventory of Depressive Symptomatology (QIDS-16)".
2   American Foundation for Suicide Prevention, facts and
    figures for depression, *http://www.afsp.org*.

Bibliography

A Woman Named Pepe. *The Adventures of Alice in Moneyland: The Magic Road to Wealth and Freedom.* Available from http://www.aliceinmoneyland.com

Aziz, Shajen Joy, and Demian Lichtenstein. *Discover the Gift: It's Why We Are Here.* New York: Harmony Books, 2011.

Brown, Brené. *The Gifts of Imperfection: Let Go of Who You Think You're Supposed to Be and Embrace Who You Are.* Center City, MN: Hazelden, 2010.

Canfield, Jack, Mark Victor Hansen, and Patty Hansen. *Chicken Soup for the Soul: Divorce and Recovery.* Cos Cob, CT: Chicken Soup for the Soul Publishing, 2008.

Canfield, Jack, with Janet Switzer. *The Success Principles: How to Get from Where You Are to Where You Want to Be.* New York: HarperCollins, 2005.

Chapman, Gary D. *The Five Love Languages: The Secret to Love That Lasts.* Chicago, IL: Northfield Publishing, 2010.

Diamond, Jed. *Male Menopause.* Naperville, IL: Sourcebooks, 1998.

Dwoskin, Hale. *The Sedona Method: Your Key to Lasting Happiness, Success, Peace, and Emotional Well-Being.* Sedona, AZ: Sedona Press, 2007.

Fisher, Bruce, and Robert Alberti. *Rebuilding When Your Relationship Ends.* 3rd edition. Atascadero, CA: Impact Publishers, 2000.

Gibbs, Nancy. "Love, Sex, Freedom and the Paradox of the Pill." *Time Magazine,* May 3, 2010.

Gibbs, Nancy. *Love, Sex, Freedom and the Paradox of the Pill: A Brief History of Birth Control.* New York: Time Inc. Home Entertainment, 2010. Kindle Edition e-book.

Gilbert, Elizabeth. *Committed: A Skeptic Makes Peace with Marriage.* New York: Viking, 2010.

George, Elizabeth E., and Darren M. George. *The Compatibility Code: An Intelligent Woman's Guide to Dating and Marriage*. 2nd ed. Garden City, NY: Morgan James, 2009.

Gottman, John M. and Nan Silver. *The Seven Principles for Making Marriage Work*. New York: Three River Press, 2000.

Hendrix, Harville. *Getting the Love You Want: A Guide for Couples*. New York: Henry Holt, 1988.

Hicks, Esther, and Jerry Hicks. *The Law of Attraction: The Basics of the Teachings of Abraham*. Carlsbad, CA: Hay House, 2006.

Karpman, Stephen B. "Fairy Tales and Script Drama Analysis." *Transactional Analysis Bulletin* 7, no. 26 (1968): 39–43.

Kingma, Daphne Rose. *Coming Apart: Why Relationships End and How to Live through the Ending of Yours*. Boston: Conari Press, 2000.

Kübler-Ross, Elisabeth. *On Death and Dying*. Scribner Classics edition. New York: Scribner, 1997.

Lerner, Harriet. *The Dance of Anger: A Woman's Guide to Changing the Patterns of Intimate Relationships*. New York: Harper-Collins, 1997.

Lovejoy, Asara. *The One Command*. Dallas: Wisdom House Books, 2007.

Masters, Robert Augustus. *Transformation through Intimacy: The Journey toward Mature Monogamy*. Ashland, OR: Tehmenos Press, 2007.

McKenna, Jed. *Spiritual Warfare*. Wisefool Press, 2010.

Moses, Barbara. *Dish: Midlife Women Tell the Truth About Work, Relationships, and the Rest of Life*. Toronto: McClelland & Stewart, 2006.

Myss, Caroline, and C. Norman Shealy. *The Creation of Health: The Emotional, Psychological, and Spiritual Responses That Promote Health and Healing*. New York: Three Rivers Press, 1998.

Parker-Pope, Tara. *For Better: The Science of a Good Marriage*. New York: Dutton, 2010.

Pease, Barbara, and Allen Pease. *Why Men Don't Listen and Women Can't Read Maps: How We're Different and What to Do About It*. New York: Broadway Books, 2000.

Quartz, Steven R., and Terrence J. Sejnowski. Liars, Lovers, and Heroes: What the New Brain Science Reveals about How We

Become Who We Are. New York: HarperCollins, 2002.

Raja, Satyen. *Living Ecstasy*. Vancouver, BC: WarriorSage, 2007.

Rath, Tom. *StrengthsFinder 2.0*. New York: Gallup Press, 2007.

Senge, Peter, C. Otto Scharmer, Joseph Jaworski, and Betty Sue Flowers. *Presence: Human Purpose and the Field of the Future*. Cambridge, MA: The Society for Organizational Learning, 2004.

Spezzano, Chuck. *If It Hurts, It Isn't Love: Secrets of Successful Relationships*. London: Hodder and Stoughton, 2001.

Spezzano, Chuck. *If It's Heartbreak, It Can be Healed: Letting Go of Hurt and Learning to Love Again*. New York: Marlowe & Company, 2007.

St. John, Noah. *The Secret Code of Success*. New York: Harper-Collins, 2009.

Stone, Tom. *The Power of How: Simple Techniques to Vaporize Your Ego and Your Pain-Body*. Carlsbad, CA: Great Life Technologies, 2008.

Talbot, Michael. *The Holographic Universe: The Revolutionary Theory of Reality*. New York: HarperCollins, 1991.

Toler, Lynn. *Making Marriage Work: New Rules for an Old Institution*. Evanston, IL: Agate Bolden, 2012.

Tolle, Eckhart. *The Power of Now: A Guide to Spiritual Enlightenment*. Vancouver, BC: Namaste Publishing, 1999.

Wattles, Wallace D. *The Science of Getting Rich*. Scottsdale, AZ: LifeSuccess Productions, 1996.

Rush, A. John, Madhukar H. Trivedi, Hicham M. Ibrahim, Thomas J. Carmody, Bruce Arnow, Daniel N. Klein, et al. "The 16-Item Quick Inventory of Depressive Symptomatology (QIDS) Clinician Rating (QIDS-C) and Self-Report (QIDS-SR): A Psychosometric Evaluation in Patients with Chronic Major Depression." *Biological Psychiatry* 54 (2003): 573-583. You can download the "Quick Inventory of Depressive Symptomatology" self-report at http://www.ids-qids.org/translations/english/QIDS-SR_AU1.0_eng-CA.pdf

Index

A

abuse, 204–211
actions, 131-132, 218-219, 324-325, 328. *see also* control
addictions, 168–170
The Adventures of Alice in Moneyland (A Woman Named Pepe), 158
affirmations, 108, 142
afformations, 255, 260
anger
  and betrayal, 107–109
  expression, 205-206
  management, 257-258
  resolving, 276-278, 287
anxiety, 221, 281
appreciation, 75-77, 243–244
attachments, 267–268, 278–279
attitude, 312-313
attributes, taking an inventory of, 67–71
awareness, 128-130, 321-322

B

behavior, 74–75, 131
betrayal, 82-83, 107–109

C

Canfield, Jack, 58, 78, 303
careers, focus on, 40–43
change, resisting, 242, 248–249, 319, 331-334
Chapman, Gary, 142, 191-193, 242–243. *see also* love languages
childhood conditioning, 129, 213-217, 233. *see also* emotional conditioning
children, 162
choice, 130–133, 138, 146-147, 301, 315
coaching, 41, 63, 150, 270, 277, 331
commitments
  in action, 170-173
  preserving, 173–175
  readiness for, 36–37
common interests, 32–36, 102-103
communication, 175-178, 334-337
conflict, 145-147, 299, 306, 316
connections to others, 77–78, 229, 285
conscious awareness, 128-130

control, 139, 228-230, 337. *see also* ego
Core Problems, 224--259, 285-297. *see also* emotional conditioning
CORE Technique, 262–264, 266, 274, 280-284, 287-297. *see also* Stone,Tom
criticism, 177–178. *see also* judgment

D

decisions, 18, 84-85, 113, 201
depression, 119-121, 279-281, 287
Diamond, Jed, 167
Divorce, principles for, 144–152. *see also* principles for divorce
Drama Triangle, 303–307, 331, 335
Dwoskin, Hale, 107–108

E

ego, 227–232. *see also* control, forcing outcomes
Eker, T. Harv, 58, 74
embarrassment, 178, 211
emotional abuse, 207, *see also* abuse
emotional baggage. *see also* childhood conditioning
  as a factor in divorce, 19- 23, 93
  letting go of, 80, 271. *see also* Core Technique
emotional conditioning. *see also* Core Problems
  within relationship, 214–216
  sources of, 216–217
Emotional Hot Button Removal techniques, 167–168, 204, 209-210, 330-331
emotional reactions. *see also* overreaction
  end of, 328–330
  vs. responses, 131–132, 306
emotional suffering, 121-122, 231, 249
emotions
  defined, 219-220
  and feelings, 213, 221-223, 311–312
  from inside 137, 141
  and the mind, 218–219
  resolving, 262, 300
energetic attachment, 267–268, 278–279
expectations, 132, 221, 250, 262

F

family, 38-40, 161-163
fear, 19, 110-113, 248-249, 286-294. *see also*
    worry
feeling
    avoiding, 86-88, 224 -226, 299-300
    and emotions, 221-223, 311-312
    physically feel 19, 122, 233, 263-269, 273-
        297, 301. *see also* emotions, resolving
feminity, 180-183. *see also* gender roles
financial fears, 111-113, 281-283. *see also*
    money
Fisher, Bruce, 112
The Five Love Languages (Chapman), 142,
    191-193, 242-243
For Better: The Science of a Good Marriage
    (Parker-Pope) 147, 157, 162-163,
    165-166, 177
forgiveness, 109, 241
forcing outcomes, 230-231, 234, 250-258
friendships 102-103, 149
frustration, 221, 300
fun, 308, 325-326

G

gratitude 76, 311
gender roles, 163-165, 180-186
Gottman, John, 162, 177
grief, 98-99, 273-275, 329
guilt, 117-119

H

happiness
    and connections to others, 77-78
    from inside, 53, 143, 233, 315
    and relationships, 13-15
health, 20, 147, 313
help, acceptance of, 148-151, 317, 325
housework, 163-165
hugs, 58-60
hurt, 84, 105-107, 215, 221, 228, 244

I

If It Hurts, It Isn't Love (Spezzano), 224,
    262, 329
independence, 85
integrity, 71-73, 106
intentions, 20, 141-142, 144-147, 307-309, 333
interests, common, 32-36

interpretations, manufacturing, 253-256. *see
    also* mind chatter
intuition, 237-239, 317-319

J

journaling, 64, 129-130, 285-298
judgment, 109, 142, 239-241. *see also*
    criticism

K

Karpman, Stephen, 303. *see also* Drama
    Triangle
kindness, towards oneself, 98-99
Kingma, Daphne, 129

L

Learning 72-73, 133-135
living
    consciously, 128-130
    from a place of love, 142-145
    principles for, 127-144. *see also* principles
        for living
loneliness, 93, 115-117, 137, 291-294
loss
    letting go, 99-101
    normal life, 100-105
    resolving, 273-275, 295
love
    fears about, 246, 286-290
    feeling, 197, 311
    languages, 142-143, 191-194, 242-243
    living from, 140-143, 338
    looking for, 226-227, 234, 241-249
    for oneself, 77, 194-197
    showing, 197-201

M

magical life, 302-308, 311-327, 337-338
mantras, 254-255
marriage. see relationships
masculinity, 183-186. *see also* gender roles
mastermind groups, 62-63
Masters, Robert, 186, 190, 202, 215, 300, 330
McKenna, Jed, 93, 133, 248, 318
menopause, male, 167
mind chatter, 65, 218-219
mirror
    effect, 129, 239
    exercise, 77

money
  and divorce, 156–161
  financial fears, 111–113, 281–284
  focus on, 40–43
  managing, 158–161
Morning Pages, 65

N

needs, unmet, 199–200, 214, 226–227, 241–249

O

outcomes, forcing, 230–231, 250–258. *see also* ego
overreaction, 256–258

P

Parker-Pope, Tara, 147, 157, 162-163, 165–166, 177
patterns of behavior, 74–75
Persecutor role, 304–305. *see also* Drama Triangle
personal development. *see also* tools, principles and techniques
  learning 17-18, 55-61, 302
  practice, 62, 271, 321 337
perspectives, excluding other's, 251–253, 259
physical abuse, 205–206. *see also* abuse
physical sensations, 222-223, 268–269
The Power of How (Stone), 224, 233, 235, 261, 262-267
Presence (Senge et al), 318–320
present, avoiding, 235–237, 318-321
principles for divorce, 144–152
  be open to help, 148
  close your relationship with ease and grace, 146
principles for living, 127–144
  choose who you want to be, 138
  everything is a learning opportunity, 134
  freedom of choice, 131
  happiness comes from inside, 149
  live from a place of love, 141
  mirror effect, 129
  practice self-observation, 136
professional support, 150. *see also* coaching
provocative questions, 64

Q

Quartz, Steven R., 115–116, 313

R

rage, resolving, 276–278
Raja, Satyen, 140
reactions, 256–258
reality, creating, 314–316
Rebuilding When Your Relationship Ends (Fisher), 112
recognition, 243–245
rejection, 93, 207, 235
relationships
  betrayal, 82–84
  emotionally letting go, 295–297
  and happiness, 13–15
  mistakes, 178-179
  purpose of, 129, 190
  reluctance, in partners, 332–334
  satisfaction with, 81–82
  stages of, 186–189, 300, 329
  vision for, 154–156
Rescuer role, 304-305. *see also* Drama Triangle
responses, vs. emotional reactions, 131–132, 146
responsibility, 303–307
romance, 43–45, 190, 193–194

S

sadness, 96–98, 136, 274
SEE Technique, 262, 264–267, 280, 282-284, 287–297. *see also* Stone, Tom
Sejnowski, Terrence J., 115–116, 315
self-awareness
  developing, 65–67, 136–140
  and loss, 104–105
  and success, 74–75
self-appreciation 75-77
self-esteem, lack of, 114–115, 207, 210, 228
self-expression, limiting, 214, 246–248, 288
self-observation, 136–138
senses, subtle, 222, 280, 265
separation, 95, 151–154, 160, 170, 202-203
The Seven Principles for Making Marriage Work (Gottman), 162, 177-178
sex, 165–168, 192-193
sexual abuse, 208–211, 270. *see also* abuse
shame, 208, 211

Spezzano, Chuck, 224, 262, 328
Spiritual Warfare (McKenna), 93, 133, 248, 318
Stone, Tom, 224, 233, 235, 261, 262–267
stress
   and depression, 119–121
   and illness, 20
   in the workplace, 46–53
success, and self-awareness, 74–75

T
Techniques
   Core Technique, 262-264, 266, 274, 280-284, 287-297
   Cutting The Cord, 267-268
   Dwoskin, Hale, 107-108
   SEE Technique, 262, 264-267, 280, 282-284, 287-297.
Toler, Lynn, 176
Tolle, Eckhert, 236, 301
tools
   affirmations, 108
   appreciation, 77
   attributes, 70
   belly laughs, 258
   critical and judgmental, 240
   feeling love, 108, 197
   forgiveness, 241
   grounding, 294
   journaling, 64
   managing the ego, 229
   mantras and afformations, 254-255
   Morning Pages, 65
   new way of being, 75
   self-observation questions, 63
   values, 73
   who are you, 67
traditions, loss of, 103–104
transference, 225
Transformation through Intimacy (Masters), 188, 192, 217
trauma, 203-204, 209, 217. see also emotional conditioning
trust, 85, 108, 143, 289

U
unmet needs, 199–200, 214, 226–227, 241–249

V
values, 71–73
verbal abuse, 205–206. see also abuse
vibrant, 137
Victim role, 303–306. see also Drama Triangle
vision
   exercises, 310–311
   for relationship, 155–156

W
workplace stress, 46–53. see also stress
worry, 114–115, 221, 236, 253. see also fear
what I want, 79, 309-311, 322-324. see also reality

Bruce County Public Library
1243 Mackenzie Rd.
Port Elgin ON N0H 2C6

CPSIA information can be obtained at www.ICGtesting.com
Printed in the USA
LVOW04s1746110914

403636LV00031B/1066/P